AF892667

ECONOMETRIC ADVANCES IN SPATIAL MODELLING AND METHODOLOGY

Essays in Honour of Jean Paelinck

Advanced Studies in Theoretical and Applied Econometrics

Volume 35

Managing Editors:
A.J. Hughes Hallet, *University of Strathclyde, Glasgow, United Kingdom*
J. Marquez, *The Federal Reserve System, Washington, D.C., U.S.A.*

Editorial Board:
F.G. Adams, *University of Pennsylvania, Philadelphia, U.S.A.*
P. Balestra, *University of Geneva, Switzerland*
M.G. Dagenais, *University of Montreal, Canada*
D. Kendrick, *University of Texas, Austin, U.S.A.*
J.H.P. Paelinck, *Netherlands Economic Institute, Rotterdam, The Netherlands*
R.S. Pindyck, *Sloane School of Management, M.I.T., U.S.A.*
H. Theil, *University of Florida, Gainesville, U.S.A.*
W. Welfe, *University of Lodz, Poland*

The titles published in this series are listed at the end of this volume.

Econometric Advances in Spatial Modelling and Methodology

Essays in Honour of Jean Paelinck

edited by

Daniel A. Griffith
Syracuse University

Carl G. Amrhein
University of Toronto

and

Jean-Marie Huriot
University of Burgundy

With Contributions by

Lay James Gibson
University of Arizona

and

Antoine Bailly
University of Geneva

Copy Editor

Neely L. Law
University of Toronto

KLUWER ACADEMIC PUBLISHERS
DORDRECHT / BOSTON / LONDON

A C.I.P. Catalogue record for this book is available from the Library of Congress.

ISBN 0-7923-4915-6

Published by Kluwer Academic Publishers,
P.O. Box 17, 3300 AA Dordrecht, The Netherlands.

Sold and distributed in North, Central and South America
by Kluwer Academic Publishers,
101 Philip Drive, Norwell, MA 02061, U.S.A.

In all other countries, sold and distributed
by Kluwer Academic Publishers,
P.O. Box 322, 3300 AH Dordrecht, The Netherlands.

Printed on acid-free paper

All Rights Reserved
© 1998 Kluwer Academic Publishers
No part of the material protected by this copyright notice may be reproduced or
utilized in any form or by any means, electronic or mechanical,
including photocopying, recording or by any information storage and
retrieval system, without written permission from the copyright owner.

Printed in the Netherlands

TABLE OF CONTENTS

LIST OF FIGURES

LIST OF TABLES

LIST OF CONTRIBUTORS

Carl G. Amrhein
Department of Geography
University of Toronto
Toronto, Ontario M5S 1A1
CANADA
carl.amrhein@utoronto.ca

Catherine Baumont
LATEC, University of Burgundy
F-2100 Dijon
FRANCE
baumonc@u-bourgogne.fr

Hubert Beguin
Department of Geography - U.C.L.
Place Louis Pasteur, 3
B-1348 Louvain-la-Neuve
BELGIUM

Reinaud A. van Gastel
Erasmus Universiteit Rotterdam
NL-3000 DR Rotterdam
THE NETHERLANDS

Arthur Getis
Department of Geography
San Diego State University
San Diego, California 92182-0381
USA
agetis@sciences.sdsu.edu

Daniel A. Griffith
Department of Geography
Syracruse University
144 Eggers Hall
Syracuse, New York 13244-1090
USA
griffith@maxwell.syr.edu

M. John Hodgson
Department of Earth and
Atmospheric Sciences
University of Alberta
Edmonton, Alberta T6G 2H4
CANADA
John.hodgson@ualberta.ca

Jean-Marie Huriot
LATEC
University of Burgundy
F-2100 Dijon
FRANCE
huriot@satie.u-bourgogne.fr

Yoshio Kimura
Faculty of Economics
Chukyo University
Nagoya
JAPAN

Hitoshi Kondo
Faculty of Economics
Nanzan University
Nagoya
JAPAN
hitoshi@ic.nanzan-u.ac.jp

Hans Kuiper
Department of Applied Economics
Erasmus Universiteit Rotterdam
Postbus 1738
NL-3000 DR Rotterdam
THE NETHERLANDS
kuiper@few.eur.nl

Michel Mignolet
Faculte des Sciences Economiques et Sociales
Notre-Dame de la Paix Namur
Rempart de la Vierge, 8
5000 Namur
BELGIUM
Michel.mignolet@fundp.ac.be

Kazuhiro Ohtani
Faculty of Economics
Kobe University
Rokkodai, Nada-ku
Kobe 657
JAPAN
ohtani@rose.rokkodai.kobe-u.ac.jp

J. Keith Ord
MSIS Department
211 Bean BAB
Pennsylvania State University
University Park, Pennsylvania 16802
USA
jko@psuvm.psu.edu

Jean H. P. Paelinck, Emeritus Professor
Erasmus University Rotterdam
& Honorary Research Fellow
Tinbergen Institute
THE NETHERLANDS
j.paelinck@pi.net

Harold Reynolds
Department of Geography
University of Toronto
Toronto, Ontario M5S 1A1
CANADA
reynolds@geog.utoronto.ca

Peter A. Rogerson
Department of Geography and National Center for Geographic Information and Analysis
Wilkeson Hall
SUNY at Buffalo
Buffalo, New York 14261
USA
Rogerson@acsu.buffalo.edu

Kenneth Earl Rosing
Erasmus University Rotterdam
Postbus 1738
NL-3000 DR Rotterdam
THE NETHERLANDS
tee-secr@few.eur.nl

Koji Shimomura
Kobe University
JAPAN
Simomura@rieb.kobe-u.ac.jp

Makota Tawada
Faculty of Economics
Nagoya City University
Mizuho-ku, Nagoya 467
JAPAN
Tawada@econ.nagoya-cu.ac.jp

PREFACE

The purpose of models is not to fit the data but to sharpen the questions.
S. Karlin, 11th R.A. Fisher Memorial Lecture, Royal Society, 20 April 1983

We are proud to offer this volume in honour of the remarkable career of the *Father of Spatial Econometrics*, Professor Jean Paelinck, presently of the Tinbergen Institute, Rotterdam. Not one to model solely for the sake of modelling, the above quotation nicely captures Professor Paelinck's unceasing quest for the best question for which an answer is needed. His FLEUR model has sharpened many spatial economics and spatial econometrics questions!

Jean Paelinck, arguably, is the founder of modern spatial econometrics, penning the seminal introductory monograph on this topic, *Spatial Econometrics*, with Klaassen in 1979. In the General Address to the Dutch Statistical Association, on May 2, 1974, in Tilburg, "he coined the term [spatial econometrics] to designate a growing body of the regional science literature that dealt primarily with estimation and testing problems encountered in the implementation of multiregional econometric models" (Anselin, 1988, p. 7); he already had introduced this idea in his introductory report to the 1966 Annual Meeting of the Association de Science Régionale de Langue Française. The impact on the profession through his work in spatial econometrics, regional science, and more conventional economics can be measured in many ways: through the work of his students (most notably Peter Nijkamp), his devotion to and activism in facilitating the diffusion of regional science to Poland, the formulation and development of his FLEUR model, his co-founding of the French-speaking Regional Science Association, the voluminous references to his scholarly publications, his many invitations to be a featured speaker at conferences and universities throughout the world, the offices he has held in scholarly and professional associations, Erasmus University Rotterdam and the Netherlands Economic Institute, and the numerous honourary degrees he has been awarded. Perhaps the easiest way to summarize Professor Paelinck's impact is to quote from the citation of his recent receipt of the Founder's Medal in Regional Science.

> Professor Jean Paelinck is the fourth recipient of the Founder's Medal of the Regional Science Association International on the occasion of its Fifth World Congress, May 2-6, 1996. ... The medal is awarded at most every five years.
>
> He has authored, co-authored or co-edited nearly 60 books and over 300 articles in French, Dutch and English; in addition, several of his works have been translated into Polish. He received honourary degrees from seven universities in Belgium, France, Switzerland and Poland.
>
> As a founder, together with Professors W. Isard, F. Perroux and later J. Boudeville, and President of the Association de Science

Regionale de Langue Française in 1991, Professor Paelinck has influenced most French-speaking Regional Scientists. In addition, he served as President of the Regional Science Association (1981) and is Honourary of Association de Science Régionale de langue Française. He was also the founding editor of *Regional and Urban Economics: Operational Methods*, now *Regional Science and Urban Economics*.

It is entirely fitting and proper that the remarkable career of Professor Paelinck be honoured by the publication of a collection of papers written in his honour.

During the period from November 1995 to November 1996, a series of special sessions in honour of Jean Paelinck were organized at the most prominent regional science meetings around the world. Under the joint leadership of Professors Lay Gibson and Antoine Bailley, a number of prominent scholars in the field organized and participated in special sessions labelled "In Honour of Professor Paelinck." These sessions reflect a truly global reach of the techniques and methods pioneered by Professor Paelinck. Scholars were invited to present papers written especially for these occasions, and with the present publication in mind. All of those papers selected for inclusion here have been subjected to the usual peer-review process. Final versions of the selection of papers drawn from this set of presentations and collected in this volume are an outgrowth of the following six conferences, listed here in chronological order:

North American Regional Science Meetings, November 1995, Cincinnati, Ohio, organized by Daniel Griffith.

Western Regional Science Meetings, February 1996, Napa Valley, California, organized by Antoine Bailly and Lay Gibson

Fifth World Congress of the Regional Science Association International, May 1996, Tokyo, Japan, organized by Lay Gibson.

European Regional Science Association Congress, August 1996, Zurich, Switzerland, organized by Jean-Marie Huriot.

Northeast Regional Science Association Meetings, April 26-27, 1997, Binghamton, New York, and had a special session in honor of Jean Paelinck, organized by Daniel Griffith

French Speaking Regional Science Meetings, September 1996, Berlin, Germany, organized by Jean-Marie Huriot.

North American Regional Science Meetings, November 1996, Washington, D.C., organized by Carl Amrhein and Daniel Griffith.

Prominent ideas contained in each of the selected contributions can be traced explicitly to work by Jean.

On a personal level, the responsibility we unhesitatingly took in editing this volume was motivated not only by scientific interests, but also by our desire to provide a token of lasting friendship and esteem for a colleague we hold in great regard. There is no question that Jean Paelinck continues to have a tremendous influence on our thinking. As colleague, teacher, adviser, and friend, Jean has managed to support our efforts, critique our findings, and somehow help us produce better results than would otherwise be the case if we were left on our own. Often after doing so, he has entertained many of us with his concert-level piano playing skills. For all of this we say thank you on behalf of the many regional scientists who share our sentiments. Le travail, c'est bien fait!

ACKNOWLEDGEMENTS

The assistance of many people made this edited collection possible. Lay Gibson deserves special thanks for conceiving "the year of the Paelinck." Each of us enjoyed the complete support of our respective departments. Finally we would like to thank those scholars who served as referees for selected papers; their thorough reviews, insightful comments, and expert recommendations greatly helped in determining the final collection of papers.

Daniel A. Griffith
(GRIFFITH@MAXWELL.SYR.EDU)

Carl G. Amrhein
(AMRHEIN@GEOG.UTORONTO.CA)

Jean M. Huriot
(HURIOT@SATIE.U-BOURGOGNE.FR)

CHAPTER 1

INTRODUCTION: FOCUS ON JEAN PAELINCK

Daniel A. Griffith and Carl G. Amrhein

The following baker's dozen of papers—constituting a unique document written by enthusiastic researchers and furnishing concrete evidence that Jean Paelinck is a very well appreciated friend of the scientific world—have been compiled as a lasting testimonial to the outstanding research, mentoring, teaching and service contributions of Jean Paelinck to science and society. Through his distinguished career and principal research accomplishments, Jean has established a legacy that should furnish a research endowment upon which regional science can draw for many years to come. Adapting a quote by Stephen Hawking, "Equations are just the boring part of [econometrics]. [Jean] attempt[s] to see things in terms of [space]." In writing to us, Professor Mignolet, who as a student first met Jean in 1975, provided an anecdote that exemplifies this very point:

> No sooner was I sitting in his office than he threw a string of equations on the blackboard. ... His proposed solution method [was based on] the consider[ation] that a policy had not been implemented.

Expressing this very same type of sentiment, Professor Ohtani wrote to us that Jean's co-authored book entitled *Spatial Econometrics* (1979) has had a profound impact upon his research program:

> Since their [Paelinck and Klaassen] book showed that shrinkage estimation can be applicable to many areas in econometrics, their book encouraged me to carry forward the study of shrinkage estimation [see Chapter 6].

Similarly, Professor Kimura wrote to us that

> The revised LIML estimator proposed in [Chapter 9] can be viewed as a generalization of Professor Paelinck's canonical coregression estimator that is ingeniously designed so as to avoid the computational difficulty that we point out. Hence, the consistency of the revised LIML estimator undoubtedly implies that of the canonical coregression estimator ... .

And, Professor Rosing wrote to us that

> An outflow of regular contacts [with Jean] was my and his increasing interest and understanding of integer programming and location allocation modelling.

The collaboration between Rosing and Paelinck over the years includes a paper investigating transport flows in Tinbergen-Bos systems, research that directly relates to Chapter 2. Jean has motivated these spatial scientists to go beyond mere equations, to capture the fascination of both quantitative and qualitative, both conceptual and empirically-based, spatial concepts within a regional science context.

Van de Snepscheut once said that "In theory, there is no difference between theory and practice. But, in practice, there is." Jean's research quest, as a regional scientist, at least in part has been directed toward operationality, too, bridging the gap between theory and practice. The mentoring he provided to us during the fall semester of 1992, when we gave a joint guest lecture at Erasmus University, was instrumental in our work on the analysis of error in geo-referenced databases, a subject of great interest to practitioners. This particular interaction with Jean impacted upon the research reported in Chapter 8. During the same semester, extensive interactions with Jean on the Box-Cox transformation problem, a data analytic subject of considerable interest to practitioners, promoted work reported in our recent book, *Multivariate Statistical Analysis for Geographers* (1997), as well as the co-authored paper appearing as Chapter 5. Along similar lines regarding mentorship, Professor Kuiper, who joined Jean's group in Rotterdam in 1979, wrote to us that

> Many original ideas came from him, helping us to understand more about spatial economics.

Certainly, although there is no question that the gap between theory and practice remains, in regional science and spatial econometrics Jean has helped narrow it.

Not surprisingly, Jean's colleagues have told us that he has been an exemplary teacher during the course of his academic career, too. Professor Kuiper wrote to us that

> All Erasmus University Rotterdam students who received a doctor's degree in the area of spatial economics worked with Jean Paelinck as their principal advisor. Most received a *cum laude* distinction for their work, and I also was granted the first "Euro-doctorate."

Also included among the ranks of these students is Peter Nijkamp! Professor Rosing, who first met Jean in 1971, conveyed to us that although he was in a different department, he came to know Jean partly because they taught the same group of students. In more recent years, at the undergraduate level Jean enthusiastically and unselfishly participated in the European-wide Erasmus student exchange program, hosting numerous student receptions at his home in Rotterdam; Professor Kuiper has recalled to us that

> I remember very well his music; especially at the well-known receptions organized by Juliette and Jean on Tuesdays in the Paelinck house, Jean played his piano [and, in the words of Professor Mignolet, "with the master's talent that all of us know"].

In a similar fashion, during one of Jean's visits to Syracuse University, he spoke informally, but elegantly and eloquently, to a freshman class about the joys and benefits of participating in student exchange programs. Of course his presentation was followed by his playing a selection of European regional piano pieces. And, with regard to students from other universities, Professor Rogerson said it best when reminiscing about his first meeting Jean in 1980:

> I was extremely impressed with his depth of knowledge, and his presentation opened my eyes to the field of spatial econometrics. Just as importantly, I remember being impressed by the kindness with which he treated me, and by the interest he took in my work. ... I truly think of Jean as a great role model for young colleagues.

This characterization of Jean holds for the first time Griffith, then a doctoral student in the mid-70s, met him, which was after Jean presented a colloquium in the Department of Geography, University of Toronto; Griffith was mesmerized by Jean's spatial econometrics lecture, so much so that he inspired part of Griffith's doctoral dissertation work in the area of spatial statistics, "and initiated a tradition of Jean's influencing [his] spatial autocorrelation research":

> Over the years we interacted at NATO Advanced Studies Institutes, during visits we hosted to each other's university, and at conferences; each time I came away with additional insights about spatial autocorrelation. These cumulative impacts culminate in the joint paper we have in [Chapter 5].

Rogerson's commentary also reflects the nature and quality of Professor Mignolet's initial experiences with Jean; in discussing modeling and analysis issues,

> When the results were good, Jean Paelinck taught me to appreciate these "windfall gifts" (in Jean's own words). When they were bad, he always had a possible explanation and "pulled out of his hat" a brilliantly thought out solution.

All of these actions were performed in a gracious and unassuming manner, a personality trait of Jean's highlighted in Amrhein's description of Jean's receptiveness to his junior colleagues:

> Jean has had an impact on my work and career [by always having] been totally accessible to young scholars. He is not at all intimidating, making it very easy to discuss ideas with him. He invariably responds with very good ideas.

Clearly over the years students have found exposures to and meetings with Jean to be very encouraging and productive! Furthermore, reiterating Rogerson's role model comment, Griffith noted that Jean provided him with "a role model … in the way a senior colleague should nurture and mentor junior colleagues."

Finally, Jean has provided considerable service to the academy. Some of his service work has impacted upon individual scholars in a very personal, positive and productive way, too. Professor Hodgson wrote to us that

> My work is linked with that of Jean mostly at the level of personal communication. As I have indicated in [Chapter 10], Jean helped me to formulate some ideas when I was at Erasmus on sabbatical leave. Moreover, he has produced a manuscript of a paper which deals with my flow capturing model.

Professor Getis wrote to us that

> [Jean's] commentaries on my papers both publicly and privately have opened my eyes to a host of considerations that have helped me through some of the more difficult stages in my research. He is immensely insightful and extremely helpful.

And Amhrein has noted that

> At conferences, Jean asks probing questions, and usually follows-up with comments (many other senior scholars are much more intimidating to the point of being frightening). This was very important to me early in my career.

Jean's more general service contribution has been to all of us, for he has provided insights into and illuminations for the discipline. Professor Kuiper wrote to us that "Jean always has been very fast in discovering new ideas and did not lose too much time in writing the exact details of his discoveries." For Jean becoming such a source of innovations and a mechanism for innovation diffusion regional science is indebted to Louis Davin, who introduced Jean to spatial problems during the second half of the fifties, as well as to Jean's keen intellect and comprehensive education, which have enabled him to exploit whatever the appropriate blend of subdisciplinary perspectives and knowledge bases is that is necessary to correctly address a spatial problem. Jean (1996, p. v) notes that

> *space* has to be explicitly present. Space is not indifferent to the workings of our systems or subsystems …

Amrhein has noted that students of Jean's work readily pick up this point, too:

> Jean has demonstrated, through his own work, the natural links and extensions that arise from a rigorous integration of economic theory with the realities imposed by space (that is "place").

This contention, especially given the manner in which Jean approaches spatial analysis, reflects Einstein's argument that "Concern for man himself and his fate must always form the chief interest of all technical endeavor. Never forget this in the midst of your diagrams and equations." Jean never does; his diagrams and equations are never pedantic!

In his 1981 Regional Science Association Presidential Address (1982, p. 1), Jean states that

> 'regional science,' as it is often called, is still poorly defined, and at its best multidisciplinary. Long experience with spatial problems—urban and regional— has taught us that partial approaches—economic, sociological, political—tend to be biased and lead to misguided conclusions and recommendations.

Amrhein has noted that students of Jean's work also realize this point:

> [Jean] presents an important and enduring example that demonstrates the futility of the partial solutions generated by holding either space or the economy "constant" so that the other may be studied more easily. In other words, Jean has proven to me that the integrated approach is the starting point, not the end point of spatial science! This was the pillar of the simulation work in my dissertation.

Jean has spent his career contributing to a wider framework of spatial analysis, one whose purpose is to promote this integrative perspective amongst spatial workers, and one that has helped to better define 'regional science.' He plans "to continue doing what I did for nearly forty years" (1996, p. iv), a contention attested to by his penning of Chapters 2 and 5. Professor Kuiper agrees, having written to us that "the productivity of Jean still is extremely high."

Jean has "retired from the Rotterdam School of Economics, the Economics Faculty of the Erasmus University," (1996, p. iv), but he has not retired from the academy, or from our lives; in the words of Professor Mignolet, we are "proud of belonging to the circle of his friends."

REFERENCES

Griffith, D., and C. Amrhein. (1997). *Multivariate Statistical Analysis for Geographers*. Englewood Cliffs, NJ: Prentice Hall.

Paelinck, J. (1982). "Presidential address: operational spatial analysis," *Papers* of the Regional Science Association, 50: 1-7.

Paelinck, J. (1996). "Founder's medal: J. H. P. Paelinck," *Papers in Regional Science*, 75: iii-v.

Paelinck, J., and L. Klaassen. (1979). *Spatial Econometrics*. Farnborough: Saxon House.

PART ONE

SPATIAL ECONOMIC THEORY AND ECONOMETRICS

CHAPTER 2

RECENT RESULTS IN TINBERGEN-BOS SYSTEMS: ON TWO PROBLEMS IN THE ANALYSIS OF TINBERGEN-BOS SYSTEMS*

Jean H.P. Paelinck

1.0 INTRODUCTION

Tinbergen-Bos Systems (TBS) continue to pose interesting problems, we recently encountered two of them, and report on the solution hereafter. The first problem concerns inadmissable systems, i.e. systems not delivering all goods and services demanded by the market. The second derives from the computation of metricised TBS, a problem in mixed integer-continuous programming.

2.0 INADMISSABLE SYSTEMS

In Paelinck (1995) an overview is given of TBS theory; briefly it considers systems i.e. sets of centers, the latter being as (spatial) clusters of plants belonging to different activity sectors. The number of possible systems for "I" activity sectors, s_I, is given as:

$$s_I = 2^{c_I} - 1 - e_I \tag{1}$$

with:

$$c_I = 2^I - 1 \tag{2}$$

c_I being the number of possible centers, and e_I that of excluded or inadmissable systems. Currently, no analytical expression is known for the latter, but hereafter we derive an upper bound.

Consider the following example for I=4; we first construct matrix **A**, linking the number of cneters (c_I=15) to the total number of possible systems ($s_I + e_I$ = 32,767).

* The results reported here have been obtained when the author was a visiting scholar to the Center for Economic Studies, University of Munich, visit gratefully acknowledged; a first version appeared in the Center's Working Paper Series No. 100.

Table 2.1. Possible center-system matrix **A**.

S_i \ C_i	1	2	3	. . .	15	
				. . .		
1	1	0	0	. . .	0	
2	0	1	0	. . .	0	all possible single
3	0	0	1	. . .	0	center systems:
.	.	.	.	. . .	.	number $=\binom{15}{1}=15$
15	0	0	0	. . .	1	
16	1	1	0	. . .	0	all possible double
	.	.	.	. . .	.	center systems:
						number $=\binom{15}{2}=105$
s_I	1	1	1	. . .	1	single system that includes
						all centers; number $=\binom{15}{15}=1$

We then construct matrix **B**, linking the number of centers to the number of activities:

Table 2.2. Possible center-activity matrix **B**.

C_I \ I_i	1	2	3	4	
1	1	0	0	0	possible single
2	0	1	0	0	activity centers:
3	0	0	1	0	number $= \binom{4}{1} = 4$
4	0	0	0	1	
5	1	1	0	0	possible two-activity
6	1	0	1	0	centers:
7	1	0	0	1	number $= \binom{4}{2} = 6$
8	0	1	1	0	
9	0	1	0	1	
10	0	0	1	1	
11	1	1	1	0	possible three-activity
12	1	1	0	1	centers:
13	1	0	1	1	number $= \binom{4}{3} = 4$
14	0	1	1	1	
15	1	1	1	1	possibel four-activity centers: number $= \binom{4}{4} = 4$
Number of zeros	7	7	7	7	

The number of zeros in each column is equal to 7, i.e. 2^3-1 = c_{I-1}; this result derives from the fact that zeros and ones are distributed in an asymmetric way inside the distribution of center types, there being one more 1 due to the absence of empty centers.

Consider now $\mathbf{C} = \mathbf{A} * \mathbf{B}$, an s_I-by-I matrix, which shows the activities present in each type of system. The rows of the first (identity) submatrix of **A** conform 7 times to the zeros of a column of **B**; the rows of the second submatrix $\binom{7}{2}$ times. It is obvious that once a row of **A** has 8 or more ones, a one in **B** will always appear in the sum of products. These combinatorial calculations yield the following table of upper bounds for inadmissable systems, as double counting is present between columns of **B**; the number in paranthesis of e(.) relates to the number of ones in the rows of the submatrices of **A**.

Table 2.3. Inadmissable systems, upper bounds.

e	Formula	I=4	Exact Number
e(1)	$I\binom{C_{I-1}}{1}$	28	14
e(2)	$I\binom{C_{I-1}}{2}$	84	66
e(3)	$I\binom{C_{I-1}}{3}$	140	?
...			
e_I	$(I(2^{C_{I-1}}-1)$	508	?

One has in general:

$$e_I < I.s_{I-1} \tag{3}$$

hence the following proposition:

Proposition 1: e_I / s_I tends towards zero as I increases.

Proof: for large I, e_I / s_I tends towards $I/2^{c_I - c_{I-1}} = I/2^{2^{I-1}}$, from which convergence to zero is obvious.

3.0 COMPUTING METRICISED TBS-EQUILIBRIA

Kuiper et al. (1993) present the equations for solving TBS metricised system. In condensed form, they may be presented as follows:

$$\min_{\mathbf{x},\mathbf{d}} \mathbf{f} = \mathbf{w}'\mathbf{x} \tag{4}$$

s.t.

$$\mathbf{Jx^* = c} \tag{5}$$

where:

$$\mathbf{x^*} \overset{\Delta}{=} [\mathbf{x'};\mathbf{d'}]', \text{ and:} \tag{6}$$

$$\mathbf{i'd_k} = n_k, \ \forall \, k. \tag{7}$$

Here **x** is a column vector of intra- and intercenter flows, **d** a vector of possible locations for the producers of each product k (numbering n_k) and **c** a vector of constants. The elements of **d** are integers.

Now from equation (5) a number of variables can be substituted via:

$$\mathbf{x_1 = J_1^{-1}(-J_2x_2^*+c)}. \tag{8}$$

Let $\mathbf{x_2^*}$ contain **d** and the vector x_{iik}s, the deliveries inside an elementary area, at transport cost zero. Substituting (8) into (4) yields:

$$\min_{\mathbf{d},\mathbf{x_{ii}},\mathbf{x_{ij}},} f = \mathbf{a'd+a_1'x_{ii} + a_2'x_{ij}}, \tag{9}$$

subject to the constraints mentioned above. Now in (4) the weights for **d** and $\mathbf{x_{ii}}$ are all zero. Consider the total differential:

$$\mathbf{dw'x = w_1dx_{ij1}+ w_2'dx_{ij2}} \tag{10a}$$

$$= \mathbf{(w_2'-v_1')dx_{ij2}} \tag{10b}$$

$$= \mathbf{a_2'dx_{ij2}}, \tag{10c}$$

where $\mathbf{v_1}'$ is the relevant part of $\mathbf{w_1'J_1^{-1}J_2}$, hence for f given, df =0, so $\mathbf{a_2= 0}$ for arbitrary $\mathbf{dx_{ij2}}$, and this holds for $\mathbf{x_{ij2}}$ given linearity.

The result leads to the following proposition:

Proposition 2: a solution to equations (4) through (7) can be obtained by solving only a linear problem in **d** and $\mathbf{x_{ii}}$ under the constraints (7), integrality for the elements of **d**, and binarity for the elements of $\mathbf{x_{ii}}$; moreover $\mathbf{d_{ik}} > 0 \Rightarrow x_{ii}=1$ (Kuiper et al. 1995).

The new system, comprising only the above-mentioned constraints (the last one being replaced by $d_i \geq x_{iik}$), can be solved with linear programming methods, which increases the possibilities of computing solutions to metricised TBS for large k and a large number of possible locations.

The following examples illustrates the foregoing. Consider three locations equally spaced on a line, with unit transport costs equal to the line-lengths to be bridged (1 and 2), in which case:

$$f = x_{21} + 2x_{31} + x_{12} + x_{32} + 2x_{13} + x_{23}. \quad (11)$$

Substituting in accordance with the arguments outlined above gives:

$$f = -1.5\mathbf{d}_2 - 2x_{11} - 2x_{33} + 5, \quad (12)$$

which for $n_1 = 2$ has a minimum equal to 1 for $x_{11} = x_{33} = 1$ (1/2 being transported from each of locations 2 and 3, to location 2). If we put the 1-3 unit transport costs equal to 3 instead of 2, the objective function becomes:

$$f = -3\,\mathbf{d}_2 + x_{22} - 3\,x_{11} - 3\,x_{33} + 7, \quad (13)$$

which has the same optimal solution as before.

4.0 CONCLUSIONS

Section 2 has shown that, even if in Tinbergen-Bos analysis some systems are inadmissable, the total number admissable systems increases very rapidly with the number of possible economic activities; that total number is in fact $O[\exp(2^I \ln 2)]$.

Section 3 gives a hint to the possibility of separating the complexity of large TBS; indeed, the implicit location-allocation problem is separable into a location and allocation part, both sequentially solvable by means of continuous linear programming. A first application is already available in Paelinck and Kulkarni (1996).

REFERENCES

Kuiper, F.J., J.H. Kuiper, J.H.P. Paelinck. (1993). "Tinbergen-Bos metricised systems: some further results." *Urban Studies*, 30(10), 1745-1761.

Kuiper, J.H., N.C.H.M. Mares, and J.H.P. Paelinck. (1995). "Alternative specifications for metricised Tinbergen-Bos systems with two industries. *Sistemi Urbani*, 1/2/3, 91-107.

Paelinck, J.H.P. 1995. Emperical Evidence on Tinbergen-Bos Systems, University of Munich, Center for Economic Studies, *Working Paper Series*, No. 100, Part 1.

Paelinck, J.H.P. and R. Kulkarni. (1996). "Location-allocation aspects of Tinbergen-Bos systems." submitted for publication.

CHAPTER 3

AN ECONOMIC DEFINITION OF THE CITY

Catherine Baumont, Hubert Beguin, Jean-Marie Huriot[*]

1.0 INTRODUCTION

Cities are a *universal* phenomenon which first appeared at several points around the planet after the Neolithic revolution (Bairoch, 1985) before spreading worldwide, growing and changing. The city-states of the ancient world, the fortified cities of the Middle Ages, the industrial cities of the 19th century and the world metropolises of the end of this millennium with their immense diversity of shape, function and development, all go by the name of city. But just what are these cities that so attract people, that fascinate and frighten, that bring progress but also nuisances, that nowadays group together the greater proportion of the world's population and the bulk of economic and cultural output? Beyond the simple fact that human societies have become urbanized, and because of the very scope and diversity of the process, there is a need for theoretical reflection if we want to understand and master the city. But understanding the city means identifying it first.

Many economists, concerned primarily with defining and analyzing agglomeration as a phenomenon, more or less implicitly define the city as the outcome of the spatial production of agglomeration. Baumont and Huriot (1996c) sought to specify the relationships between city and agglomeration by showing that while the city is the end-product of a process of agglomeration, not every agglomeration necessarily gives rise to a city.

In an explicit attempt to define the city, Beguin (1996) provided the alternative between a catch-all definition whereby the city is merely a part of geographic space identified by specific attributes such as a minimum density or a minimum level of agglomeration economies, and a « non-definition », or refusal to define, i.e. to identify sub-spaces within geographic space that are clearly of a different nature from others.

This paper is an extension of two earlier contributions. We put forward a definition of the city from a specific standpoint and using instruments of economic analysis, drawing on suggestions from Beguin for a general definition and on the

[*] The authors are grateful to Florence Goffette-Nagot for her comments on an earlier version.

analysis of the city in terms of agglomeration processes by Baumont and Huriot. We accept the following set of propositions as a starting point.

(1) We think that the many definitions available conceal a minimum of common features justifying the use of the same word for objects that vary so greatly in space and time.
(2) We think that these features refer both to a process of spatial organization of human interaction and to a degree of complexity in such organization.
(3) We assume that a definition reached on this basis can cover, as individual cases, a large number of more or less partial definitions to be found in economic and geographic literature.

First we set out a few methodological remarks about the definition of a complex concept: why and how do we define the city? (Section 2), then show what obstacles complicate such research (Section 3). We next attempt to lay down a definition which seems to achieve a certain degree of generality. To do this we take a detailed look at the general definition of Beguin (1996) from the analysis of the agglomeration process (Section 4) and end by showing both how different concepts and definitions of the city can be tied in with our proposition (Section 5).

2.0 A FEW METHODOLOGICAL PRINCIPLES

Defining things is not an end in itself. It is part and parcel of the actual theoretical process on which it is supposed to cast light. But it is not always easy to say just what a definition is or should be.

2.1 The need for a definition

The need to know what the city is can be more or less clearly perceived.

On the one hand, empirical and theoretical analyses provide a wide array of proposals as to what makes a city. The city may be viewed as a large concentration of population, as a space with a high density of population and activities. It is often defined as a space that is built up in a continuous or near-continuous way, with a permanent and monumental character. It is sometimes taken as an agglomeration of industrial firms or more usually of services, a market center, and also a place where economic and political power is concentrated. It is readily considered as the seed bed of technical, economic, cultural and political innovation. It is seen as the cradle of civilization, the means by which it progresses, but also as the symbol of its bounds or the harbinger of its fall. It is held up as a miniature of society, a true microcosm, a place of diversity, of integration and exclusion, as the vector of social progress or on the contrary the means of replicating inequalities or exploitation. It raises all kinds of hopes, but all manner of fears too.

On the other hand, we can live in the city, benefit from its advantages and suffer from its drawbacks, without feeling the need for a definition. We can even discuss the city scientifically without proposing a definition, because we judge it impossible to define the city in a few words or because we think that the diversity of its appearances means that an « objective definition is impossible » (Pumain, 1994). We may also consider that the meaning of the term city is clear enough and does not need explaining. When Fujita wrote his *Urban Economic Theory* (1989), he did not define his subject of analysis. It could be deduced implicitly that the city is what urban theories deal with, much as for Viner economics is what economists do.

2.2 Why define the city?

We have several reasons for wanting to define the city. We may want to understand why the city is increasingly at the heart of economic theory. In defining the city, we may also wish to opt for a specific conception of the ties between the city and the remainder of space. Lastly, we may use a definition as a means of evaluating urban theories.

- The city is present in the thought of 18th century economists (e.g. Cantillon, Smith) both as a fundamental form of spatial organization and a key element of economic growth. However, urban economics develops at a late date, and oddly enough as an outlier from the mainstream of economic analysis. It seems that we are now seeing a form of *revolution in the economic theory of cities*.

This growing interest in the city is probably due to certain characters in the recent development of cities, which is sometimes evoked by reference to the urban crisis, an ill-defined expression that lumps together the uncontrolled expansion of megalopolis, the multiplication of urban nuisances, the development of an urban social fringe, etc.

This theoretical renewal is also related to awareness of the significance of both local and world scales in the analysis of economic growth. This is thought to depend on local forces, but also on world constraints, or on the way that local impulses fit into the worldwide mesh of interdependence. The local-world relationship is especially relevant in the current analysis of metropolization. Urban analysis is recovering the place it should never have lost in economic theory. Urban economics is not only a chapter of Economic Geography (Krugman, 1995), but becomes integrated in international economics (Krugman, 1993b) in theories of endogenous growth (Glaeser, 1994; Baumont, 1997) and even in organization theory (Cappellin, 1988).

In these different theoretical frameworks, reflection on the city is developed at the two levels of the organization of city networks and of the formation and internal structuring of cities. In all of these approaches, and at both of these levels, the city is related to the theory of agglomeration which seems to be a key element in the renewal of urban economics. One way of understanding how the city enters increasingly in economic analysis is to grasp the nature of this spatial concentration: this is what we expect first from a definition.

- Defining is specifying (Foulquié, 1962), which means pinning down what makes the difference. Attempting to formulate definitions involves finding out whether there is anything to distinguish one type of space that is the city and something else, that is whether there is continuity or change between urban space and the rural world. But defining things is already answering by opting for change rather than continuity. Admitting a specific feature also means accepting that the concept of the city exists by comparison with something that is not the city. Economic and geographic literature provides us with this interesting paradox: while it is remarkably rich in demonstrations of the non-relevance of differentiation between urban and rural areas it contains a growing number of theories and models applied to the city, which assumes that there are such things as specifically urban features.

By attempting to define things, we make the assumption that the increasingly apparent continuity between the descriptive characters of the rural world and those of the urban world do not cancel out all of the specific features of the city and any discontinuity in the meaning of these spaces, i.e. in the way they are organized and the way the operate. The idea is that a continuous quantitative variation in the parameters making up human space may, above certain levels, engender phenomena of a different nature, as in a catastrophic process. Then what is true of the city is not necessarily true of space in general.

- Defining also means, as a consequence, evaluating theories from several standpoints. First we may want to judge the relevance of certain theories of the city. For instance, are micro-economic theories that reduce the city to an agglomeration of productive activities capable of accounting for the complexity and diversity of urban phenomena (Baumont and Huriot, 1996b)? Is it relevant to use the same theories of agglomeration interchangeably to investigate urban concentration and to analyze the inter-regional distribution of economic activities? If the city is different from other spaces, other concentrations of population and activities, if it stands apart from other forms of organization of relations between economic agents, that means that it is amenable to specific theories.

Next, if what we have said is true, identifying the city should also suggest the limits to the validity of specifically urban theories. One issue, for example, is how far the residential location models in a monocentric city, developed as part of New Urban Economics, can be used to analyze the peri-urbanization of rural areas in a relevant way (Goffette-Nagot, 1996). A positive answer would not mean there was no break between rural and urban, but that the break point had moved in space.

2.3 How can the city be defined?

« Definition: a proposition indicating the essential characters of a thing » (Foulquié, 1962). Two classical, and not necessarily independent distinctions may be introduced to clarify matters, between definitions that create an object on the one side and those that identify an existing object on the other. A definition of the city is necessarily nominal, it is invariably a creation and must obey certain quality criteria.

- *Nominal* definitions consist in replacing a word of which we do not know the meaning with an equivalent word or group of words with a known meaning. *Real* definitions describe an object completely so that it can be recognized. A real definition seems relatively easy to lay down for a simple object. But the city is a highly complex object, and it is impossible to describe it completely. In addition, if we accept that all cities are to a greater or lesser degree different one from another, a complete description can only identify a single city. We are therefore necessarily led to look for a nominal definition.

- Some definitions create an object from scratch, which is what happens in mathematics, while others attempt to identify an existing object. Defining the city involves identifying an existing object. However, we are confronted with the impossible task of describing the object completely. To understand the nature of the city, we must first simplify the city so that it fits into a theoretical framework. In this sense, defining is part of the same procedure as theorizing or representing. In all of these cases, the object is seen through a filter which only retains the characters that we perceive as being important. Any definition of the city will therefore necessarily be a simplification, an abstraction, and therefore a *creation*. As such, it is likely to lead to different representations, depending on the personality of the person doing it, his or her culture, and intentions in proposing the explanation or in acting (Bailley et al., 1995). This explains the multiplicity of conceptual definitions of the city and raises the question of what a good definition should be.

- If we go along with Poincaré, a « good » definition « applies to all of the objects defined and to them alone », which means that it is « necessary and sufficient » for designating such objects. We might add, by reference to the axiomatic approach, that a good definition should achieve this objective with the minimum possible elements and allow us to find all of the known properties of the object defined. This cannot be achieved therefore either by collecting descriptive features, or by amassing theoretical representations. It may be that we take a list of the properties of the city as a definition. But a definition is incomplete by nature, it cannot and should not say everything. We could transpose to the city what Valéry said of the circle: « I know what it is. But *what it is* includes all of the possible properties and who can claim to know them? » (Valéry, 1973). Finally, there is no *single* good definition. The criteria we have just evoked may lead to very different definitions. The items we have elected to highlight in the definition are closely dependent on what is to be done with the definition. In this sense, a good definition, for us, would be one which would allow us to answer the questions set out in the section « Why define the city? ».

3.0 ON THE DIFFICULTY OF DEFINING THE CITY

We seek to emphasize two sets of problems here: first, none of the most commonplace definitions of the city satisfy Poincaré's criterion of being necessary and sufficient. We shall take just a few examples. Then we shall see why the contemporary development of cities reinforces the difficulty in producing a definition.

3.1 Flawed criteria

The most widely accepted definitions call on a number of criteria which are relevant but flawed with respect to the conditions proposed in the previous section.

- Defining the city by the level of population concentrated in an « agglomeration » runs up against the double problem of the spatial framework in which the number of inhabitants is computed and the limit of population to be selected as a definition of the city. We sometimes refer to an agglomeration of relatively small size as a city, whereas a larger agglomeration may in some cases be merely a village. This ground is familiar enough and does not need to be covered again (the Chicago School had already addressed the question: Wirth, 1938).

- Intuitively, the idea of high density pretty well covers that of concentration of people and activities which is necessary, but not sufficient, for the concept of the city. However, this criterion raises an identical problem. It could easily be shown that the density of some spaces that we agree to call cities may be far less than that of very closely packed villages as in some small « bastides » of South-West France. In addition, the average density depends very much on the spatial basis of the calculation (François et al., 1995): there may be very high local densities within an urban space of low average density. Fouchier (1994) showed that depending on the spatial basis and the means of computation, the density of Paris could vary from 55,400 to 3,600 inhabitants per square kilometer. Finally, density should be combined with other criteria and at least with some degree of permanence: a rock festival bringing together several thousand young people in a small area for several days is not a city...

- The criterion of continuity of the built area is flawed by imperfections of the same type. Such continuity is seldom perfect, and we again require an arbitrary criterion such as the maximum distance between dwellings (200 m in the definition of urban agglomerations of the French Statistics Institute INSEE). Once again, it could be shown that the continuity and the distribution of the built area vary tremendously from city to city, and throughout history. Fractal analysis of urban structures provides us with valuable leads on this point (Frankhauser, 1994).

- A city can further be identified by the composition of the active population, made up essentially of non-farmers, and sometimes reduced to people living from retailing and services (Brunet et al., 1992). However, Bairoch (1985) provides several examples that remove its necessary and sufficient character from this criterion. At the beginning of civilization, a mode of urban life developed in units that were too small to be called cities (e.g. in Israel) and large cities (probably of more than 100,000 inhabitants) inhabited mainly by farmers (especially in pre-Colombian America).

- In a more theoretical approach, the definition of the city as an agglomeration of productive activities is frequently used in spatial microeconomics and in the analyses developed in economic geography. Most analyses of agglomerations in economic geography examine the spatial concentration of production and more or less implicitly assume that when the mechanisms of such concentration are correctly understood, the formation and development of cities has been understood. Now agglomeration economies sometimes apply to places that are completely lacking in specificity as they may equally well be regions as cities. Furthermore, the majority of theoretical analyses of agglomeration, while claiming to explain the city or letting us suppose that they do, concentrate only on partial forms of agglomeration: either the city comprises solely households and the role of social interaction alone is examined, or the city comprises firms and households, but only certain economic interactions between firms and sometimes between firms and households are examined. These are models of partial cities. Thus a degree of ambiguity or confusion is often maintained in agglomeration theories between the spatial concentration of production and the city (Baumont and Huriot, 1996b).

It may be that the productive dimension of the city is important. But a city is not made up just of firms and the people who work for them. The city exists at least as much in its social, cultural, political and even symbolic and imaginary dimensions (Bailly et al., 1995; Baumont and Huriot, 1997). This should not lead to economic theories of productive agglomeration being rejected, but should simply encourage us to consider them as theories that are both highly elaborate and partial.

3.2 Unbounded cities

Brunet et al. (1992) propose the following definition: « City: agglomeration of buildings and people of some size, *which originally was distinctive from farmland*[1] ». Here we hit on a significant source of difficulties nowadays encountered in defining the city. In the past, as in mythology or in urban utopia, the city was often bounded by a surrounding wall. The Greek term « polis » first meant « surrounding wall ». The Latin word « urbs » or « walled city » is related to « orbis », that is « the circle ». The original meaning of the English word « town » which was « circular palisade », is derived from the same root as the German « Zaun » meaning « hedge » (Kerbat, 1995).

This linguistic exercise casts light on the significant separation of the city from everything that was not the city. This separation was signalled in two main ways: by a material boundary and by a legal distinction, the boundary being, in addition to its defensive purpose, the symbol of the second. Historians agree that the specific legal status was a major criterion for identifying the city at least until the end of the Middle Ages and sometimes later (e.g. Duby, 1980).

This clear-cut separation no longer exists. The legal status has become uniform, except for minor exceptions, at least within each national area, or increasingly in the international arena. Urban activities have little by little extended

[1] Our italics.

beyond the physical boundaries of the city, first to create « faubourgs » and then suburbs, which are very much part of the city, but of a more dispersed city with indistinct boundaries. The development of suburbs has not pushed the city limits outwards, it has erased them by creating an indeterminate space (Kerbat, 1995).

To illustrate this dispersal, the Poet inspires the geographer; Verhaeren wrote of « Tentacular cities » (Verhaeren, 1895): « The plain is drab and dreary –and the city eats into it » and Reclus spoke of « our immense cities [...] like giant squids, stretching their tentacles into the surrounding countryside » (Reclus, 1895). This dispersed character is even more flagrant for major cities. « Bursting through its ancient walls, the city spreads over the surroundings and in some instances forms urban regions, some of which already extend over whole countries, over large areas where all land use and labor force activities are derived from the urban phenomenon » (Gottman, 1962). « Looking down from a plane, or on any map, at London, Buenos Aires, Chicago or Sidney, we wonder what shape the city is and where it stops. [...] There is nothing to show where the city stops and where the countryside begins. » (Mumford, 1961).

Beyond the dispersed city, the city that can be seen « eating away » at the surrounding countryside, spreads again what Mumford calls the « invisible City » which symbolizes the influence the « visible » city exerts over consumption, culture, and life styles of the smallest remote villages, because of advances in transport and telecommunications. This may be the same idea evoked by Serre in the « invisible city, the center of which is everywhere and the perimeter nowhere. » (Serre, 1993). More concretely, one manifestation of the « invisible City » is periurbanization or the growth of « commuterland » (Goffette-Nagot, 1996).

All of this can suggest leads. It seems inadequate nowadays to define a city by its visible characters, and to attribute to it a space with precise limits, except for statistical requirements. Which is why we look for a definition based on the processes and behavior patterns related to human interaction.

4.0 CITY, SPACE AND INTERACTION

The city is the most remarkable manifestation of the uneven distribution of people and activities in geographical space, so much so that the fundamental theory of spatial heterogeneity is sometimes confused with that of the formation of cities. Our definition is therefore to be based on the concept of agglomeration and the fundamental theory of agglomeration processes. The concept of interaction will play a fundamental part here. Other basic concepts will be involved such as proximity, information and the rational behavior of individuals.

But not every agglomeration is a city. The difference between the two lies especially in the difference between simplicity and complexity. The process leading to cumulative agglomeration of different agents and diversified activities will therefore be highlighted.

We propose here a three-stage definition leading successively from the most general spatial framework to spatial agglomeration and then to the city which is a specific form of it. We shall show in the final section how a large number of current definitions of the city may be considered to be special instances of the one we propose.

4.1 Space and the city

Cities enter into the process of space formation from in a double point of view. Each city appears both as an element of a larger spatial organization and as a spatial organization of smaller elements. On the one hand, the city is part of a larger system: the city within a system of cities (i.e. within a city network: Pumain and Robic, 1996) and the city in relation to the surrounding rural space. On the other hand, it is difficult to grasp the deep nature of the city without examining its internal properties and therefore without attributing to it a true spatial dimension, presenting a specific form and structure (Baumont and Huriot, 1996a).

Urban space, as *geographical space*, can be described using the axiomatic definition of Beguin and Thisse (1979). Pre-geographical space is first reduced to a mathematical set S made up of elements s, which are location supports, separated by distances or, generalizing, by proximity measurements. We shall name these elements here *pre-geographic places*. We obtain geographical space proper when these elements are characterized by attributes. These ones are defined for stocks (population, predominant social status, level of local public services, etc.), or flows (migrations, exchanges, sundry interaction), whether simple or compound (density is compounded from population and surface area), quantitative or qualitative. Each pre-geographical place, with all of its quantitative and qualitative attributes, becomes a geographical place or simply a *place*.

This definition provides a simple analytic framework which can act as a methodological safety barrier. But it is not invested with any particular meaning as to the space defined and cannot therefore be the basis of a specific urban feature. The distinction between the « pre-geographic » and « geographic » levels supposes that at the first level a place can be defined as a neutral support regardless of its attributes. This amounts to accepting the separation between an abstract and universal container-space and the attributes that fill it. It might on the contrary be thought that space only exists independently of its content. In which case we would consider the « geographic » space as an indivisible whole.

To define the city on these bases, we could however consider within S a subset T made up of the cities of S. Each city would be a connex part of T. Subset T would be determined on the basis of specific attributes and « it could be required that part of these attributes were specific to the city: that they constituted a necessary and sufficient condition for justifying the name "city" and the qualification "urban" » (Beguin, 1996). More generally, the city could appear as an original combination of places, proximities and attributes. But the question of determining adequate qualitative attributes or suitable levels of quantitative attributes and of the way they are combined with the notion of proximity would remain unanswered.

4.2 From space to agglomeration

The question of the formation of cities is related to how the heterogeneity of human space can be explained. The answers provided by economists involve the concept of agglomeration[2].

In an agglomeration, economic agents are close together. In a free society, such proximity results from each seeking geographic proximity with others. But why do agents seek to be close to others? Because it is in their interests. Why? Because they need to interact, and it is generally easier to interact when in close proximity.

Thus the search for proximity seems to be a leading principle for the formation of cities. But it only takes on its full meaning when tied in with the fundamental idea of indivisibility and the phenomenon of increasing returns that follows from it. It creates *agglomeration economies*, by facilitating interaction of various types, whether or not the market is involved. It is thus the source of a *cumulative agglomeration phenomenon* which may be thwarted by the perverse effects of proximity, namely the exogenous dispersive forces or those produced by the actual phenomenon of agglomeration and which, by combining with forces of concentration determine a spatial equilibrium, that is termed « agglomeration equilibrium ».

One particularly important property of agglomeration is therefore its *cumulative* character (Baumont and Huriot, 1996b). An endogenous agglomeration process may develop from an exogenous source, namely a « first nature » cause (Krugman, 1993a) or a « historical accident » (Arthur, 1990). Endogenous, first because the agglomeration results from the behavior of agents, more especially from the fact that they seek to achieve agglomeration economies by locating close to one another. Endogenous, above all, in the sense that the agglomeration process, once underway, has the capacity to develop by itself: *agglomeration entails agglomeration*. This snowball effect is the result of « circular causality » (Myrdal, 1957) or « positive feedback » which is found both in Arthur (1990) and Krugman (1991, 1993a). It might be illustrated by the interaction between firms and workers: firms tend to set up where there is a large skilled labor market and the market is to be found where industrial production is concentrated.

This dynamic agglomeration mechanism does not always develop in a regular way. It sometimes proceeds by qualitative leaps or *bifurcations*, following constant development of the quantitative parameters of the models. Agglomeration in one place or on the contrary the appearance of other places of agglomeration may occur only beyond certain *threshold values* of key parameters such as transport costs, the economies of scale indicator and, for a model where an agricultural sector and an industrial sector are present, the proportion of spending on industrial goods (Krugman, 1991). The point of transition from one urban center to several is also a

[2] Analysis of agglomeration has given rise to several recent publications (e.g. Baumont and Huriot, 1996b; Fujita and Thisse, 1997) and a more detailed presentation is not called for here.

bifurcation. Such bifurcations also appear in the models of urban structure formation of Fujita and Ogawa (1982) and in the mono or multi-center agglomeration model of Fujita and Krugman (1995).

It is also possible to conceive that individuals agglomerate for purely exogenous causes: each comes to find a comparative advantage, a resource or a natural amenity in the same place and does not seek the proximity of others *per se*. Such spatial concentration does not necessarily engender a cumulative agglomeration process. Interactions between individuals may be too weak to engender a cumulative process.

It is possible to imagine a concentrated human settlement that remains too small, or for which the above parameters do not have sufficient values, to create a system of interaction capable of developing by itself and attracting new individuals: that may be the case of a village that will never become a city. A concentration of gold prospectors does not form a city unless it is the source of sufficient interaction. *A fortiori*, if the two previous circumstances arise simultaneously, it may be that no endogenous cumulative mechanism appears.

We might then make a first step towards a definition by proposing provisionally to *call a city a human concentration capable of forming the consequence and/or origin of a cumulative agglomeration process*. But this is still incomplete.

4.3 From agglomeration to city

Among these cumulative agglomerations, spatial microeconomics studies in particular the agglomeration of firms and/or industries. It also studies other more-or-less partial agglomerations, but these agglomerations are always relatively simple ones, and reflect systems of interaction between fairly similar agents: firms, in the same or different industrial sector, or individuals often with the same utility function, or firms and households.

On the contrary, the city is the place of *diversity*. Diversity prompts the need for interactions and emphasizes the cumulative character of the processes of interactions. Thus urban interactions occur between diversified agents: consumers and/or producers. The city is therefore an organization of diversity: it results from the concentration of different agents in a single place. It seems to us that defining the city solely in terms of concentration or of density is to overlook the point that the city is a composition of *necessarily* heterogeneous agents and activities satisfying a *minimum degree of differentiation*. It is, in part, in this that its complexity lies.

The *diversity* of agents may be manifested more or less intensely. We may be in the presence of a single type of agent, all identical, say firms producing the same good with identical production functions. There may also be differences between such agents of the same type. Several levels of differentiation then appear. They may be differentiated by their endowments (in goods, human capital, etc.), by different objective functions: utility or production functions, or by introducing differences in income, or production of different goods of the same type (as in monopolistic competition), or production of different goods. Lastly agents from different categories may be combined: producers, consumers, and the State.

If the city is a spatial organization of diversity, it does not result from a single elementary agglomeration process, but combines different simple processes by what is a still poorly understood process (Papageorgiou, 1983).

The city now seems to be a human concentration in space resulting from the organization of diversity, and where interactions are of sufficient size to take place in a complex endogenous agglomeration process.

5.0 RELATED CONCEPTS AND DEFINITIONS

This definition *implicitly* contains other important concepts related by the idea of agglomeration: *external effects*, *proximity*, *information*, *collective good*, *rationality*, and *centrality*. In itself, it covers a whole set of more or less partial definitions which emphasize these concepts.

5.1 External effects

Agglomeration economies which engender the formation and development of cities are one form of *external effect*. The conceptual origin of agglomeration economies lies in Marshall's external economies (Marshall, 1890) and in the location theory of Weber (1909). Agglomeration economies measure the gains made in production operations by the geographic proximity of firms. They are a source of external increasing returns which appear, all things being equal, when the size of the localized productive complex in which a firm of a given size fits increases. They may still be linked to indivisible factors, but ones that are external to the firm. But the idea of external effect is not only related to production. It is at the basis of the most general presentations of the agglomeration process, whatever the agents concerned. Papageorgiou and Smith (1983) determine under what circumstances the existence of externalities between individuals entails spatial concentration, all of the other causes of agglomeration being eliminated. The utility of individuals depends on the intensity of these externalities (decreasing with distance) and on the congestion entailed by spatial concentration. The existence of positive externalities leads to agglomeration provided that the marginal effect of such externalities is greater than the marginal effect of congestion.

It goes without saying that any definition of the city that emphasizes the impact of the creation of spatial external effects comes down to a definition based on the endogenous agglomeration phenomenon.

5.2 Proximity

Proximity is implied in the idea of concentration, as an end-result, as well as in the idea of agglomeration, which includes organizing proximity for the purpose of deriving benefits from it (monetary or other). Proximity is a spatial relation that includes and generalizes the notion of distance; but it is also a relation of resemblance, of complementarity of common objective that is sometimes summarized by the term of organizational or relational proximity and which is not incompatible with the diversity of actors. If spatial concentration is conveyed in terms of spatial proximity, the agglomeration process and the interactions it initiates concern organizational proximity too (Huriot, 1997).

Our definition thus covers the definitions that make the city a place of organization of proximity, or of organization of individuals to benefit from the advantages of proximity. This recalls the idea that the city is the outcome of combining spatial proximity and organizational proximity (Cappelin, 1988). However, the city is necessarily based on spatial proximity: it differs in this from the network, which is also an organization designed for the purpose of taking advantage of relational proximity but independently of spatial proximity.

5.3 Information

Information occupies an increasing and better recognized share in the processes of production and innovation. Despite very rapid advances in the possibilities for remote information exchange, and notwithstanding what is sometimes called the « information revolution », people and economic activities still feel at least as acutely a need for proximity, for direct contact. As information is a good that is particularly sought after by « face to face » contact, it is at the root of the agglomeration processes that form the city (Baumont et al., 1997).

Since cities offer a large variety of proximity forms, geographical and relational, they constitute privileged places of creation, exchange, dissemination of informations. This is in complete agreement with our proposal.

5.4 Collective good

The idea of a collective good is intimately tied in with that of agglomeration and with the foregoing concepts. Agglomeration as an endogenous process can be sustained by concentrating collective goods in space. The facilities for collective services, information distribution and transport allow agglomeration economies to be made or transmitted. Firms and households seek to locate close together in order to benefit from these facilities, but these only arise in places where agents are already concentrated, which gives rise to a cumulative agglomeration process. The city has at times been defined as a simple spatial concentration of collective goods.

But the capacity of spatial concentration to engender and distribute agglomeration economies entails considering the set of agglomeration economies that the city makes available at any given time as a collective good. This one is impure if each new agent benefits from lesser economies and lowers the level of agglomeration economies enjoyed by the others. The city is then simply a collective good (Papageorgiou, 1983). This collective good appears as the privileged means of action in creating external effects and implementing the agglomeration process. Our definition thus implies the conception of the city as a collective good.

This conception itself includes definitions that involve politics: the city as a collective good is the city as a community of interests, as the concentration and symbol of power, the city as a political organization or as an instrument of regulation of a larger space. It also links up with the conception of the city as a concentration of creation and cultural conservation.

5.5 Rationality

Rationality is present in the way agents organize themselves to take advantage of proximity. The agglomeration phenomenon that engenders the city creates interdependences between the location choices of the different actors, the households and firms but also a political authority representing a collective interest and which may be the local authority. Individual rationality is present in the objective functions of the agents. It is revealed in the way that they react to the advantages and drawbacks of agglomeration. It can be expressed by the way individuals integrate more or less complete information into their behavior, or by the way each can take into account the reactions of others to his/her own behavior through learning or inertia effects. Such behavior may be interpreted in terms of strategic interaction.

When Claval (1968), for example, defined the city as an organization for « maximizing » interaction in society, surely he was suggesting the importance of individual or collective rationality which enables such maximization? Whether the city is considered as a spontaneous arrangement of individuals or as a planned collective construction, whether it results from cooperative behavior or not, the question of rationality is to the fore, even if economists have paid it scant attention as yet.

5.6 Centrality

A spatial concentration of diverse economic and social agents capable of generating a cumulative agglomeration cannot survive by itself. It is necessarily linked with other cities and/or with its hinterland for several reasons of which we shall give examples here. First our definition emphasizes diversity and the agglomeration process. That means in particular the division of labor and increased productivity, and which implies the production of commodities that cannot be sold only at the production place. Industrial and then tertiary specialization of the city has made external supplying from the surrounding countryside necessary. Information is produced by the same rules of specialization, not only for internal use but is also distributed to other external agents. The political role of regulation and domination supposes further relations with a greater area.

All of this makes the city as we have defined it a *center*, as illustrated by the terms « center-city » and « central place ». The word concentration also contains the word center and literally means the act of bringing together at a center. The following characterization of a center leaves no doubt as to the fact that our definition contains the idea of center: « The center is a place of assembly and concentration, a place where what happens is important, a place of action and maximum interaction. It concentrates population, employment, wealth, knowledge, information, culture, capacity for economic, scientific and cultural innovation, but also the resources for political, legal and economic action, power and decision making. [...] The center maintains with other places asymmetrical relations of complementarity and conflict [...] it is a highly accessible place, a focal point, a point of convergence and radiation, a place that attract and/or emits flows of people, and material and immaterial entities. » (Huriot and Perreur, 1994). Just as the city differs from rural areas, the center contrasts with something else, the periphery.

6.0 CONCLUSION

The definition we propose has a degree of generality, but is neither universal nor definitive. It is conditioned by a microeconomic perception of the world based on the need for interaction between individuals, and even if some ideas about rationality, organization and information lead us to « new microeconomics », therefore to the enlargement of hypotheses that are broadly accepted in microeconomics, it is not sure that everybody accept this definition.

We attempted to find the « necessary and sufficient » conditions for the existence of a city, but the fact remains that our proposal does not necessarily concern *all* cities and *only* cities. It is clearly direct at characterizing contemporary cities of the industrialized world. It seems difficult to find a definition that rigorously satisfies Poincaré's condition, unless we decide that our definition creates the city as an object.

Finally, the search for a definition of the city is inevitably related to all of the investigations into the formation and nature of cities. It is therefore necessarily *provisional*.

REFERENCES

Arthur, W.B. (1990). "Silicon valley locational clusters: when do increasing returns imply monopoly?" *Mathematical Social Science*, 19, 235-251.

Bailly A., C. Baumont, J.-M. Huriot, and A. Sallez. (1995). *Représenter la Ville*. Paris: Economica (Géopoche).

Bairoch, P. (1985). *De Jericho à Mexico - Villes et Économie dans L'histoire*. Paris: Gallimard.

Baumont, C. (1997). "Croissance endogène des régions et espace." In *L'intégration Régionale des Espaces*, edited by F. Célimène and C. Lacour, pp. 33-61. Paris: Economica.

Baumont, C., R. Guillain and J.-M. Huriot. (1997). "Proximités et formation des villes : le rôle des externalités d'information." In *Proximités Urbaines*, edited by J.-M. Huriot. Cahier du PIR-Villes, Paris, Editions du CNRS.

Baumont, C. and J.-M. Huriot. (1996a). "La ville et ses représentations formelles." In *Penser la Ville. Théories et Modèles* , edited by P.-H. Derycke, J.-M. Huriot, and D. Pumain, pp.7-51. Paris: Anthropos (Collection Villes).

Baumont, C. and J-M. Huriot. (1996b). Modèles d'agglomération et ville, Annual Meeting of the Western Regional Science Association, February 26-28.

Baumont, C. J.-M. Huriot. (1997). "La ville, la raison et le rêve: entre théorie et utopie." *L'espace Géographique*, 2, 99-117.

Beguin, H.. (1996). "Faut-il définir la ville?" In *Penser la ville. Théories et Modèles*, edited by P.-H. Derycke, J.-M. Huriot, and D. Pumain, pp. 301- 320. Paris: Anthropos (Collection Villes).

Beguin, H. and J.-F. Thisse. (1979). "An axiomatic approach to geographical space." *Geographical Analysis*, II, 4, 325-341.

Brunet, R., R. Ferras, and H. Théry. (1992). *Les Mots de la Géographie*. Paris: Reclus-La Documentation Française.

Cappellin, R. (1988). "Transaction costs and urban agglomeration." *Revue d'Economie Régionale et Urbaine*, 2, 261-278.

Claval, P. (1968). "La théorie des villes." *Revue Géographique de l'Est*, 1-2, reprinted in M. Roncayolo and T. Paquot. 1992. *Villes et Civilisation Urbaine - XVIIIe-XXe Siècle*, 195-222. Paris: Larousse.

Duby, G. (1980). *Histoire de la France Urbaine*, Paris, Seuil, vol. 1.

Fouchier, V. (1994). "Penser la densité." *Etudes Foncières*, 64, 7-12.

Foulquié, P. (1962). *Dictionnaire de la langue philosophique*, Paris:PUF.

François, N., P. Frankhauser P., and Pumain D. (1995). "Villes, densité et fractalité." *Les Annales de le Recherche Urbaine*, 67, 55-64.

Frankhauser, P. (1994). *La Fractalité des Structures Urbaines*, Paris: Anthropos (Collection Villes).

Fujita, M. (1989). *Urban Economic Theory - Land Use and City Size*. Cambridge: Cambridge University Press.

Fujita, M. and P. Krugman. (1995). "When is economy monocentric? Von Thünen and Chamberlin unified." *Regional Science and Urban Economics*, 25, 505-528.

Fujita, M. and H. Ogawa. (1982). "Multiple equilibria and structural transition of non-monocentric urban configuration." *Regional Science and Urban Economics*, 12, 161-196.

Fujita, M. and J.-F. Thisse. (1997). "Economics of agglomeration." In *Economics of Cities*, edited by J.-M. Huriot and J.-F. Thisse. (forthcoming).

Glaeser, E.L. (1994). "Economic Growth and Urban Density: a Review Essay." Working Paper No. E-94-7, Hoover Institution, Stanford University.

Goffette-Nagot, F. (1996). "Un modèle radioconcentrique pour l'analyse des espaces ruraux périurbains." *Revue d'Economie Régionale et Urbaine*, 4, 813-832.

Gottmann, J. (1962). "Mégalopolis, région-laboratoire de l'urbanisme moderne." *Les cahiers de la République*, 7, 46, reprinted in M. Roncayolo and T. Paquot. 1992. *Villes et Civilisation Urbaine - XVIIIe-XXe siècle*, pp. 587-592. Paris: Larousse.

Huriot, J.-M., ed. (1997). *Proximités Urbaines*. Cahier du PIR-Villes, Paris: Editions du CNRS.

Huriot, J.-M. and J. Perreur. (1994). "La centralité." In *Encyclopédie d'économie Spatiale*, edited by J.-P Auray, A. Bailly, P.-H. Derycke P.-H., and J.-M. Huriot, pp. 47-53. Paris: Economica.

Kerbat, M.-C. (1995). *Leçon Littéraire sur la Ville.* Paris: PUF (Collection Major).

Krugman, P. (1991). "Increasing returns and economic geography." *Journal of Political Economy*, 99, 483-499.

Krugman, P. (1993a). "First nature, second nature and metropolitan location." *Journal of Regional Science*, 33, 129-144.

Krugman, P. (1993b). "On the relationship between trade theory and location theory."*Review of International Economics*, 1, 110-122.

Marshall, A. (1890). *Principles of Economics*, 1st ed.. London: Macmillan.

Mumford, L. (1961). *The City in History.* New York:Harcourt Brace Jovanovich.

Myrdal, G. (1957). *Economic Theory and Under-Developed Regions.* London: Duckworth.

Papageorgiou, Y.Y. (1983). "Models of agglomeration." *Systemi Urbani*, 3, 391-410.

Papageorgiou, G.J. and T. Smith. (1983). "Agglomeration as local instability of spatially uniform steady-states." *Econometrica*, 51, 1109-1119.

Pumain, D. (1994). "Villes et agglomérations urbaines." In *Encyclopédie d'économie Spatiale*, edited by J.-P. Auray, A. Bailly, P.-H. Derycke, and J.-M. Huriot, pp.111-125. Paris: Economica (Bibliothèque de Science Régionale).

Pumain, D. and M.-C. Robic. (1996). "Théoriser la ville." In *Penser la Ville. Théories et Modèles*, edited by P.-H. Derycke, J.-M. Huriot, D. Pumain D., 107-161. Paris:Anthropos (Collection Villes).

Reclus, E. (1895). "The Evolution of cities." *Contemporary Review*, French translation reprinted in Roncayolo M., Paquot T., 1992, *Villes et Civilisation Urbaine - XVIIIe-XXe Siècle*, 158-173. Paris: Larousse.

Serre, M. (1993). *La Légende des Anges.* Paris: Flammarion.

Valéry, P. (1973). *Cahiers.* Paris: Gallimard (Bibliothèque de la Pléiade).

Verhaeren, E. (1895). *Les Villes Tentaculaires*, reprinted in Verhaeren E., 1982, *Les Campagnes Hallucinées - Les Villes tentaculaires*, Paris, Gallimard.

Weber, A. (1909). *Uber den Standort der Industrien*, Tübingen, Verlag Mohr, English translation, C.J. Friedrich, 1929-1957, *Alfred Weber's Theory of the Location of Industries.* Chicago: University of Chicago Press.

Wirth, L. (1938). "Le phénomène urbain comme mode de vie." In M. Roncayolo and T. Paquot,1992, *Villes et Civilisation Urbaine - XVIIIe-XXe Siècle*, 312-326. Paris: Larousse.

CHAPTER 4

ON THE HECKSCHER-OHLIN ANALYSIS AND THE GAINS FROM TRADE WITH PROFIT-MAXIMIZING AND LABOUR MANAGED FIRMS

Makota Tawada and Koji Shimomura

1.0 INTRODUCTION

Although much attention has been paid to labour-managed firms or economies, almost none of the studies focused on the analysis of general equilibrium trade theories. The only exceptions are the work of Ishii (1986, 1990). In particular, Ishii (1986) dealt with the Heckscher-Ohlin analysis in an economy with two countries, one of which is a labour-managed country and the other is a capitalist country. Under the assumption of constant returns to scale technologies, he showed that the traditional trade theorems such as the Rybczynksi, the factor price equalization, the Stolper-Samuelson and the Heckscher-Ohlin theorems prevail.

In this paper we re-examine his analysis in a two-country, two-commodity and two-factor general equilibrium model but under a different assumption regarding the production technologies. As often assumed in the theory of labour-managed firms, we incorporate a fixed cost in production at the firm's level and give up the constant returns to scale techologies. Each firm behaves as an average labour-income maximizer or, alternatively, a profit-maximizer. Except for these two points, all other assumptions are the same as in the traditional Heckscher-Ohlin model.

We then show that the standard theorems of international trade mecessarily hold regardless of whether firms are profit maximizing or labour-managed. In fact, the various theorems prevail for any mixture of profit-maximizing and labour-managed firms in any industries of either countries. Moreover, we extend our analysis to the gains from trade. In Ishii's framework (1986), the gains from trade are obviously obtained. Under our assumption of the existence of the fixed costs in production, however, the number of the firms is crucial to the gains from trade. We show that trade is gainful under certain circumstances. Though this is our main result, we can also point out one further significant aspect arising from our model: in responses to price changes, all firms change their factor inputs but never change the levels of their outputs.

The paper consists of the following sections: the next section presents the model. The Heckscher-Ohlin analysis is given in Section 3. Section 4 is devoted to the analysis of the gains from trade. The last section summarizes our finding with an interpretation of the model.

2.0 MODEL

Consider a world economy with two countries, each of which produces two commodies with two primary factors. Concentrating on one country, for the time being, we suppose that each industry consists of only labour-managed firms. Later, we wiill relax it and incorporate profit-maximizing firms as well in any industry. A labour-managed firm produces output by the use of two primary factors, which are labour and capital, in order to maximize the average income of labour. Thus, under perfect competition, a typical labour-managed firm in industry i maximizes,

$$\frac{p_i F^i(L_i, K_i) - rK_i - p_i T_i}{L_i}, i = 1,2,$$

by the choice of L_i and K_i, which are labour and capital inputs, respectively, where p_i is the price of the ith commodity, $p_i T_i$ (>0) is the fixed cost incurred by a firm in industry i, r is the rental price on capital, and $F^i(\cdot)$ is the production function of a firm in industry i and is assumed to have positive but diminishing marginal productivities. In this formulation, we implicitly assume that the fixed cost of a firm is charged in terms of the firm's output. In this sense, T_i, can be thought of as the fixed amount of output to be used up in order to produce any positive amount of the same good. We make the following assumption on the production functions:

Assumption 1

$F^i(L_i, K_i)$, i = 1,2, are strictly quasi-concave, but not linearly homogeneous.[1]

Two steps are taken to solve the above optimization problem of the labour-managed firms. First, we consider Y_i as given and maximize $w \equiv (p_i Y_i - rK_i - p_i T_i)/L_i$ subject to $Y_i \leq F^i(L_i, K_i)$, with respect to L_i and K_i i = 1,2. Solving this optimization problem, we have

$$w \equiv lL_i F^i_L \text{ and } r = \lambda L_i F^i_K, i = 1,2,$$

where $F^i_K \equiv \partial F^i / \partial K_i$ and $F^i_L \equiv \partial F^i / \partial L_i$, i = 1,2, and λ is the Lagrangean multiplier. Hence, $r/w = F^i_K / F^i_L$ is established. Therefore, taking account of $Y_i = F^i(L_i, K_i)$, we can define the cost function of a firm in the ith industry as

[1] Haruna (1986) verified that a labour-managed firm does not operate if the production function is homogeneous with degree α not equal to one. In constrast, in our model, a labour-managed firm does operate under the homnogeneous production function of this sort. Conversely, our model does not allow a linear homogeneous property to yield any positive solution. This is because a positive fixed cost is incorporated into the model.

$C^i(w,r,Y_i) \equiv wL_i + rK_i$, where $C^i(w,r,Y_i)$ satisfies the property of linear homogeneity with respect to w and r. Moreover, the zero profit condition assures

$$p_i Y_i = p_i T_i + C^i(w,r,Y_i), i = 1,2. \tag{1}$$

In the second step, for given p_i, T_i and r we maximize w with respect to Y_i in (1). The first order condition of the problem is described as

$$dw/dY_i = (p_i - C_Y^i)/C_w^i = 0,$$

where, $C_Y^i = \partial C^i/\partial Y_i$ and $C_w^i \equiv \partial C^i/\partial w$ which in turn implies

$$p_i = C_Y^i(w,r,Y_i), i = 1,2. \tag{2}$$

Now, we suppose that the produced commodities are internationally mobile but the primary factors are only domestically mobile. Hence, assuming full employment, the factor market equilibrium conditions can be introduced as

$$n_1 L_1 + n_2 L_2 = L, \tag{3}$$

$$n_1 K_1 + n_2 K_2 = K, \tag{4}$$

were n_i is the number of firms in industry i, for i= 1,2, and L and K are, respectively, the labour and capital endowments. Both factor endowments are assumed to be given and constant.

Let p_i be numeraire and equal to unity. Then, the general equilibrium system of this small open economy consists of the following equations:

$$Y_1 - T_1 = C^1(w,r,Y_1), \tag{5}$$
$$p(Y_2 - T_2) = C^2(w,r,Y_2), \tag{6}$$
$$1 = C_Y^1(w,r,Y_1), \tag{7}$$
$$p = C_Y^2(w,r,Y_2), \tag{8}$$
$$L = n_1 C_w^1 + n_2 C_w^2, \tag{9}$$
$$K = n_1 C_r^1 + n_2 C_r^2, \tag{10}$$

where $p \equiv p_2/p_1$ and $C_r^i \equiv \partial C^i/\partial r$, i = 1,2. Equations (9) and (10) are obtained from (3) and (4) since Shephard's Lemma assures $C_w^i = L_i$ and $C_r^i = K_i$. This equation system determines Y_i, n_i, w and r, once p, L and K are given.

3.0 THE ANALYSIS OF TRADE THEOREMS

In this section, we examine the Rybczynski, the factor price equalization, the Stolper-Samuelson, and the Heckscher-Ohlin theorems.

Equations (9) and (10) can be solved for n_1 and n_2, if w, r, and Y_i, $i = 1,2$, are determined by equations (5)-(8). Hence the solutions of n_1 and n_2 are given by

$$\left.\begin{aligned} n_1 &= \frac{C_r^2 L - C_w^2 K}{C_w^1 C_r^1 - C_w^2 C_r^2} = \frac{L}{C_w^1}\left(\frac{k_2 - k}{k_2 - k_1}\right), \\ n_2 &= \frac{C_w^1 K - C_r^2 L}{C_w^1 C_r^1 - C_w^2 C_r^2} = \frac{L}{C_w^2}\left(\frac{k - k_1}{k_2 - k_1}\right), \end{aligned}\right\} \tag{11}$$

where $k_i \equiv K_i / L_i = C_r^i / C_w^i$ and $k \equiv K/L$.

Suppose that unique and positve solutions of w, r, and Y_i, $i = 1,2$, are obtained from (5)-(8). Then equations (11) assure positive n_i, $i = 1, 2$, and if and only if the factor endowment ratio is strictly in between the factor intensities of two industries. So we impose the following assumption on factor intensities throughout our analysis.

Assumption 2

The factor endowment ratio is strictly in between the factor instensities of two industries, namely, $k_1 < k < k_2$ or $k_2 < k < k_1$.

As for the Rybczynski theorem and the factor price equalization theorem, their validity is obvious by the fact that the factor endowments do not affect each firm's output and the factor prices. Let the total output of industry i be denoted as $X_i \equiv n_i(Y_i - T_i)$. Then, changes in X_i caused by the shifts of factor endowments are summarized as follows: If $k_i > k > k_j$ for i, $j = 1,2$, and $i \neq j$, then we have $\partial X_i / \partial L = (Y_i - T_i)(\partial n_i / \partial L) < 0$, $\partial X_j / \partial L = (Y_i - T_i)(\partial n_i / \partial L) > 0$, $\partial X_i / \partial K = (Y_i - T_i)(\partial n_i / \partial K) > 0$ and $\partial X_j / \partial K = (Y_j - T_j)(\partial n_j / \partial K) < 0$, by (11). Moreover, equations (11) assure Jones' magnification effect. That is, $\hat{X}_i > \hat{K} > 0 > \hat{X}_j, \hat{X}_j > \hat{L} > 0 > \hat{X}_i, \hat{X}_j > 0 > \hat{K} > \hat{K}_i$ and $\hat{X}_i > 0 > \hat{L} > \hat{X}_j$, for $k_i > k_j$, where '^' denotes percentage change, i.e., $\hat{X}_i = dX_i / X_i$.

So we may state

Theorem 1

The Rybczynski theorem with Jones' magification effect holds under Assumptions 1 and 2. This is

$\hat{X}_i(\hat{X}_j) > \hat{K}(\hat{L}) > 0 > \hat{X}_j(\hat{X}_i)$ and $\hat{X}_i(\hat{X}_j) > 0 > \hat{L}(\hat{K}) > \hat{X}_j(\hat{X}_i)$ if $k_i >$ (<) k_j.

The factor prices w and r are determined by equations (5)-(8), independently of (9) and (10). Hence w and r are not dependent on L and K, which means that the factor price equalization is also valid.

Theorem 2

Suppose that the production technologies are the same between countries. Then, under Assumptions 1 and 2, the factor prices are equalized between countries.

Now we proceed with our analysis to the Stolper-Samuelson theorem. To do this, differentiate equations (5)-(8) totally. Then, we obtain

$$C^1_{Yw}dw + C^1_{Yr}dr + C^1_{YY}dY_1 = 0 \tag{12}$$

$$C^2_{Yw}dw + C^2_{Yr}dr + C^2_{YY}dY_2 = dp \tag{13}$$

$$\theta_{1w}\hat{w} + \theta_{1r}\hat{r} = 0, \tag{14}$$

$$\theta_{2w}\hat{w} + \theta_{2r}\hat{r} = \hat{p}, \tag{15}$$

where $C^i_{Yw} \equiv dC^i_Y/dw, C^i_{Yr} \equiv \partial C^i_Y/dr, C^i_{YY} \equiv \partial C^i_Y/dY_i, \theta_{iw} \equiv wC^i_w/C^i$ and $\theta_{ir} \equiv rC^i_r/C^i$, for $i = 1,2$.

In view of (14) and (15), the analysis can assure the validity of the Stopler-Samuelson theorem with Jones' magnification effect. So we can state

Theorem 3

Under Assumptions 1 and 2, the Stopler-Samuelson theorem with Jones' magnification effect holds, namely,

$\hat{w}(\hat{r}) > \hat{p}_1 > 0 > \hat{r}(\hat{w})$ and $\hat{r}(\hat{w}) > 0 > \hat{p}_2 > \hat{w}(\hat{r})$ if $k_1 > (<) k_2$.

In order to examine whether the Heckscher-Ohlin pattern of trade holds or not, we need to analyze the price-output relation. For this purpose, we restrict the production functions to the homothetic type. So the following assumption is made.

Assumption 3

$F^i(L_i, K_i), i = 1,2$ are homothetic as well as strictly quasi-concave.

Then, with the use of linear homogeneous function $f(\cdot)$and an increasing function $g^i(\cdot)$, $F^i(L_i, K_i)$ can be expressed as $g^i(f^i(L_i, K_i))$. Hence the cost function becomes separable between factor prices and output, which yields

$$C^i(w,r,Y_i) \equiv c^i(w,r)h^i(Y_i). \tag{16}$$

where $c^i(w,r)$ is linear homogenous with respect to w and r and

$$h^i(Y_i) \equiv (g^i)^{-1}(Y_i)/Y_i.$$

Bearing (16) in mind, we can rewrite (12) and (13) as

$$\theta_{1w}\hat{w}+\theta_{1r}\hat{r}+\varepsilon_1\hat{Y}_1 = 0, \tag{17}$$

$$\theta_{2w}\hat{w}+\theta_{2r}\hat{r}+\varepsilon_2\hat{Y}_2 = \hat{p}, \tag{18}$$

where $\varepsilon_i \equiv Y_i(d^2h^i/dY_i^2)/(dh^i/dY_i)$. Combining (14), (15), (17) and (18) together, we obtain $\hat{Y}_i = 0, i = 1,2$. This implies that the level of each firm's output does not depend on the commodity prices.[2]

Theorem 4

Under Assumptions 2 and 3, the firm's output of any industry is not influenced by any commodity price change.

Thus, the commodity prices affect the output of each industry level through the number of firms in the industry. Equations (9) and (10) can be rewritten as

$$n_1c^1_w(w,r)h^1(Y_1)+n_2c^2_w(w,r)h^2(Y_2) = L, \tag{19}$$

$$n_1c^1_r(w,r)h^1(Y_1)+n_2c^2_r(w,r)h^2(Y_2) = K, \tag{20}$$

[2] Under a homogeneous production function, a similar phenomenon comes out in the analysis of the rate-of-return regulation on a labour-managed firm. Okamura, et al. (1994) showed that the degree of the rate-of-return regulation does not affect the firm's output level under homogeneous production technologies.

from which the standard analysis of the price-output relation gives $d(n_1h^1(Y_1))/dp < 0$ and $d(n_2h^2(Y_{21}))/dp > 0$. SinceY_i, i = 1,2, are insenstive to price changes, it obvisously holds that $dn_1/dp < 0$ and $dn_2/dp > 0$. As a result we have $dX_1/dp < 0$ and $dX_2/dp > 0$.

Theorem 5

Under Assumptions 2 and 3, the price-output relation is normal. That is, $dX_i/dp_i > 0$ and $dX_i/dp_j < 0$, for i, j = 1,2, and $i \neq j$.

Now we are in a position to present our conclusion on the validity of the Heckscher-Ohlin pattern of trade. Suppose that technologies and preferences are identical between two countries and that the preferences are homothetic. Then, in view of Theorems 1 and 5, we can apply the usual analysis of the Heckscher-Ohlin type to our present discussuion and obtain the following result:

Theorem 6

Under Assumptions 2 and 3, if production technologies and consumption preferences are identical between the two countries and if the preferences are homothetic, the Heckscher-Ohlin pattern of trade prevails. Namely, the country which is endowed with more labour (capital) relative to capital (labour) exports the labour-intensive (capital-intensive) commodity and imports the other.

4.0 GAINS FROM TRADE

The traditional Heckscher-Ohlin analysis ensures from (7), (8), (19) and (20) that the equlibrium locus of (n_1, n_2) is concave to the origin because changes in p do no affect Y_i. In Figure 4.1, this equilibrium locus is drawn and a price line is tangential to this locus, thus,

$$\frac{dn_1}{dn_2} = -p$$

Bearing $X_i = (Y_i - T_i)n_i$ in mind, we have

$$\frac{dX_1}{dX_2} = \frac{Y_1 - T_1}{Y_2 - T_2}\frac{dn_1}{dn_2} = -\frac{Y_1 - T_1}{Y_2 - T_2}p,$$

where the equilibrium locus of (X_1, X_2) is also concave to the origin. Therefore, as shown in Figure 4.2, trade is gainful if $Y_1 - T_1 > Y_j - T_j$ and $(p_j^0/p_i^0) > (p_j^1/p_i^1)$, for i, j = 1,2, and $i \neq j$, where p_i^0 and p_i^1, are, respectively, autarkic and international prices of the ith commodity, for i = 1,2.

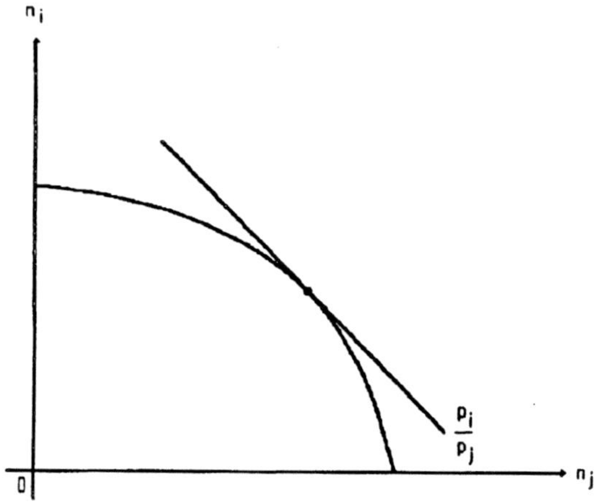

Figure 4.1. Equilibrium locus on a production possibility curve for a number of firms in industries *i* and *j*.

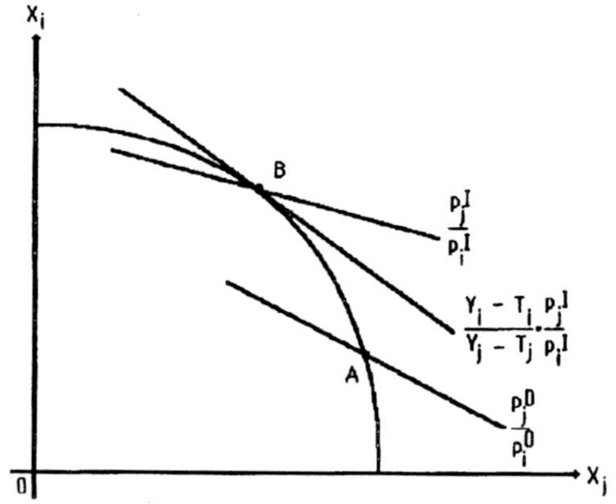

Figure 4.2. Autarik (A) and international PRICE (B) equilibria for commodities *i* and *j*.

In Figure 4.2, let point A be an autarkic equilibrium. Then, since,

$$\frac{Y_i - T_i}{Y_j - T_j}\frac{p_j^0}{p_i^0} > \frac{Y_i - T_i}{Y_j - T_j}\frac{p_j^I}{p_i^I},$$

the post-trade equilibrium production unit, say point B, is somewhere upward from point A in the locus. As the line $((Y_i - T_i)/(Y_j - T_j))\cdot(p_j^I/p_i^I)$ is tangential to the concave locus at B and $Y_i - T_i > Y_j - T_j$, the budget line after trade, which is indicated by the line p_j^I/p_i^I passing through B covers point A clearly. Hence the consumption at the autarkic equilibrium is possible even after trade.

It is also clear that the price line p_j/p_i approaches to the line $((Y_i - T_i)/(Y_j - T_j))/(p_j/p_i)$ tangential to the locus of (X_1, X_2) as $(Y_i - T_i)/(Y_j - T_j)$ becomes close to unity. So trade becomes more likely to yield gains. As an extreme case, suppose that $Y_i - T_i = Y_j - T_j$. Then trade is always gainful.

Our discussion in this section can be summarized as

Theorem 7

If, after the opening of trade, the price of the commodity whose net output at the firm's level is larger than that of the other commodity becomes relatively high, the country will gain from trade. If the net output at the firm's level is equal between industries, then trade is always gainful.

Based on this theorem together with Theorem 6, we can extend the analysis a little further. Consider a two-country economy and suppose a country which is endowed with relatively abundant labour. Then, if the net output per firm of the labour-intensive commodity is less than that of the other commodity, trade between two countries is gainful for this country. This is obvious because the price of the labour-intensive commodity facing this country becomes realtively higher after trade. Thus, we generally state

Theorem 8

Consider a two-country economy. A country has gains from trade if the relatively abundant factor for this country is intensively used in the industry where the net output per firm is not less than that of the other industry.

5.0 CONCLUDING REMARKS

We have three concluding remarks.

First, up to the previous section, we assumed that all industries of all countries consist of labour-managed firms only. Now we relax this assumption and allow profit-maximizing firms to operate in any industries of any countries. Consider a profit-maximizing firm operating in an industry, for instance. This firm's profit-maximizing conditions are expressed by (2). Moreover (1) can be interpreted as the zero-profit condition for this firm which should be satisfied under perfect competition in the commodity market. Therefore nothing is changed by the introduction of a profit-maximizing firm. So all of our results in this section can be extended as follows.

All Theorems 1 to 8 are still valid if some or all of the firms in any industry in either countries are of profit-maximizing type.

The implication of the above statement is that whether firms are of the labour-managed or the profit-maximizing type in any industry in either countries, the Heckscher-Ohlin pattern of trade and other theorems of trade continue to be valid. In Komiya's (1988) discussion which is cited by a number Japanese economists, some Japanese firms are pointed out to be of rather the labour-managed type than the profit-maximizing type.[3] However, it does not matter for the pattern of trade as long as the Heckscher-Ohlin framework holds in other respects.

Secondly, as shown in Section 3, the theorems of international trade carry over in our economy where labour-managed firms and profit-maximizing firms co-exist. This conclusion is essentially the same as Ishii's, though he only considered the trade between capitalist and labour-managed countires. In our model, however, the constant returns to scale technologies are given up and fixed costs are incorporated, by which our present model differs from Ishii's and reveals an interesting aspect: the output of the firm level is influenced by neither commodity prices nor factor endowments, while commodity prices affect the factor employment at the firm's level. Therefore, the number of the firms is crucial to the validity of the Heckscher-Ohlin Theorem.

More importantly, fixed costs affect the validity of the gains from trade in the Heckscher-Ohlin framework. In Theorem 7, we presented a sufficient condition for the gainful trade that the price of the commodity whose net output of the firm's level is larger becomes relatively high after opening trade. This condition can be intuitively interpreted as follows: If the relative price of one commodity rises, then the number of the firms producing that commodity increases. So national income is likely to increase, if firms in that industry produce more in net amount than those of the other industry. This is because production becomes more efficient by concentrating on a more productive industry.

Finally, our model is somewhat similar to the standard Heckscher-Ohlin model with decreasing returns to scale technologies, where the firms behave as profit maximizers. In that case, the firms gain a positive profit which is endogenously determined. In our model, this positive profit is substituted to a fixed cost which is exogenously given. The firm's production level is determined so as to satisfy the zero profit condition under a given fixed cost, whatever the amounts of factor endowments there are. In order to attain market clearing in factor markets, the number of firms adjust in each industry.

---

[3] There have been several papers which treat theoretical extensions of a labour-managed firm in favor of Komiya's work. See, for example, Iwai (1988), Kishimoto (1989) and Miwa (1992).

REFERENCES

Haruna, S. (1986). "Long-run supply resources under self-management: comment." *Journal of Comparative Economics*, 10,338-341.

Ishii, Y. (1986). "On the theory of international trade between capitalist and labour-managed countries." *Economic Letters*, 21, 195-198.

Ishii, Y. (1990). "On the theory of east-west trade under uncertainty." *Journal of Economics*, 267-283.

Iwai, K. (1988). "Japanese firms as a labour-managed firm (in Japanese). In *Nihonkeizai Kenkya (Studies in Japanese Economy)*, edited by K. Iwata and T. Ishikawa. University of Tokyo Press.

Kishomoto, T. (1989). "Public enterprises: focusing on electric power and gas industries (in Japanese). In *Nihon no Kigyo(Japanese Firms)*, edited by K. Imai and R. Komiya. University of Tokyo Press.

Komiya, R. (1988). *The Japanese Economy: Trade, Industry, and Government*. University of Tokyo Press.

Miwa, Y. (1992). "Labour-managed firms and regulation by government: rate of return regulation and price-cap regulation (in Japanese)." *Keizaigaku Ronshui*, 58, 2-26.

Okamura, M., M. Tawada, and K. Mizuno. (1994). *Rate of Return Regulation and a Labour-Managed Firm*. Discussion Paper No. F-068, Tezukayama University.

CHAPTER 5

THE BOX-COX TRANSFORMATION: COMPUTATIONAL AND INTERPRETATION FEATURES OF THE PARAMETERS

Daniel A. Griffith, Jean H. P. Paelinck, and Reinaud A. van Gastel

> It seems that if one is working from the point of view of getting beauty in one's equations, and if one has really a sound insight, one is on a sure line of progress. If there is not complete agreement between the results of one's work and experiment, one should not allow oneself to be too discouraged, because the discrepancy may well be due to minor features that are not properly taken into account and that will get cleared up with further development of the theory.
>
> P. Dirac, *Scientific American*, May 1963.

1.0 INTRODUCTION

Recently attention has returned in spatial statistics and spatial econometrics to the Box-Cox and Box-Tidwell families of power transformations (e.g., van Gastel and Paelinck, 1995; Kobayashi and McAleer, 1995). In part this renewed interest arises from geo-referenced data sets almost always falling under the heading of small sample theory. In such cases design-based inference cannot rely upon the conventional central limit theorem, and model-based inference risks confusing specification and sampling error. Power transformations offer a remedy for retaining the symmetry, constant spread, and linearity assumptions typifying conventional statistical analyses. These transformations often preserve the target parameter, and produce a change in measurement scale that better characterizes the population under study. Power transformations are monotone--changing only the distance between successive numbers along a measurement scale--tend to offer modest gains in statistical efficiency and to introduce no difficulties with the consistency of inferences.

In Bailly et al. (1992, Ch. 5), results were reported on estimation of the parameters of the linear model in Box-Cox/Box-Tidwell transformed variables, which result in a multiple regression equation being rewritten as

$$y_i^{\sigma} = \sum_{k=1}^{K} a_k\, x_{ik}^{\rho_k} + b + \varepsilon_i ; i = 1,2,\ldots,n \qquad (1.1)$$

The principal innovation in the work by Bailly et al., and its extension by van Gastel and Paelinck (1995), concerns taking elasticities as a starting point for developing a new estimation method. The partial elasticities derivable from equation (1.1) may be expressed as

$$E_{ik} = \frac{a_k \rho_k}{\sigma} \frac{x_{ik}^{\rho_k}}{y_i^{\sigma}} \tag{1.2}$$

This paper extends this work, emphasizing interpretation of the parameters, treating the spatial autoregressive counterpart to equation (1.1), and further investigating equation (1.2) for the bivariate regression case.

2.0 APPROXIMATING ELASTICITIES

For a single exogenous variable, the following four test cases were explored in van Gastel and Paelinck (1995):

$$y_i = 2x_i + 1 \tag{2.1}$$
$$y_i = 2x_i^{0.6} + 1 \tag{2.2}$$
$$y_i^{-1} = 2x_i^{-1} + 1 \tag{2.3}$$
$$\ln(y_i) = 2\times\ln(x_i) + 1 \tag{2.4}$$

The sample data presented in Table 5.1 have been used for exploratory purposes here.

Table 5.1. Numerical examples data, with random error.

x_i	$2x_i + 1 + \epsilon_i$	$2x_i^{0.6} + 1 + \epsilon_i$	$[2x_i^{-1} + 1]^{-1} + \epsilon_i$	$\exp[2\times\ln(x_i) + 1] + \epsilon_I$
1	3.300	3.100	0.358	2.465
2	5.200	3.831	0.532	11.242
3	6.900	4.866	0.559	26.065
4	8.500	5.695	0.689	40.593
5	10.800	6.653	0.656	70.257
6	13.100	6.560	0.667	101.858
7	15.900	7.628	0.771	122.196
8	18.200	7.864	0.872	181.970
9	18.000	8.174	0.859	216.181
10	22.500	9.262	0.776	267.328
11	24.000	9.251	0.894	332.912
12	27.000	10.083	0.892	404.433
13	25.000	10.120	0.886	468.390
14	27.400	10.343	0.923	557.783
15	30.000	10.925	0.823	579.613

The ϵ_i terms included in Table 5.1 were chosen at random so as to not exceed, in absolute value, 10% of the exact values of the y_is. Figures 5.1(a-d), which present y_i-x_i scatterplots, portray the apparent relationships latent in this table.

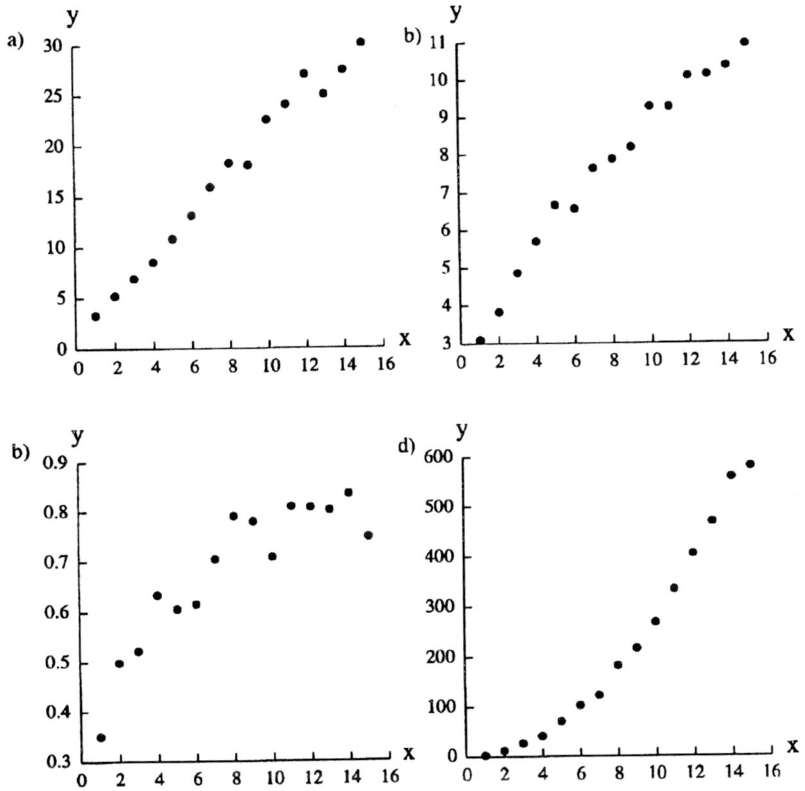

Figure 5.1. Graphs of data appearing in Table 5.1: a) equation 2.1; b) equation 2.2; c) equation 2.3; d) equation 2.4.

The principal outcomes of this exercise may be summarized as follows:

a) if σ is exactly known, then the value of ρ can be estimated correctly;
b) when the analytically computed elasticities, E_is, are used, then the proposed estimation algorithm performs identically--this execution was run as a test of the model itself; and,

c) as far as experience goes, as the magnitude of the error terms increases, their disturbance of the estimated values tends to increase.

Especially points (b) and (c) suggest a procedure to get analytically correct elasticities. One way to perform this task is to step away from the (sometimes highly perturbed) arc-elasticities used. An elementary study of equation (1.2) shows that, for increasing x, the elasticity approaches an asymptote equal to either 0 or ρ_k/σ. This result suggests that the following function (index k has been omitted for the sake of simplicity) may be substituted without compromising this property:

$$E_i = \begin{cases} \alpha\,(1 - e^{-\gamma x}), & \text{for} |E_i| \text{ increasing} \quad (2.5a) \\ \alpha\, e^{\gamma x}, & \text{for} |E_I| \text{ decreasing} \quad (2.5b) \end{cases}$$

with α equal to either the value for $x \to \infty$ or for $x = 0$, which means an estimate of ρ/σ.

As functions (2.5a) and (2.5b) are not analytically integrable to y_i, and as there is no prior knowledge as to the functional form [e.g., (2.5a) or (2.5b)] to be preferred, the following mixed solution was explored:

$$E_i = \alpha\left[\mu\frac{x}{x+1} + (1-\mu)\frac{1}{x+1}\right], \tag{2.6}$$

which integrates to:

$$\ln(y_i) = \alpha\left[(2\mu - 1)\times\ln(x+1) + (1-\mu)\times\ln(x)\right] + \delta \tag{2.7}$$

allowing calculation of the two parameters necessary for deriving equation (2.6).

Applied to the aforementioned sample data (Table 5.1) accompanying equations (2.1) through (2.4), and equation (2.7) respectively yield R^2s in excess of 0.99, 0.99, 0.94 and 0.99. The following tabulation summarizes the main results of this analysis:

Table 5.2. Computational results.

Eq. #	μ	α	μ = est(ρ/σ)	true ρ/σ
(2.1)	0.971	1.193	1.039	1
(2.2)	0.694	0.788	0.547	0.6
(2.3)	0.138	1.141	0.973*	1
(2.4)	0.457	4.249	1.943**	2

* denotes $(1-\mu)\alpha$; ** denotes constant elasticity

Of note is that each of the four estimates deviates little from its parameter value counterpart.

Reported in the next tabulation are results obtained by introducing the $\hat{y}_i$ and $\hat{E}_i$ values into equations (16) though (20) and (28) of van Gastel and Paelinck (1995). The truncated regression is the consequence of the location of μ in the [0,1]-range; one could infer the dominant tendency for E_i either to increase ($\mu > 0.5$), to decrease ($\mu < 0.5$) or to remain constant ($\mu \approx 0.5$).

Table 5.3. Estimation results.

Eq #	Complete Regression			Truncated Regression			True Values		
	σ	ρ	$\hat{a}$	σ	ρ	$\hat{a}$	σ	ρ	$\hat{a}$
(2.1)	0.852	0.896	1.549	0.928	1.000	1.530	1	1	2
(2.2)	1.309	0.732	3.005	1.648	1.000	3.319	1	0.6	2
(2.3)	0.465	-0.225	-0.727	-0.675	-1.000	1.035	-1	-1	2
(2.4)	0.235	.446	1.389	0.030	-0.061	0.971	0	0	2
						or*:	1	2	

* the double logarithmic form can be written as a homogeneous function when exponentiating

These results confirm entirely the working hypothesis previously expressed as a basis for this section. An additional illuminating remark is that

> in the above calculations no use was made of the excellent approximations to ρ/σ (see Table 5.2); equation (28) of van Gastel and Paelinck (1995) can easily be generalized to:

$$\left(\ln|E_i| \ln(y_i) - \mu\alpha \ln(x_i)\right)\begin{pmatrix}1\\ \sigma\end{pmatrix} = \ln|\mu\alpha| \,, \tag{2.8}$$

> and the same holds for equation (4.1) reported in §4 of this paper.

3.0 PARAMETER INTERPRETATION

Noting that the mean equals the median for a symmetric distribution, Hinkley (1977) proposes a useful heuristic for quickly selecting a power transformation, namely computing $\hat{\rho}_k$ such that $\frac{\sum_{i=1}^{n} x_i^{\hat{\rho}_k}}{n} = x_{median}^{\hat{\rho}_k}$; a precise solution here requires nonlinear regression analysis. While this heuristic yields good results, its explicit objective is to optimize symmetry rather than conformity to a normal frequency distribution, whose explicit objective is to either shrink or inflate relatively large values of an attribute. Johnson and Wichern (1992, p. 165) state the necessary equation to be optimized with respect to ρ_k, which results from the logarithm of a normal frequency distribution likelihood function after maximizing it with respect to μ and σ^2.

Following Johnson and Wichern, Griffith and Amrhein (1997, pp. 19-32) promote a method of analytically selecting a power transformation that attempts to optimize symmetry, and moves the subjected measurement scale as close as possible to that for a normal frequency distribution. This method is based upon the Shapiro-Wilk test statistic for normality. Specifically, for a given variable y, the value at rank r, y_r, needs to relate to the normal score $\Phi^{-1}\left(\frac{r-\frac{3}{8}}{n+\frac{1}{4}}\right)$, where Φ denotes the normal probability density function[1]. Accordingly, in order to optimally select a power transformation, in terms of normality of the resulting frequency distribution, the following nonlinear regression problem has to be solved:

$$\Phi^{-1}\left(\frac{r_y-\frac{3}{8}}{n+\frac{1}{4}}\right)=\alpha_y+\beta_y\left(y_r+\delta_y\right)^{\gamma_y}+\varepsilon_{r,y}\,, \qquad (3.1)$$

where the two parameters of interest are the power transformation exponent, γ_y, and the shifting additive constant, δ_y. This second parameter, δ_y, enhances reexpression of a measurement scale, especially in cases where zeroes and/or negative values originally appear, and is most commonly encountered in logistic regression work.

A similar expression can be constructed for variable x in a bivariate regression:

$$\Phi^{-1}\left(\frac{r_x-\frac{3}{8}}{n+\frac{1}{4}}\right)=\alpha_x+\beta_x\left(x_r+\delta_x\right)^{\gamma_x}+\varepsilon_{r,x}\,. \qquad (3.2)$$

Substituting equations (3.1) and (3.2) into the bivariate version of equation (1.1) yields

$$\left[\left(y_i+\delta_y\right)^{\gamma_y}\right]^{\sigma*}=a\left[\left(x_i+\delta_x\right)^{\gamma_x}\right]^{\rho*}+b+\xi_i \qquad (3.3)$$

---

[1]Two alternative arguments to the inverse-normal probability density function may be considered. Preferable in the case of censored data are the Kaplan-Meir method, which replaces the argument $\frac{r_i-\frac{3}{8}}{n+\frac{1}{4}}$ with $\frac{r_i}{n}$, or the Herd-Johnson method, which replaces this argument with $\frac{r_i}{n+1}$. Results rendered by all three of these arguments are very similar.

where, in terms of equation (1.1), $\sigma = \gamma_y\sigma^*$ and $\rho = \gamma_x\rho^*$. In other words, the individual power transformations for variables x and y can be interpreted as reexpressing the respective measurement scales in such a way that normality of the frequency distribution for each variable is optimized. Next, parameter components σ^* and ρ^* bring the two adjusted measurement scales into better alignment with each other. The serendipitous nature of these power transformations is that they also tend to stabilize spread, resulting in homogeneity of variance tending to improve. Of course, other objective functions could be optimized with equations (3.2) and (3.3).

Equations (3.2) and (3.3) render a new version of equation (1.2), namely, for bivariate regression,

$$E_i = a\frac{\gamma_x}{\gamma_y}\frac{\rho^*}{\sigma^*}\frac{(x_i+\delta)^{\gamma_x\rho^*}}{(y_i+\delta_y)^{\gamma_y\sigma^*}}. \tag{3.4}$$

The estimation procedure outlined in §2 can be used here to estimate σ^* and ρ^* now.

Next consider the simple bivariate spatial autoregressive response model, which actually is a trivariate regression model, whose form following equations (1.1), (3.2) and (3.3) would be

$$(y_i+\delta_y)^\sigma = \rho_s\left[\sum_{j=1}^{n} c_{ij}(y_i+\delta_y)^\sigma\right]^1 + a(x_i+\delta_x)^\rho + b + \xi_i; i = 1,2,\dots,n, \tag{3.5}$$

where ρ_s is the spatial autocorrelation parameter. The explicitly stated exponent of 1 for the autoregressive term here means that the elasticity for this term becomes

$$E_{i\rho_s} = \rho_s\frac{1}{\gamma_y}\frac{1}{\sigma^*}\frac{\sum_{i=1}^{n} c_{ij}(y_j+\delta_y)^{\gamma_y\sigma^*}}{(y_i+\delta_y)^{\gamma_y\sigma^*}} \tag{3.6}$$

The extreme right-hand term, $\frac{\sum_{i=1}^{n} c_{ij}(y_j+\delta_y)^{\gamma_y\sigma^*}}{(y_i+\delta_y)^{g_y\sigma^*}}$, alludes to statistics such as the Getis-Ord (1992, 1995) one.

An illustrative exploration of the bivariate situation can be conducted by inspecting results based upon the four selected cases given by equations (2.1) through (2.4), which cover a wide range of empirical possibilities. Sample data for this exploration are as follows (the Table 5.1 data, minus the error terms):

Table 5.4. Numerical examples data, without random error.

x_i	$2x_i + 1$	$2x_i^{0.6} + 1$	$(2x_i^{-1} + 1)^{-1}$	$EXP[2\times ln(x_i) + 1]$
1	3	3.00000	0.333333	2.718
2	5	3.08493	0.500000	10.873
3	7	3.13628	0.600000	24.465
4	9	3.17347	0.666667	43.493
5	11	3.20277	0.714286	67.957
6	13	3.22699	0.750000	97.858
7	15	3.24769	0.777778	133.196
8	17	3.26577	0.800000	173.970
9	19	3.28184	0.818182	220.181
10	21	3.29631	0.833333	271.828
11	23	3.30948	0.846154	328.912
12	25	3.32157	0.857143	391.433
13	27	3.33274	0.866667	459.390
14	29	3.34314	0.875000	532.783
15	31	3.35286	0.882353	611.613

These values constitute the various populations, and are treated here (in contrast to §2) without an error term.

Estimations of equations (3.2) and (3.3) for the data appearing in Table 5.4 yield the following results:

equation	δ	γ	RESS
x_i	0.00000	0.88885	1.80×10^{-2}
$2x_i + 1$	0.00000	0.88990	1.80×10^{-2}
$2x_i^{0.6} + 1$	0.40161	1.63088	1.72×10^{-2}
$(2x_i^{-1} + 1)^{-1}$	0.01869	6.17588	4.31×10^{-2}
$EXP[2\times ln(x_i) + 1]$	0.00000	0.44443	1.80×10^{-2}

where RESS denotes the relative error sums of squares. These calculations reveal that relatively good data fits can be achieved with equations (3.2) and (3.4); but, this apparent close correspondence is somewhat misleading, since it is based upon two sets of values that are ranked separately. In addition, the results for x_i and $(2x_i + 1)$, which should be exactly the same, deviate slightly due to the inability of nonlinear optimization to be perfectly precise in all cases.

Accompanying diagnostic statistics for the data presented in Table 5.4 include

	original data				transformed data			
equation	S-W	B	L	F_{max}	S-W	B	L	F_{max}
x_i	0.9658	0.094	0.227	1.313	0.9670	0.354	0.683	1.669
$2x_i + 1$	0.9658	0.094	0.227	1.313	0.9670	0.324	0.636	1.633
$2x_i^{0.6} + 1$	0.9627	7.376	4.795	12.708	0.9680	7.038	4.771	11.837
$(2x_i^{-1} + 1)^{-1}$	0.8252	14.290	5.588	48.901	0.9381	0.949	1.974	2.305
$EXP[2\times ln(x_i) + 1]$	0.9132	3.904	4.598	5.190	0.9672	0.354	0.683	1.669

where the data have been divided into two groups (i = 1, 2, ..., 8 and i = 9, 10, ..., 15) for assessment purposes, S-W denotes the Shapiro-Wilk normality test statistic, B denotes the Bartlett and L denotes Levene's homogeneity of variance test statistics, and F_{max} denotes the F-ratio between the two groups. These diagnostic results reveal that for the population as a whole, equations (3.2) and (3.4) move the frequency distributions closer to ones mimicking a normal distribution, even if only slightly (e.g., x_i), and that often this induced symmetry is accompanied by a more homogeneous spread [e.g., $(2x_i^{-1} + 1)^{-1}$].

Plots of the original population data, without stochastic error added (variable y on the vertical axis and variable x on the horizontal axis) appear in Figures 5.2(a-d). By construction only x versus (2x + 1) displays a linear relation. Plots of the power-transformed data, in accordance with equations (3.2) and (3.3), appear in Figures 5.3(a-d). Dramatic improvement is attained for the two cases of $y = (2x^{-1} + 1)^{-1}$ and $y = EXP[2 \times ln(x) + 1]$; only very slight improvement is attained for the case of $y = 2x^{0.6} + 1$ (see Figure 5.4, which portrays a superimposed plot of the standardized original and power transformed data).

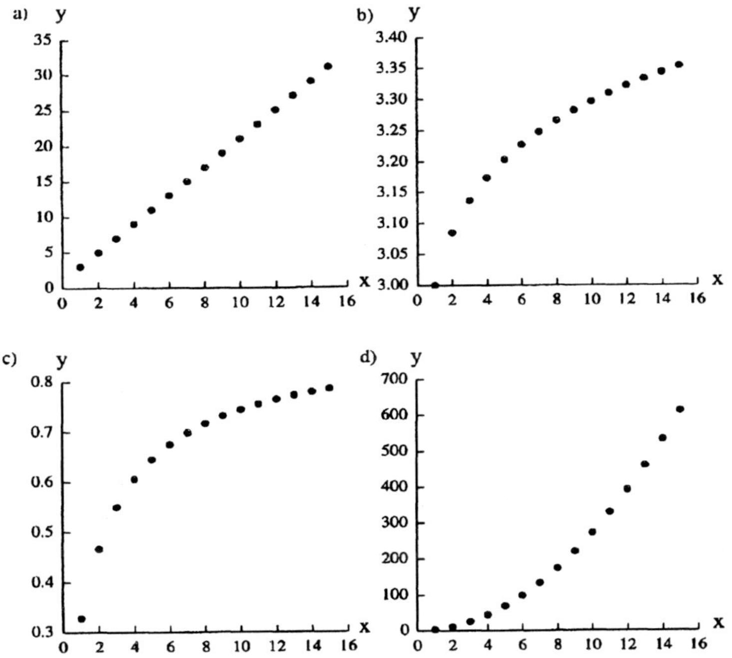

Figure 5.2. Graphs of data appearing in Table 5.4: a) equation 2.1; b) equation 2.2; c) equation 2.3; d) equation 2.4.

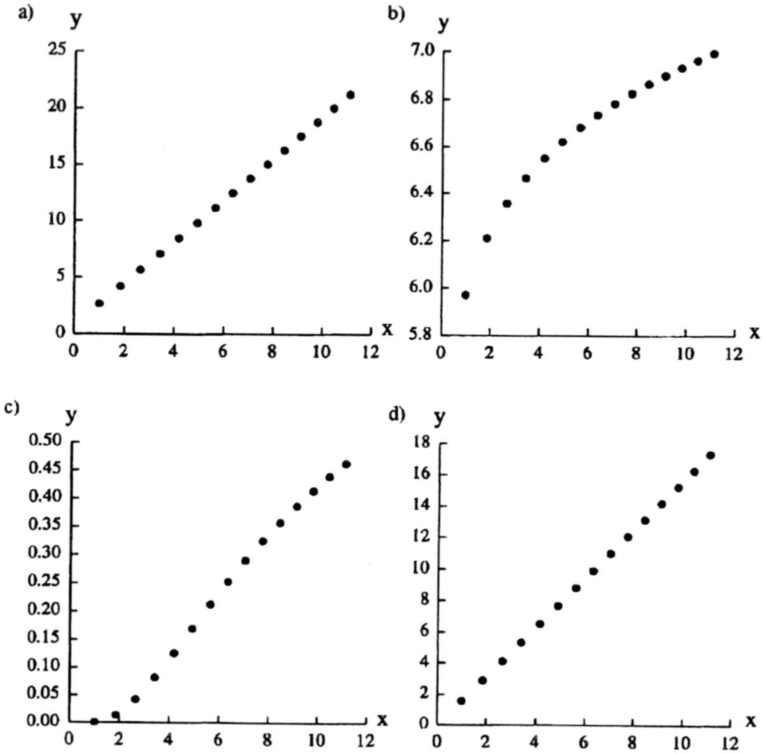

Figure 5.3. Graphs of power-transformed versions of data appearing in Table 5.4: a) equation 2.1; b) equation 2.2; c) equation 2.3; d) equation 2.4.

The results reported in this section for population data suggest that a considerable portion of each of the exponents σ^* and ρ^* is accounted for by their respective components γ_y and γ_x; but in cases like $y = 2x^{0.6} + 1$, the components σ^* and ρ^* can play an important role. Of course this picture becomes less clear with the introduction of an error term into the data, as was the case in §2.

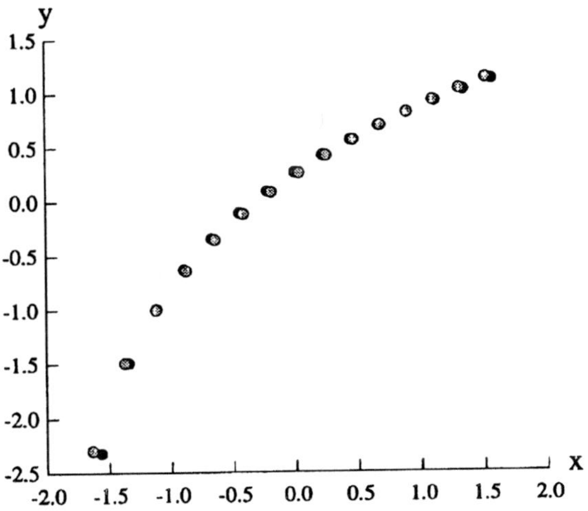

Figure 5.4. Superimposition of graphs 5.2.b) and 5.3b).

4.0 CONCLUSIONS

In conclusion, individual Box-Cox/Box-Tidwell power transformations for variables x and y can be reliably estimated using the concept of elasticity, and can be interpreted as reexpressing the respective measurement scales in such a way that normality of the frequency distribution for each variable is optimized, with parameter components σ^* and ρ^* bringing the two adjusted measurement scales into better alignment with each other. This elasticity formulation reveals how spatial autocorrelation enters into the problem, and in part links this work to LISA (e.g., Anselin, 1995).

The method presented in §2 can be easily generalized to the multiple exogenous variable case, by treating each variable separately (i.e., without cross-terms). A simultaneous estimation would be substantially more difficult than the individual estimations, and more than likely would not yield remarkably better results. In practice these individual solutions may be good enough; if not, they could serve as initial values for a simultaneous estimation solution. Of note is that σ is common to all elasticities in this more complex case. Equation (28) from van Gastel and Paelinck (1995) could, however, be generalized to

$$\begin{bmatrix} \vdots & \vdots \\ \ln|E_{ik}| & \ln y_i \\ \ln|E_{il}| & \ln y_i \\ \vdots & \vdots \end{bmatrix} \begin{bmatrix} 1 \\ \sigma \end{bmatrix} = \begin{bmatrix} \cdot & & & & \cdot \\ & 1 & 0 & x_k & 0 \\ & 0 & 1 & 0 & x_l \\ \cdot & & & & \cdot \end{bmatrix} \begin{bmatrix} \vdots \\ \ln\left|\frac{\alpha_K \rho_K}{\sigma}\right| \\ \ln\left|\frac{\alpha_l \rho_l}{\sigma}\right| \\ \vdots \\ \rho_k \\ \rho_l \\ \vdots \end{bmatrix} \tag{4.1}$$

allowing the simultaneous estimation of all parameters (except of course b).

REFERENCES

Anselin, L. (1995). "Local indicators of spatial autocorrelation," *Geographical Analysis.* 27: 93-115.

Bailly, A., W. Coffey, J. Paelinck, and M. Polèse. (1992). *The Spatial Econometrics of Services.* Aldershot: Avebury.

Getis, A., and J. Ord. (1992). "The analysis of spatial association by use of distance statistics," *Geographical Analysis.* 24: 189-206.

Griffith, D., and C. Amrhein. (1997). *Multivariate Statistical Analysis for Geographers.* Englewood Cliffs, NJ: Prentice Hall.

Hinkley, D. (1977). "On a quick choice of power transformation," *Applied Statistics.* 26: 67-9.

Johnson, R., and D. Wichern. (1992). *Applied Multivariate Statistical Analysis*, 3rd ed. Englewood Cliffs, NJ: Prentice Hall.

Kobayashi, M., and M. McAleer. (1995). "Power comparisons of tests of linear and loglinear regression models," *TRACE Discussion Paper* TI 95-68. Amsterdam-Rotterdam: The Tinbergen Institute.

Ord, J., and A. Getis. (1995). "Local spatial autocorrelation statistics: distributional issues and an application," *Geographical Analysis.* 27: 286-306.

van Gastle, R., and J. Paelinck. (1995). "Computation of Box-Cox transform parameters: a new method and its application to spatial econometrics," in L. Anselin and R. Florax (eds.), *New Directions in Spatial Econometrics.* Berlin: Springer, pp. 136-155.

CHAPTER 6

IMPROVING THE STEIN-RULE ESTIMATOR OF EACH INDIVIDUAL REGRESSION COEFFICIENT USING THE STEIN VARIENCE ESTIMATOR*

Kazuhiro Ohtani

1.0 INTRODUCTION

A substantial body of literature on regression has focused on estimators which are biased but more precise than the ordinary least squares (OLS) estimator. As is discussed in Paelinck and Klaasseen (1979), estimation of regression parameters is important in spatial econometric models, and the precision of estimation is often measured by the mean square error (MSE). It is well known that when three or more coefficients are estimated simultaneously, the Stein-rule (SR) estimator proposed by Stein (1955) and James and Stein (1961) dominates the OLS estimator in terms of MSE. [Exactly speaking, in terms of predictive MSE.] Further, the positive-part Stein-rule (PSR) estimator dominates the SR estimator in terms of MSE. [See, for example, Judge and Yancey (1986).

However, as is shown in Efron and Morris (1972), and Rao and Shinozaki (1978), the SR estimator does not necessarily dominate the OLS estimator when each individual coefficient is estimated separately. Also, Ohtani and Kozumi (1996) showed that although the PSR estimator dominates the SR estimator even if each individual coefficient is estimated separately, the PSR estimator does not necessarily dominate the OLS estimator.

When our main concern is to estimate the normal variance, the Stein variance estimator proposed by Stein (1964) dominates the usual variance estimator. Following George's (1990) suggestion, Berry (1994) showed that the modified SR (MSR) estimator for the normal mean vector which incorporates the Stein variance estimator in stead of the usual variance estimator dominates the usual SR estimator. Also, in the context of regression, Ohtani (1996) showed that Berry's (1994) MSR estimator is a pre-test estimator after a pre-test for the null hypothesis that all the regression coefficients are zeros, and it can be further modified if a critical value of the pre-test is chosen appropriately.

In this paper, we examine the MSE performance of the MSR estimator for each individual regression coefficient when the Stein variance estimator is used instead of the usual variance estimator. The MSR estimator is a pre-test estimator after a pre-test for the null hypothesis that all the regression coefficients are zeros. As is shown

* The author is grateful to Professors Jean Paelinck, Tony E. Smith and Gustav Kristensen for their useful comments.

later, the MSR estimator reduces to the usual SR estimator when a critical value of the pre-test is zero. It is exactly shown that the MSE of the MSR estimator for each individual regression coefficient decreases as a critical value of the pre-test increases from zero to a certain value. This indicates that the usual SR estimator can be improved by conducting the pre-test with an appropriate critical value even when our concern is to estimate each individual regression coefficient. It is also shown by numerical evaluations that neither the PSR estimator nor the MSR estimator dominates each other in terms of MSE. However, if a particular critical value of the pre-test which guarantees the dominance of the MSR estimator over the SR estimator is used, the MSR estimator has the middle MSE among the SR, PSR and MSR estimators. In final section, we carry out some Monte Carlo experiments, and show that the density function of the MSR estimator with the particular critical value mentioned above is located between the density function of the SR estimator and that of the PSR estimator.

2. 0 ESTIMATORS AND MSE

Consider a linear regression model

$$y = X\beta + \varepsilon, \quad \varepsilon \sim N(0, \sigma^2 I_n), \qquad (1)$$

where y is an $n \times 1$ vector of observations on a dependent variable, X is an $n \times k$ matrix of full rank of observations on nonstochastic independent variables, β is a $k \times 1$ vector of regression coefficients, and ε is an $n \times 1$ vector of normal error terms with $E[\varepsilon] = 0$ and $E[\varepsilon\varepsilon'] = \sigma^2 I_n$.

Following Judge and Yancey (1986), we reparameterize the model (1) as follows:

$$y = Z\gamma + \varepsilon \qquad (2)$$

where $Z = XS^{-1/2}$, $\gamma = S^{1/2}\beta$, and $S^{-1/2}$ is a symmetric matrix such that $S^{-1/2}X'XS^{-1/2} = Z'Z = I_k$. The ordinary least squares (OLS) estimator, the Stein-rule (SR) estimator, and the positive-part Stein-rule (PSR) estimator for γ are respectively

$$c = Z'y, \qquad (3)$$
$$c_{SR} = (1 - ae'e/c'c)c, \qquad (4)$$
$$c_{PSR} = max[0,\ 1 - ae'e/c'c]c, \qquad (5)$$

where $e = y - Zc$, and a is a constant such that $0 \le a \le 2(k-2)/(n-k+2)$ for $k \ge 3$.

If the null hypothesis is $H_0 : \gamma = 0$ and the alternative is $H_1 : \gamma \ne 0$ (*i.e.*, $H_0 : \beta = 0$ and $H_1 : \beta \ne 0$ since $S^{-1/2}$ is nonsingular), then the test statistic for H_0 is

$$F = \frac{c'c/k}{e'e/v'} \qquad (6)$$

where $v = n - k$. Since the residual vector is y itself if the null hypothesis is accepted and it is e if the null hypothesis is rejected, the residual vector after the pre-test for H_0 is

$$e^* = I(c'c/e'e \geq \tau)e + I(c'c/e'e < \tau)y, \tag{7}$$

where $\tau = kF_{k,v}(\alpha)/\upsilon$, $F_{k,v}(\alpha)$ is the upper $100 \times \alpha\%$ critical value of the F distribution, and $I(A)$ is the indicator function such that $I(A) = 1$ if an event A occurs and $I(A) = 0$ otherwise. Noting that $y'y = c'c + e'e$, the modified SR (MSR) estimator which is an extension of Berry's (1994) estimator is

$$\begin{aligned} \hat{\gamma}^* &= I(c'c/e'e \geq \tau)(1 - a_1 e'e/c'c)c \\ &\quad + I(c'c/e'e < \tau)(1 - a_2 y'y/c'c)c \\ &= I(c'c/e'e \geq \tau)(1 - a_1 e'e/c'c)c \\ &\quad + I(c'c/e'e < \tau)[1 - a_2(1 + e'e/c'c)]c, \end{aligned} \tag{8}$$

where $a_1 = (k - 2)/(v + 2)$ and $a_2 = (k - 2)/(n + 2)$. When $\tau = 0$, the MSR estimator reduces to the usual SR estimator.

Let h' be an $1 \times k$ vector with known elements. If h' is the i th row vector of $S^{-1/2}$, then $h'c$, $h'c_{SR}$, $h'c_{PSR}$ and $h'\hat{\gamma}^*$ are the OLS, SR, PSR and MSR estimators for the i th regression coefficient in the original model. Thus, we examine the MSE performance of $h'\hat{\gamma}^*$ etc. hereafter. Since the elements of h' are known, we assume $h'h = 1$ without loss of generality.

The MSE of $h'\hat{\gamma}^*$ is

$$\begin{aligned} MSE(h'\hat{\gamma}^*) &= E[(h'\hat{\gamma}^* - h'\gamma)^2] \\ &= E[(h'\hat{\gamma}^*)^2] - 2h'\gamma E[h'\hat{\gamma}^*] + (h'\gamma)^2. \end{aligned} \tag{9}$$

The first two moments of $\hat{\gamma}^*$ are written as

$$\begin{aligned} E[h'\hat{\gamma}^*] &= E[I(c'c/e'e \geq \tau)(1 - a_1 e'e/c'c)h'c \\ &\quad + I(c'c/e'e < \tau)(1 - a_2(1 + e'e/c'c)h'c)] \\ &= E[I(c'c/e'e \geq \tau)\{h'c - a_1(e'e/c'c)h'c\} \\ &\quad + I(c'c/e'e < \tau)\{(1 - a_2)h'c - a_2(e'e/c'c)h'c\}], \end{aligned} \tag{10}$$

$$\begin{aligned} E[(h'\hat{\gamma}^*)^2] &= E[\{I(c'c/e'e \geq \tau)(1 - a_1 e'e/c'c)h'c \\ &\quad + I(c'c/e'e < \tau)(1 - a_2(1 + e'e/c'c)h'c\}^2] \\ &= E[I(c'c/e'e \geq \tau)\{(h'c)^2 - 2a_1(e'e/c'c)(h'c)^2 + a_1^2(e'e/c'c)^2(h'c)^2\} \\ &\quad + I(c'c/e'e < \tau)\{(1 - a_2)^2(h'c)^2 - 2a_2(e'e/c'c)(h'c)^2 \\ &\quad + 2a_2^2(e'e/c'c)(h'c)^2 + a_2^2(e'e/c'c)^2(h'c)^2\}]. \end{aligned} \tag{11}$$

If we define the funtion $H(m,r;\tau)$ as

$$H(m,r;\tau) = E[I(c'c/e'e) \geq \tau)(e'e/c'c)^m(h'c)^r], \tag{12}$$

then the first two moments of $h'\hat{\gamma}^*$ are written as

$$E[h'\gamma^*] = H(0,1;\tau) - \alpha_1 H(1,1;\tau) + (1-a_2)[H(0,1;0) - H(0,1;\tau)] - a_2[H(1,1;0) - H(1,1;\tau)], \quad (13)$$

$$E[(h'\gamma^*)^2] = H(0,2;\tau) - 2a_1 H(1,2;\tau) + a_1^2 H(2,2;\tau)] + (1-a_2)^2[H(0,2;0) - H(0,2;\tau)] - 2a_2(1-a_2)[H(1,2;0) - H(1,2;\tau)] + a_2^2[H(2,2;0) - H(2,2;\tau)]. \quad (14)$$

As is shown in Ohtani and Kozumi (1995), the explicit formula of $H(m,r;\tau)$ for $r = 2p + \delta(\delta = 0 \text{ or } 1)$ is written as

$$H(m,2p+\delta;\tau) = (2\sigma^2)^p (h'\gamma)^\delta \sum_{i=0}^{\infty} \sum_{j=0}^{\infty} w_i(\theta) w_j(\lambda) G_{i,j+\delta}(m,p;\tau), \quad (15)$$

where

$$G_{ij}(m,p;\tau) = \frac{\Gamma(p+j+1/2)\Gamma(\nu/2+m)\Gamma(k/2+p+i+j-m)}{\Gamma(j+1/2)\Gamma(\nu/2)\Gamma(k/2+p+i+j)} \times I_{1/(1+\tau)}(\nu/2+m, k/2+p+i+j-m), \quad (16)$$

$$w_i(\theta) = \exp(-\theta/2)(\theta/2)^i/i!, \quad \theta = \gamma'(I_k - hh')\gamma/\sigma^2,$$
$$w_j(\lambda) = \exp(-\lambda/2)(\lambda/2)^j/j!, \quad \lambda = (\gamma'h)^2/\sigma^2,$$

and $I_x(a,b)$ is the incomplete beta function ratio defined as

$$I_x(a,b) = [1/B(a,b)] \int_0^x t^{a-1}(1-t)^{b-1} dt. \quad (17)$$

Substituting (13) and (14) in (9), we obtain the formula of $MSE(h'\gamma^*)$. Since $E[h'\gamma^*]$ includes $h'\gamma$ through $H(m,1;\tau)$ and the second term in (9) is $2h'\gamma E[h'\gamma^*]$, the MSE of $h'\gamma^*$ normalized by σ^2 (i.e., $MSE(h'\gamma^*)/\sigma^2$ depends on only λ and $\gamma'\gamma/\sigma^2$ because $\lambda + \theta = \gamma'\gamma/\sigma^2$. In a similar way, the MSE of $h'c_{PSR}$ is obtained:

$$MSE(h'c_{PSR}) = H(0,2;a_1) - 2a_1 H(1,2;a_1) + a_1^2 H(2,2;a_1) - 2(h'\gamma)[H(0,1;a_1) - a_1 H(1,1;a_1)] + (h'\gamma)^2. \quad (18)$$

3. 0 MSE PERFORMANCE

To examine the MSE performance of $h'\gamma^*$, the following formula is useful:

$$\frac{\partial H(m,2p+\delta)}{\partial\tau} = -(2\sigma^2)^p(h'\gamma)^\delta \sum_{i=0}^{\infty}\sum_{j=0}^{\infty} w_i(\theta)w_j(\lambda)$$
$$\times\frac{\Gamma(p+j+\delta+1/2)\Gamma((k+v)/2+p+i+j+\delta)}{\Gamma(j+\delta+1/2)\Gamma(v/2)\Gamma(k/2+p+i+j+\delta)}$$
$$\times\frac{\tau^{k/2+p+i+j-m+\delta-1}}{(1+\tau)^{(v+k)/2+p+i+j+\delta}}. \tag{19}$$

Using (19) and noting that $\lambda = (h'\gamma)^2/\sigma^2$, we have:

$$\frac{\partial MSE(h'\hat{\gamma}^*)}{\partial\tau} = [1-(1-a_2)^2]\frac{\partial H(0,2;\tau)}{\partial\tau}$$
$$-[2a_1-2a_2(1-a_2)]\frac{\partial H(1,2;\tau)}{\partial\tau}$$
$$+[a_1^2-a_2^2]\frac{\partial H(2,2;\tau)}{\partial\tau}$$
$$-2h'\gamma\left\{[1-(1-a_2)]\frac{\partial H(0,1;\tau)}{\partial\tau}-[a_1-a_2]\frac{\partial H(1,1;\tau)}{\partial\tau}\right\}$$
$$= 2\sigma^2\sum_{i=0}^{\infty}\sum_{j=0}^{\infty} w_i(\theta)w_j(\lambda)$$
$$\times\frac{\Gamma((k+v)/2+1+i+j)}{\Gamma(v/2)\Gamma(k/2+1+i+j)}\frac{\tau^{k/2+i+j-2}}{(1+\tau)^{(k+v)/2+i+j+1}}D(\tau) \tag{20}$$

where

$$D(\tau) = -(j+½)\{[1-(1-a_2)^2]\tau^2 - 2[a_1-a_2(1-a_2)]\tau + (a_1^2-a_2^2)\}$$
$$+ a_2\lambda\tau^2 - (a_1-a_2)\lambda\tau$$
$$= D_1(\tau)D_2(\tau), \tag{21}$$

where

$$D_1(\tau) = a_2\tau - (a_1-a_2), \tag{22}$$

$$D_2(\tau) = -(j + ½) \{(2 - a_2)\tau - (a_1 + a_2)\} + \lambda\tau. \tag{23}$$

Since $\lambda\tau \geq 0$, we have

$$D_2(\tau) \geq -(j + ½) [(2 - a_2)\tau - (a_1 + a_2)]. \tag{24}$$

Let τ_1 and τ_2 be the solutions of $D_1(\tau) = 0$ and $(2 - a_2)\tau - (a_1 + a_2) = 0$:

Since $(2 - a_2)\tau - (a_1 + a_2) < 0$ if $\tau < \tau_2$, $D_2(\tau) > 0$ if $\tau < \tau_2$. Also, $D_1(\tau) < 0$ if $\tau < \tau_1$.

$$\tau_1 = \frac{k}{\nu+2}; \qquad \tau = \frac{k-2}{\nu+2}\frac{2n-k+4}{2n-k+6}.$$

Since $\tau_2 < \tau_1$, we see that $D_1(\tau) < 0$ and $D_2(\tau) > 0$ if $\tau < \tau_2$, and thus $\partial MSE(h'\gamma^*)/\partial\tau < 0$ if $\tau < \tau_2$. This indicates that the MSE of the MSR estimator decreases as τ increases from zero to τ_2. Since the MSR estimator reduces to the SR estimator when $\tau = 0$, we have the following theorem.

Theorem 1. The SR estimator is dominated by the MSR estimator with $\tau = \tau_2$.

Although $\tau = \tau_1$ is a necessary condition for the MSE of the MSR estimator to have an extreme point, it is ambiguous whether the MSE has a local maximum or a local minimum at $\tau = \tau_1$. Since more analytical study of the MSE of the MSR estimator seems to be very difficult, we examine the MSE performance of the MSR estimator and the PSR estimator by numerical evaluations.

The parameter values used in the numerical evaluations are:

$k = 3, 5, 8$; $\quad n = 10, 20, 30$
$\gamma'\gamma/\sigma^2 = 0.5, 1.0, 2.0, 5.0, 10.0, 20.0$; $\quad \lambda$ = various values.

The numerical evaluations were executed on an NEC personal computer, using FORTRAN code. The infinite series in (15) converged rapidly with the convergence tolerance of 10^{-12}. The results for $k = 5$ and $n = 20$ are shown in Table 6.1. Since the results in Table 1 are qualitatively typical, we omit to show the results for other values of k and n. Since the MSE of the OLS estimator is unity, the MSR estimator has smaller MSE than the OLS estimator if the entry in Table 6.1 is smaller than unity.

We can confirm from Table 6.1 that the MSR estimator has uniformly smaller MSE than the SR estimator. When $\gamma'\gamma/\sigma^2 \leq 1$, the MSR estimator has smaller MSE than the OLS estimator. However, when $\gamma'\gamma/\sigma^2 \geq 2$, the MSE of the MSR estimator gets larger than unity as λ increases. Although the MSE of the MSR estimator decreases as τ increases from zero to τ_2, it depends on the values of $\gamma'\gamma/\sigma^2$ and λ whether the MSE has a local minimum or a local maximum at $\tau = \tau_1$. For example, when $\gamma'\gamma/\sigma^2 = 0.5$ and $\lambda = 0.0$, the MSE seems to have a local maximum. However, when $\gamma'\gamma/\sigma^2 = 2.0$ and $\lambda = 2.0$, the MSE seems to have a local minimum.

Table 6.1. MSE's of the modified SR estimator and the PSR estimator.

MSE's of the modified SR estimator and the PSR estimator

		τ (size of the pre-test)						
$\frac{\gamma'\gamma}{\sigma^2}$	λ	∞ (.0)	.97 (.05)	.76 (.10)	.29(τ_1) (.52)	.17(τ_2) (.76)	.0(SR) (1.0)	PSR
0.5	.000	.3615	.3844	.3980	.4304	.4281	.4725	.3779
	.050	.3828	.4062	.4198	.4514	.4497	.4962	.3961
	.100	.4040	.4280	.4416	.4723	.4713	.5199	.4142
	.150	.4253	.4498	.4634	.4933	.4929	.5437	.4323
	.200	.4465	.4715	.4852	.5143	.5145	.5674	.4505
	.250	.4678	.4933	.5070	.5353	.5361	.5911	.4686
	.300	.4890	.5151	.5288	.5563	.5577	.6148	.4868
	.350	.5103	.5369	.5506	.5773	.5793	.6385	.5049
	.400	.5315	.5587	.5724	.5983	.6009	.6623	.5230
	.450	.5528	.5804	.5942	.6193	.6225	.6860	.5412
	.500	.5740	.6022	.6160	.6403	.6441	.7097	.5593
1.0	.000	.3691	.3961	.4108	.4437	.4417	.4776	.4013
	.100	.4079	.4359	.4506	.4817	.4808	.5203	.4348
	.200	.4466	.4757	.4904	.5198	.5199	.5629	.4682
	.300	.4854	.5155	.5301	.5578	.5590	.6055	.5016
	.400	.5241	.5553	.5699	.5958	.5981	.6481	.5350
	.500	.5629	.5951	.6097	.6339	.6372	.6908	.5684
	.600	.6016	.6349	.6494	.6719	.6763	.7334	.6019
	.700	.6404	.6746	.6892	.7099	.7154	.7760	.6353
	.800	.6791	.7144	.7290	.7479	.7545	.8187	.6687
	.900	.7179	.7542	.7687	.7860	.7935	.8613	.7021
	1.000	.7566	.7940	.8085	.8240	.8326	.9039	.7355
2.0	.000	.3868	.4224	.4393	.4724	.4708	.4944	.4447
	.200	.4519	.4894	.5060	.5353	.5354	.5638	.5016
	.400	.5170	.5565	.5726	.5981	.5999	.6332	.5584
	.600	.5821	.6235	.6393	.6610	.6644	.7026	.6153
	.800	.6472	.6905	.7059	.7238	.7289	.7720	.6722
	1.000	.7123	.7576	.7726	.7867	.7935	.8414	.7291
	1.200	.7773	.8246	.8392	.8495	.8580	.9108	.7859
	1.400	.8424	.8916	.9059	.9124	.9225	.9802	.8428
	1.600	.9075	.9586	.9725	.9752	.9870	1.0496	.8997
	1.800	.9726	1.0257	1.0392	1.0381	1.0516	1.1190	.9565
	2.000	1.0377	1.0927	1.1058	1.1009	1.1161	1.1885	1.0134

Table 6.1. (continued).

$\frac{\gamma'\gamma}{\sigma^2}$	λ	τ (size of the pre-test)						PSR
		∞	.97	.76	.29(τ_1)	.17(τ_2)	.0(SR)	
		(.0)	(.05)	(.10)	(.52)	(.76)	(1.0)	
5.0	.000	.4446	.5082	.5288	.5586	.5578	.5645	.5507
	.500	.5483	.6146	.6323	.6523	.6535	.6641	.6405
	1.000	.6520	.7209	.7358	.7460	.7491	.7638	.7302
	1.500	.7557	.8272	.8393	.8397	.8447	.8634	.8199
	2.000	.8594	.9336	.9428	.9334	.9403	.9630	.9097
	2.500	.9631	1.0399	1.0463	1.0270	1.0360	1.0627	.9994
	3.000	1.0667	1.1462	1.1498	1.1207	1.1316	1.1623	1.0892
	3.500	1.1704	1.2526	1.2532	1.2144	1.2272	1.2620	1.1789
	4.000	1.2741	1.3589	1.3567	1.3081	1.3228	1.3616	1.2687
	4.500	1.3778	1.4653	1.4602	1.4018	1.4185	1.4613	1.3584
	5.000	1.4815	1.5716	1.5637	1.4955	1.5141	1.5609	1.4482
10.0	.000	.5218	.6310	.6506	.6698	.6696	.6704	.6688
	1.000	.6416	.7455	.7570	.7621	.7629	.7650	.7604
	2.000	.7614	.8600	.8633	.8545	.8562	.8596	.8521
	3.000	.8813	.9745	.9696	.9468	.9495	.9541	.9438
	4.000	1.0011	1.0889	1.0760	1.0392	1.0428	1.0487	1.0354
	5.000	1.1210	1.2034	1.1823	1.1315	1.1362	1.1432	1.1271
	6.000	1.2408	1.3179	1.2886	1.2239	1.2295	1.2378	1.2188
	7.000	1.3606	1.4324	1.3950	1.3162	1.3228	1.3324	1.3104
	8.000	1.4805	1.5469	1.5013	1.4085	1.4161	1.4269	1.4021
	9.000	1.6003	1.6614	1.6076	1.5009	1.5094	1.5215	1.4938
	10.000	1.7202	1.7759	1.7140	1.5932	1.6027	1.6161	1.5854
20.0	.000	.6049	.7767	.7857	.7906	.7906	.7906	.7905
	2.000	.7327	.8611	.8604	.8575	.8576	.8577	.8575
	4.000	.8605	.9455	.9350	.9245	.9247	.9248	.9245
	6.000	.9883	1.0299	1.0097	.9914	.9917	.9919	.9915
	8.000	1.1161	1.1144	1.0843	1.0584	1.0588	1.0590	1.0585
	10.000	1.2440	1.1988	1.1590	1.1254	1.1258	1.1262	1.1255
	12.000	1.3718	1.2832	1.2337	1.1923	1.1929	1.1933	1.1925
	14.000	1.4996	1.3676	1.3083	1.2593	1.2600	1.2604	1.2595
	16.000	1.6274	1.4520	1.3830	1.3263	1.3270	1.3275	1.3265
	18.000	1.7553	1.5364	1.4577	1.3932	1.3941	1.3946	1.3935
	20.000	1.8831	1.6208	1.5323	1.4602	1.4611	1.4617	1.4605

Comparing the MSR estimator with $\tau = \tau_2$ and the PSR estimator, the PSR estimator dominates the MSR estimator with $\tau = \tau_2$. However, comparing the MSR estimator with $\tau \geq 0.76$ (i.e., $\alpha \leq 0.1$) and the PSR estimator, neither the MSR estimator nor the PSR estimator dominates each other. For example, the MSR estimator with $\tau = \infty$ has smaller MSE than the PSR estimator when λ is close to zero. However, as λ increases from zero, the MSE of the MSR estimator gets larger than that of the PSR estimator.

Although the MSR estimator with $\tau = \tau_2$ dominates the MSR estimator with $\tau < \tau_2$ which includes the SR estimator as a special case, the MSE performance of the MSR estimator with $\tau > \tau_2$ cannot be examined analytically. Thus, if we want to select the best MSR estimator among the class of the MSR estimators which are theoretically guaranteed to dominate the SR estimator, we may select the MSR estimator with $\tau = \tau_2$. In this case, the MSR estimator has the middle MSE among the SR, PSR and MSR estimators.

4.0 SOME MONTE CARLO EXPERIMENTS

In the previous section, it is shown that the MSR estimator is the middle MSE among the SR, PSR and MSR estimators in terms of MSE if $\tau = \tau_2$ is used. Although there are so many studies of the bias and MSE performances of the SR estimator and its variants, the studies of the distribution of the SR estimator itself are rather limited. Some examples are Ullah (1982) and Phillips (1984). Ullah (1982) derived the asymptotic distribution of the SR estimator, and Phillips (1984) derived the exact density function of $h'c_{SR}$. However, the formula shown in Phillips (1984) is very complicated and it is very difficult to execute numerical evaluations because he derived the density function using the fractional calculus. Also, the exact density functions of the PSR and MSR estimators have not been derived yet. Thus, we examine the shapes of the density functions of the SR, PSR, and MSR estimators by Monte Carlo experiments. Since it is shown theoretically that the MSR estimator with $\tau = \tau_2$ dominates the MSR estimator with $\tau < \tau_2$, we consider only the MSR estimator with $\tau = \tau_2$ in this section, except for the usual SR estimator *(i.e.,* $\tau = 0$*)*. Also, we examine the density functions for the first component of γ *(i.e.,* γ_1*)*.

The method of Monte Carlo experiments is as follows:

(1) For $n = 20$, $k = 5$, $\gamma'\gamma/\sigma^2 = 5$ and $\sigma = 1$, two sets of the values of γ_i are used:

$$\text{Case of } \lambda = 0.5; \gamma_1 = \sqrt{0.5} \doteq 0.707, \gamma_2 = \gamma_3 = \gamma_4 = \sqrt{4.5/4} \doteq 1.061.$$

$$\text{Case of } \lambda = 4.5; \gamma_1 = \sqrt{4.5} \doteq 2.121, \gamma_2 = \gamma_3 = \gamma_4 = \sqrt{0.5/4} \doteq 0.354.$$

(2) Using the above parameter values, the values of the dependent variable are generated from $y_t = \Sigma^k_{i=1} x_{it}\beta_i + \varepsilon_t$ where ε_t's are drawn from a standard normal random number generator, and x_t's are generated by the same random number generator. The number of replications is 1,000,000, where x_t's are fixed in each replication.

(3) The interval [-4, 6] are divided into 50 sub-intervals with equal length of 0.2. We count the frequency with which the estimates of the first components of the SR, PSR, and MSR estimators fall within each sub-interval, and draw the polygons from the frequency distributions whose total areas are adjusted to unity. These polygons are the empirical density functions of the estimators.

The results are shown in Figures 6.1 and 6.2. For comparison, the exact density function of the OLS estimator is also shown in the figures. Since the empirical density function of the OLS estimator almost overlaps with the exact one, we do not show it. The empirical MSE's of the OLS, SR, PSR and MSR estimators were also calculated. The results are as follows: 1.0033(OLS), 0.6654(SR), 0.6430(PSR), 0.6522(MSR) for $\lambda = 0.5$; and 1.0068(OLS), 1.4690(SR), 1.3626(PSR), 1.4241(MSR) for $\lambda = 4.5$. Comparing these values with the corresponding entries in Table 6.1, the Monte Carlo results seem to be reasonably accurate. We also calculated the total MSE of the estimators (*i.e.*, $E(C_{SR}-\gamma)'(C_{SR}-\gamma)$, *etc.*) and obtained the following results: 5.0266(OLS), 3.8299(SR), 3.6665(PSR), 3.7573(MSR) for $\lambda = 0.5$; *5.0175*(OLS), 3.8317(SR), 3.6601(PSR), 3.7561(MSR) for $\lambda = 4.5$. Although the MSE's of the first component of the SR, PSR, and MSR estimators are larger than that of the OLS estimator for $\lambda = 4.5$, the total MSE'S of the SR, PSR and MSR estimators are less than that of the OLS estimator. This result coincides with the well known dominance results of the SR, PSR and MSR estimators over the OLS estimator.

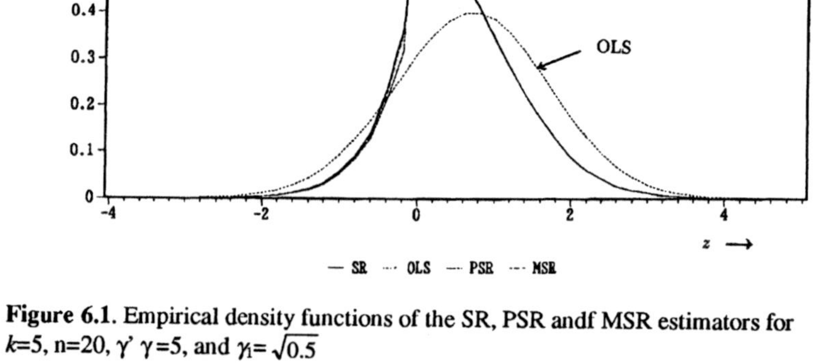

Figure 6.1. Empirical density functions of the SR, PSR andf MSR estimators for k=5, n=20, $\gamma'\gamma$=5, and $\gamma_1=\sqrt{0.5}$

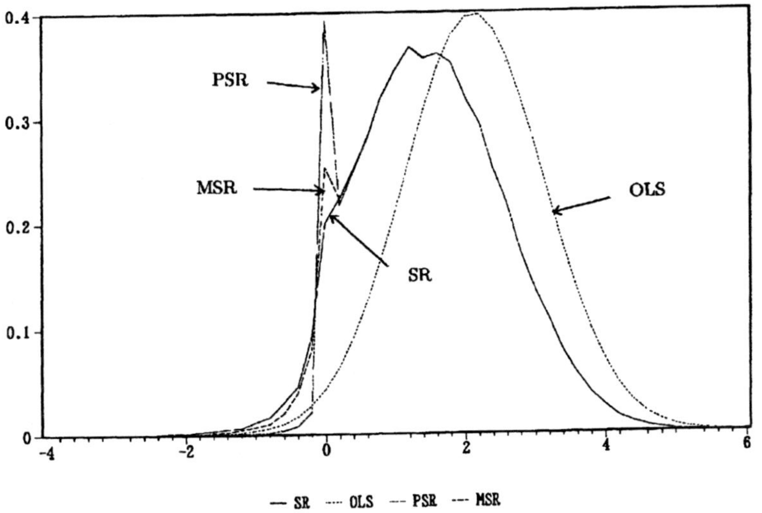

Figure 6.2. Empirical density functions of the SR, PSR and MSR estimators for k=5, n=20, $\gamma'\gamma$=5, and $\gamma_1=\sqrt{4.5}$

From Figure 6.1, we see that when $\gamma_1 = \sqrt{0.5}$, the distributions of the SR, PSR and MSR estimators are skewed to the right, and the distribution of the PSR estimator concentrates most in the mode and the SR estimator least. Since the biases of these three estimators are almost the same and the PSR estimator has the most sharp mode, the PSR estimator has the smallest MSE and, similarly, the MSR estimator has the smaller MSE than the SR estimator.

From Figure 6.2, we see that when $\gamma = \sqrt{4.5}$, the distributions of the SR, PSR and MSR estimators are skewed to the right, and the density funtions are almost the same for $z \geq 0.6$. Also, the distributions of the PSR and MSR estimators have the second mode at $z = 0$. The second mode of the PSR estimator seems to be caused by the truncation at $z = 0$ (*i.e.*, $max[0,1 - a_1e'e/c'c]$), and the second mode of the MSR estimator seems to be caused by the pre-test for H_0: $\gamma = 0$. Since the second mode of the PSR estimator is much higher than that of the MSR estimator, the effect of the truncation in the PSR estimator seems to be stronger than that of the pre-test in the MSR estimator. Although the SR estimator does not have the second mode at $z = 0$, the left tail of the SR estimator is fattest, and that of the PSR estimator is thinnest. This may be the reason that the PSR estimator has the smallest MSE and the MSR estimator has the smaller MSE than the SR estimator, while the PSR and MSR estimators have the second mode at $z = 0$.

Figures 6.1 and 6.2 show that the density function of the MSR estimator is located between the density function of the SR estimator and that of the PSR estimator. This fact seems to be the reason that the MSR estimator has the middle MSE among the SR, PSR, and MSR estimators.

REFERENCES

George, E.I. (1990). Comments on "Decision theoretic varience estimation," by Maata and Casella, *Statistical Science*, 5, 107-109.

Berry, J.C. (1994). Improving the James-Stein estimator using the Stein varience estimator, *Statistics and Probability Letters*, 20, 241-245.

Efron, B. and C. Morris. (1973). Combining possibly related estimation problems, *Journal of the Royal Statistical Society*, Series B 35, 379-402.

James, W. and C. Stein. (1961). Estimation with quadratic loss, *Proceedings of the Fourth Berkeley Symposium on Mathematical Statistics and Probability* 1, (Berkeley, University of California Press), 361-379.

Judge, G.G. and T.A. Yancey. (1986). *Improved Methods of Inference in Econometrics*, (Amsterdam, North-Holland).

Ohtani, K. (1996). Further improving the Stein-rule estimator using the Stein varience estimator in a misspecified linear regression model, *Statistics and Probability Letters*, 29, 191-199.

Ohtani, K. and H. Kozumi.(1996). The exact general formulae for the moments and the MSE dominance of the Stein-rule estimator and positive-part Stein-rule estimators, *Journal of Econometrics*, 74, 273-287.

Paelinck, J.H.P. and L.H. Klaassen. (1979). *Spatial Econometrics*, (Westmead, Saxon House).

Phillips, P.C.B. (1984). The exact distribution of the Stein-rule estimator, *Journal of Econometrics*, 25, 123-131.

Rao, C.R. and N. Shinozaki. (1978). Precision of individual estimators in simultaneous estimation of parameters, *Biometrika*, 65, 23-30.

Stein, C. (1956). Inadmissibility of the usual estimator for the mean of a multivariate normal distribution, *Proceedings of the Third Berkeley Symposium on Mathematical Statistics and Probability* 1, (Berkeley, University of California Press), 197-206.

Ullah, A. (1974). On the sampling distribution of improved estimators for coefficients in linear regression, *Journal of Econometrics*, 2, 143-150.

PART TWO

SPATIAL ANALYSIS AND METHODS

CHAPTER 7

A SPATIAL VERSION OF THE CHI-SQUARE GOODNESS-OF-FIT TEST AND ITS APPLICATION TO TESTS FOR SPATIAL CLUSTERING

Peter A. Rogerson

1.0 INTRODUCTION

Whether observed spatial data conform to our expectations has long been a central question of spatial analysis. Departures of observations from complete spatial randomness may be tested in a number of ways, for both point data and area data. A useful review is provided by Bailey and Gattrell (1995).

Tests of spatial clustering may be categorized as either "general" tests that are designed to detect departures from randomness in the study region as a whole, or "focused" tests, which are designed to detect unusually high or low values of a variable around a predefined point (Besag and Newell 1991). Examples of the former include global statistics, such as the nearest neighbor statistic and Moran's I; examples of the latter include tests described by Diggle (1990) and Lawson (1993). Besag and Newell also refer to tests for the detection of clustering -- here the objective is to detect localized "hotspots" in the data, with no *a priori* specification of where they might occur. An early test for the detection of clustering is the exploratory, geographical analysis machine of Openshaw (1987); subsequent refinements are described by Besag and Newell (1991), and by Fotheringham and Zhan (1996). Kulldorf and Nagarwalla (1994) describe a spatial scan statistic based on the likelihood ratio that is also aimed at the detection of clusters. Local statistics (Anselin, 1995), such as the G_i statistic developed by Getis and Ord (1992) are also well suited for this purpose.

In this paper, a global statistic for general tests of spatial clustering is developed. The statistic is related to Oden's (1995) recent modification of Moran's I, and is a special case of the test recently suggested by Tango (1995). The form of this statistic represents a generalization of the well-known chi-square goodness-of-fit test.

The remainder of the paper is organized as follows. The next section summarizes both Oden's revision of Moran's I to account for regional variations in population density and Tango's test for the detection of general clustering. The third section focuses upon the development of a spatial chi-square test, and its application to general tests for clustering. The final section contains a summary of the results and discussion.

Much of the discussion that follows is phrased in terms of the study of disease patterns, though application may easily be extended to other phenomena.

2.0 ODEN'S I_{pop} AND TANGO'S C_G STATISTICS

Oden's I_{pop}

In studying the spatial pattern of disease, it is common to use Moran's I statistic:

$$I = \frac{m \sum\sum z_i z_j w_{ij}}{(\sum\sum w_{ij}) \sum z_i^2},$$

where $z_i = x_i - \bar{x}$, and x_i is the disease rate in subregion i. A weight w_{ij} is assigned to each pair of subregions, in accordance with that pair's importance in measuring spatial autocorrelation. By convention, w_{ii} is set equal to zero. The observed statistic is then compared with the critical values associated with the null distribution of I. The derivation of the null distribution of I and the appropriate critical values depend upon one of two assumptions about the x_i values -- either they all come from a particular parent distribution, or every permutation of the x_i values across regions is taken to be equally likely. Neither of these assumptions will hold in most cases. The primary culprit is varying regional population sizes. Even when all regions have identical expected values, disease rates in smaller regions will be more variable. This implies that regional rates come from different parent distributions, and that permutations of regional rates are not equally likely[1]. The consequence of this is that the null distribution is no longer valid, and conclusions based on Moran's I may be misleading.

Oden supplies a solution to the problem, considering a modified Moran statistic that includes not only terms related to spatial pattern but also a term related to within subregion variability. Oden's statistic is

$$I_{pop} = \frac{n^2 \sum\sum w_{ij}(r_i - p_i)(r_j - p_j) - n(1 - 2\bar{b}) \sum w_{ii} r_i - n\bar{b} \sum w_{ii} p_i}{S_0 \bar{b}(1 - \bar{b})},$$

where

$$S_0 = x^2 A - xB,$$
$$A = \sum\sum p_i p_j w_{ij},$$
$$B = \sum p_i w_{ii},$$

and where $p_i = x_i / x$ is the expected proportion of cases in region i (taken, e.g., as the proportion of the population residing in county i), and $r_i = n_i / n$ is the observed proportion of all disease cases found in region i. The quantity $\bar{b}$ is defined as the overall

[1] Besag and Newell provide a thorough discussion of this point.

prevalence rate, and is equal to n/x. The expected value and variance of I_{pop} are as follows:

$$E[I_{pop}] = -\frac{1}{x-1}$$

and

$$V[I_{pop}] \approx \frac{2A^2 + C/2 - E}{A^2 x^2},$$

where

$$A = \sum\sum p_i p_j w_{ij}$$

$$C = \sum\sum p_i p_j (w_{ij} + w_{ji})^2$$

$$E = \sum_i p_i \left[\sum_j p_j (w_{ij} + w_{ji}) \right]^2$$

The null hypothesis of no clustering is then tested by assuming that I_{pop} has a normal distribution under H_0.

Oden designed his test by first constructing a Moran's I statistic that was based upon individuals, rather than regional values, thereby also capturing "within region" variation. He then simplified the resulting expression to get the equation above. The merits of the test include its ability to capture both within region variability and the spatial covariation of nearby regions. Oden finds that I_{pop} is more powerful than both Moran's I and the chi-square goodness-of-fit test. Griffith (1992) also discusses this case where the variable of interest has a non-constant varaince across regions.

Tango's C_G Statistic

Tango has suggested a test for general clustering that is based upon the observed and expected proportion of cases in each region. For a study area with n subregions and a disease rate of λ across the entire population, the expected number of cases is proportional to ξ_i, the population size of region i:

$$H_0: E[N_i] = l x_i, \quad i = 1,2,\ldots,m,$$

Let $\mathbf{r}$ and $\mathbf{p}$ be mx1 vectors containing the observed and expected proportions of cases in regions 1,2,...,m, respectively. Tango's statistic is

$$C_G = (\mathbf{r}-\mathbf{p})' W (\mathbf{r}-\mathbf{p}),$$

where $\mathbf{W}$ is an mxm matrix containing elements w_{ij} that measure the closeness of region i to region j. These elements could be, for example, either zero or one depending on contiguity (as is commonly done in measuring spatial autocorrelation), or they might be taken as a function of distance between region centroids. Tango adopts the latter approach, defining

$$w_{ij} = exp(-d_{ij} / t), \quad i \neq j$$

with w_{ii}=1, and d_{ij} equals the distance between i and j. The parameter τ is related to "friction of distance" and hence the size of the cluster, with larger values of τ corresponding to larger clusters. In summation form,

$$C_G = \sum_i \sum_j w_{ij} \left(r_i - p_i \right) \left(r_j - p_j \right)$$

Thus C_G is a weighted sum, across pairs of regions, of the deviations between observed and expected proportions. Tango gives the expected value and variance of C_G as

$$E[C_G] = \frac{1}{N} Tr(W V_{.p})$$

and

$$V[C_g] = \frac{2}{N^2} Tr(W V_p)^2 ,$$

where N is the total number of cases. Also,

$$V_p = D(p) - pp'$$

with Δ(p) defined as an mxm diagonal matrix containing the elements of **p** on the diagonal.

Under the null hypothesis, C_G is approximately distributed as chi-square. In particular, the quantity

$$n + \frac{C_G - E[C_G]}{\sqrt{V[C_G]}} \sqrt{2n}$$

has approximately a chi-square distribution with υ degrees of freedom, where υ is equal to

$$n = \left(\frac{Tr(W V_p^2)^{1.5}}{Tr(W V_p^3)} \right)^2 .$$

In both cases, the matrix conveying information on connectivity between regions is given a priori.

3.0 A SPATIAL VERSION OF THE CHI-SQUARE GODDNESS-OF-FIT STATISTIC

In this section, the merits of the following statistic are explored:

$$R = \sum_i \sum_j w_{ij} \frac{(r_i - p_i)(r_j - p_j)}{\sqrt{p_i \; p_j}} .$$

The statistic R is both a simplification of Oden's I_{pop} and a special case of Tango's C_G statistics. R may be viewed as a special case of C_G, where the original weight matrix **W** is modified to contain elements equal to their original value, each divided by the quantity $\sqrt{p_i p_j}$ R is also a simplification of I_{pop}; in particular, Oden notes that R is a major contributor to the numerator of I_{pop} for the case where the original weights have been divided by $\sqrt{p_i p_j}$. Oden refers to this quantity as a "spatialized chi-square," though he does not discuss the statistical distribution of R.

Note that the R may be decomposed as follows:

$$R = \sum_i w_{ii} \frac{(r_i - p_i)^2}{p_i} + \sum \sum_{i \neq j} w_{ij} \frac{(r_i - p_i)(r_j - p_j)}{\sqrt{p_i p_j}}$$

$$= R_{X^2} + R_I .$$

In measuring deviations from expected values in a spatial pattern, the statistic R thus counts contributions from two separate sources: (a) differences between observed and expected values within each region, and (b) covariation in the differences between observed and expected values across pairs of regions (where the weight associated with each pair is w_{ij}). Accounting for these two sources of variation was the rationale for Oden's original derivation of I_{pop}. Source (a) is identical to the aspatial chi-square goodness-of-fit statistic when the w_{ii} are equal, while source (b) is captured by Moran's I. For example, consider the two maps in Figure 7.1. Both maps could conceivably yield identical chi-square values, since each map has three regions that contribute heavily to the chi-square statistic and four regions that make only small contributions to it. But the usual chi-square goodness-of-fit does not account for *where* the individual contributions to its sum come from; thus spatial patterns at the regional scale may not be detected with it. Similarity of the contributions made by adjacent or nearby regions is not information that is included in the calculation of the aspatial chi-square statistic. The statistic, does, however, pick up patterns when there are sufficient regional differences between observed and expected values (regardless of the spatial pattern of the differences).[2]

---

[2] Fingleton (1983, 1986) discusses how the aspatial chi-squared test can be corrected to account for spatial observations that are not dependent.

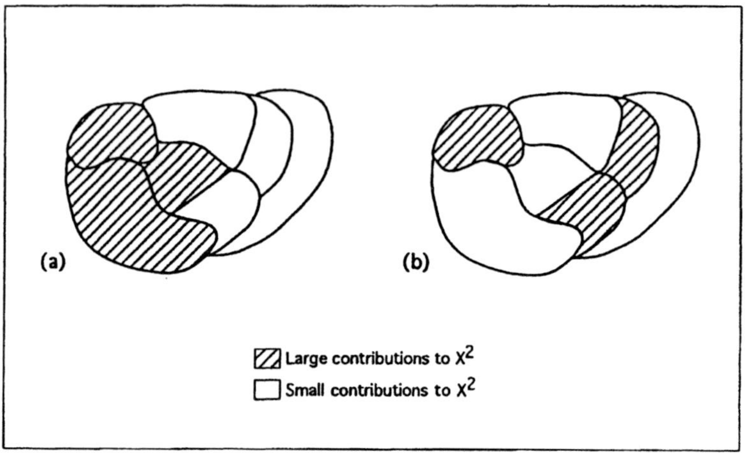

Figure 7.1. Example of similar chi-square values obtained from differing regional patterns of deviations between observed and expected values.

Moran's I has just the opposite characteristics -- it can detect similarity (or dissimilarity) among the nearby pairs of regions, but by convention does not account for the magnitude of deviations between observed and expected values *within* regions. The two scenarios in Figure7.2 could lead to very similar I values, yet in panel (a) the pattern is not far from random, while in panel (b) it is.

Oden's I_{pop}, Tango's C_G, and R all have the advantage of accounting for both of these elements of pattern. R is conceptually appealing as a special case of C_G and a simplification of I_{pop} since it is a natural generalization of the aspatial chi-square goodness-of-fit test.

The Null Distribution of R

Since R may be viewed as a special case of C_G, we have the following for the mean and variance of R:

$$E[R] = \frac{1}{n} Tr(\mathbf{W} \mathbf{V}_p)$$

$$V[R] = \frac{2}{n^2} Tr(\mathbf{W} \mathbf{V}_p)^2$$

where the elements of the weight matrix **W** are now taken as the set of original elements, each divided by the quantity $\sqrt{p_i p_j}$. Two possibilities for the distribution of R under the null hypothesis suggest themselves. Oden uses the mean and variance of I_{pop} and takes I_{pop} to be normally distributed under H_0; since R is a major component of I_{pop}, it is

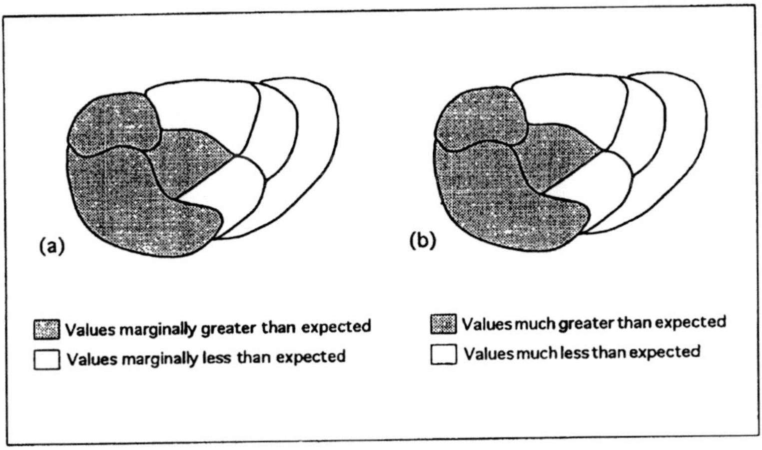

Figure 7.2. Example of similar *I* values obtained from differeing magnitudes of deviation between observed and expected values.

natural to explore whether the normal distribution can be used as an approximation to the sampling distribution of *R*. Alternatively, we can consider Tango's argument that the distribution of $(\mathbf{r}-\mathbf{p})'\mathbf{W}(\mathbf{r}-\mathbf{p})$ may have substantial skewness, and consequently we can consider Tango's chi-square approximation for the null distribution of *R*.

Several Monte Carlo experiments were carried out to assess the relative merits of these two alternatives. Centroids of regions were chosen by randomly locating points within a square. Populations were assigned to centroids by randomly drawing them from a lognormal distribution. Weights were chosen to be negative exponential functions of distance. Finally, disease cases were assigned to centroids at random, and in proportion to population size.

Table 7.1 summarizes the results from these experiments. Each scenario described in the table was replicated 500 times, and the proportion of times the null hypothesis was rejected is reported. In most cases, these proportions are quite close to their nominal values. In addition there is no clearcut "winner" -- the normal and chi-square approximations yield roughly similar, satisfactory results. Figure 7.3 depicts probability plots for the normal and chi-square approximations. The 1,000 observations in the figure represent 1,000 simulated values of *R* under H_0. Although the chi-square approximation provides a better fit to the entire distribution, both the normal and the chi-square distributions fit the upper tail well. Though Figure 7.3 represents the outcome of 1,000 repetitions of a particular scenario (characterized by given population location and sizes), it is typical of the outcome for other scenarios. These findings suggest that on the basis of simplicity, the normal distribution may be employed to test the null hypothesis.

Table 7.1. Results of Monte Carlo simulations of the distribution of R Under H_0.

Regions	No. of Cases	Proportion of Null Hypotheses Rejected	
		Using Normal	Using Chi-Square
10	50	.044	.050
10	50	.062	.062
10	100	.052	.054
10	100	.050	.060
20	100	.044	.046
20	100	.052	.058
20	200	.042	.052
50	50	.056	.044
50	50	.056	.048
50	50	.088	.096
50	100	.052	.058
50	200	.052	.066
50	200	.042	.044
50	500	.062	.032

Comparative Power of C_G, I^*_{pop}, and R

Monte Carlo simulation was also used to assess the relative power of each statistic. This time, the relative likelihood of a case being assigned to a particular centroid was raised threefold at a single prespecified centroid. Relative risk was then assumed to decline exponentially with distance away from the centroid. Following a similar experiment conducted by Tango, when the relative risks assigned to centroids in this manner were less than 1.5, these centroids were reassigned relative risks equal to the background value of 1.0. Six scenarios, each characterized by particular centroid locations and population sizes, were examined. For each scenario, 500 replications of the disease process were simulated, and the statistics R, I_{pop}, and C_G were calculated for each repetition. Each of the six scenario has 50 regions, defined by their randomly placed centroid locations.

Table 7.2 displays for each of the several scenarios the proportion of times that the null hypothesis of no pattern was rejected. In all cases, R performed similarly to I^*_{pop} (defined as I_{pop}, where the weights have been divided by $\sqrt{p_i p_j}$. This is not surprising, since R is a major component of I^*_{pop}. The comparison of the relative merits of R and C_G is more complex, since there were cases where R performed better (scenarios A through D) and cases where C_G performed better (scenarios E and F).

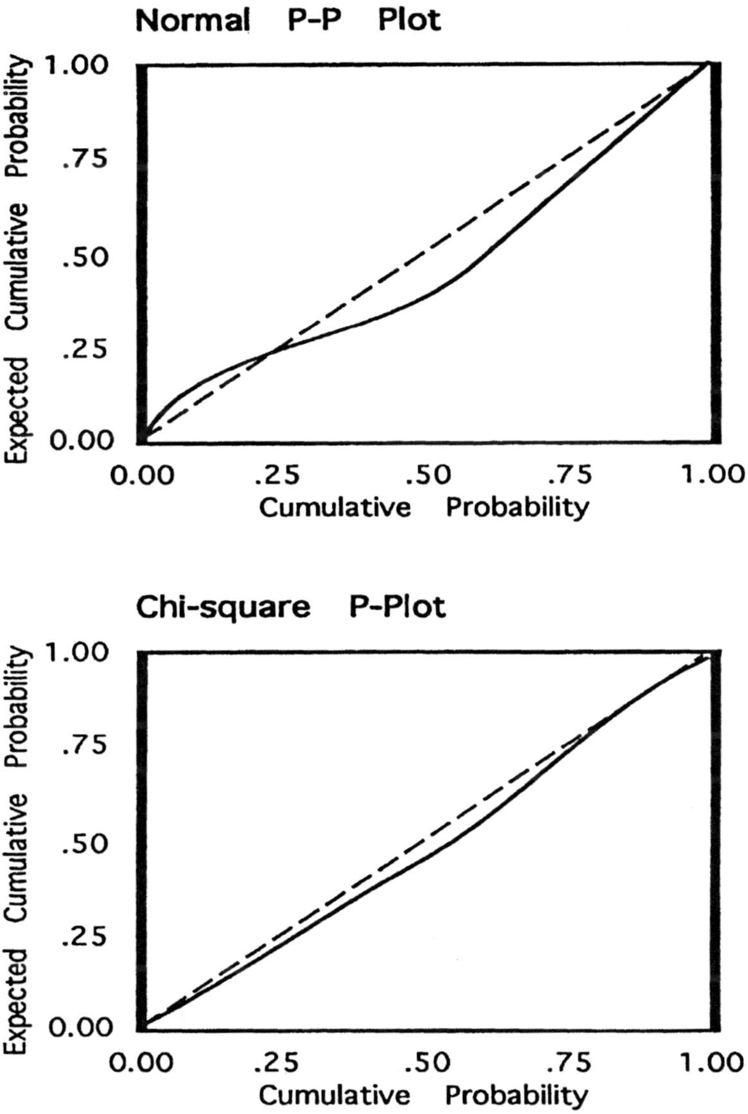

Figure 7.3. Probability plots for the normal and chi-square distributions.

Table 7.2. Comparative Power of R, I_{pop}, and C_G

Cases	R	C_G	I_{pop}	
50	.146	.074	.104	
100	.230	.138	.136	Scenario A
200	.372	.194	.364	
600	.858	.596	.864	
50	.192	.142	.172	
100	.262	.176	.258	Scenario B
200	.500	.328	.510	
600	.954	.846	.966	
50	.278	.130	.284	
100	.444	.242	.478	Scenario C
200	.738	.478	.708	
600	.998	.948	.996	
50	.164	.088	.144	
100	.232	.126	.264	Scenario D
200	.394	.212	.408	
600	.872	.634	.854	
50	.362	.662	.368	
100	.702	.926	.732	Scenario E
200	.972	.998	.966	
600	1.00	1.00	1.00	
50	.176	.594	.168	
100	.412	.890	.408	Scenario F
200	.816	.994	.802	
600	1.00	1.00	1.00	

Comparison of the scenario characteristics reveals that C_G fares better when the relative population size of the centroid of highest relative risk is relatively large. R performs better when the deviations between observed and expected numbers of cases is largest in small population centers. The relative locations and population sizes for scenarios C and F are shown in Figures 7.4 and 7.5. In each figure, a circle is centered upon the centroid where the relative risk is raised threefold, and in each figure the circle encompasses all surrounding centroids where the relative risk is greater than 1.5.

These differences in performance can also be seen for the case of aspatial frequency data. The usual aspatial chi-square goodness-of-fit test is relatively better at rejecting alse hypotheses when the deviations between observed and expected values are largest in those categories where the expected value is small. In contradistinction, using the sum of squared deviations between observed and expected values (analogous to the aspatial

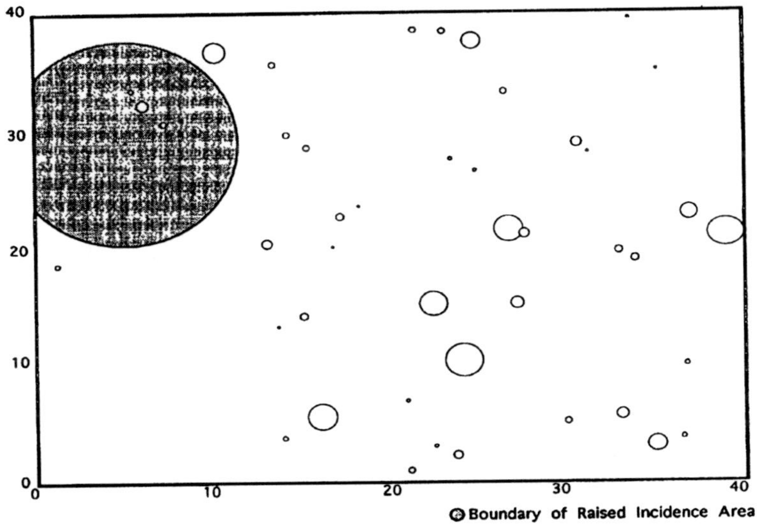

Figure 7.4. Relative locations and sizes of centroids: Scenario F.

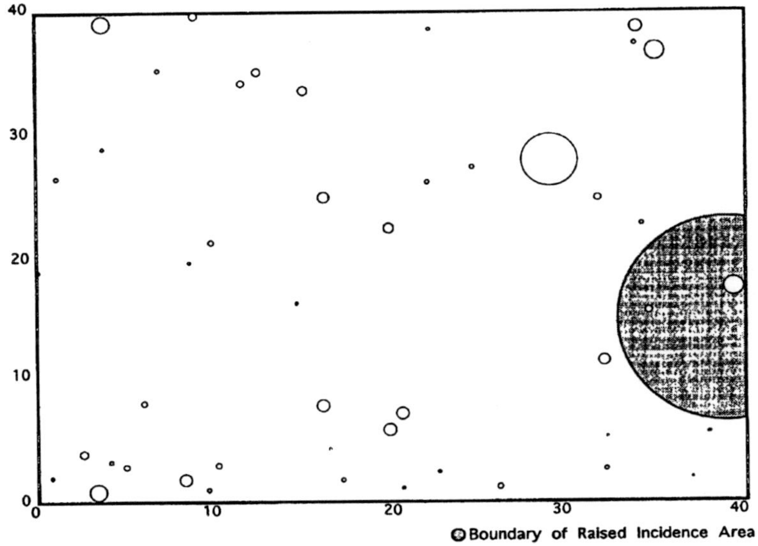

Figure 7.5. Relative locations and sizes of centroids: Scenario C.

between observed and expected values are largest for those categories with relatively high expected values.

Components of R

When the observed value of R is greater than its critical value and the null hypothesis is rejected, it may be of interest to explore the relative size of the contributions made by the two sources of deviations from the expected values described earlier in this section.

To illustrate, the results of three selected simulated scenarios are reported; each scenario consisted of 20 regions and 100 cases. In each scenario, the disease rate was increased threefold around a designated center, with the magnitude of the risk decaying exponentially away from the center. Scenarios 1 and 2 have a relatively steeper exponential decline in the risk (τ=20) than does scenario 3 (τ=5). Table 7.3 reveals that in all three scenarios, the observed value of R is significant; the null hypothesis is rejected since p<0.05. In scenario 1, each of the components has observed values near its respective critical value, indicating that both components contribute roughly equally to the rejection of H_0. In scenario 2, the aspatial chi-square component is the overwhelming contributor to the rejection of H_0. Finally, in scenario 3, where the cluster is larger due to a flatter exponential decay, the covariation of the deviations between observed and expected values between nearby places is the primary contributor to the significant value of R.

Table7.3. p-values for R and its components for three scenarios.

Scenario	p-values		
	Overall R	R_{x^2}	R_I
1	.010	.062	.082
2	.012	.003	.626
3	<.001	.457	<.001

When the aspatial chi-square component is the only strong contributor to R, then the cluster or clusters responsible for rejecting H_0 are small in its/their spatial extent -- strong covariations between regions do not appear, while the deviations within regions are substantial. Similarly, when regional covariations among the deviations are the primary contributor to a large observed value of R, then a larger cluster or set of clusters is responsible for the rejection of H_0.

An alternative way to assess the relative importance of the components for a number of replications would be to regress R on R_{x_2}, R_I and an interaction term, $R_{x_2} * R_I$. The coefficients would not be of particular interest, but the relative partitioning of the variance would reveal which component was most important in explaining the variation in R across replications.

4.0 SUMMARY AND DISCUSSION

The statistic R is a spatial version of the chi-square goodness-of-fit statistic, accounting for deviations between observed and expected values within regions, and also for the covariation of the deviations among nearby pairs of regions. Oden originally noted that R is a spatial chi-square statistic, but left its behavior unexplored. R may also be interpreted as a special case of Tango's C_G, where the weights are appropriately defined.

In the simulations examined, R consistently performed in a manner similar to I^*_{pop}. Given that R is both simpler and has a natural conceptual interpretation as a spatial chi-square statistic, it would seem preferable to I_{pop} (though simulations covering a more extensive range of scenarios would of course be desirable to lend further weight to this conclusion). C_G and R are best at detecting clusters in quite different situations, with the former best when clustering occurs around relatively large centers, and the latter best when clustering occurs around relatively smaller centers.

It would be interesting to explore spatial generalizations of other goodness-of-fit measures, such as those related to entropy and information (see, e.g., Knudsen and Fotheringham, 1986). In this regard, it would be useful to ascertain which goodness-of-fit statistics had the greatest statistical power against certain types of alternative hypotheses. The present paper has done this for C_G and R, but other types of spatial goodness-of-fit measures may work better for particular types of clustering.

Also of interest is how the work described here might be extended to the case of focused tests such as Tango's. Here the statistic of interest is the distance-weighted fit, using a chi-square type statistic (or other goodness-of-fit stat) viewed from a point). In this case, a poor "fit" would result either from a large deviation between the observed and expected values at the point of interest, or from a large and positive covariation between the deviations of the point of interest and nearby points. These focused tests could carried out in either a confirmatory mode a la Tango (e.g., around a small number of sites of interest), or in an exploratory mode a la Fotheringham's recent work, which results in maps indicating where the fit is good and where it is not.

REFERENCES

Anselin, L. (1995). "Local indicators of spatial association – LISA." *Geographical Analysis*, 27, 93-115.

Bailey, T., and A. Gattrell. (1995). *Interactive spatial data analysis*. New York: Longman Scientfic and Technical

Besag, J., and J. Newell. (1991). "The detection of clusters in rare diseases." *Journal of the Royal Statistical Society, Series A*, 154, 143-55.

Diggle, P.J. (1990). "A point process modelling approach to raised incidence of a rare phenomenon in the vicinity of a prespecified point." *Journal of the Royal Statistical Society, Series A*, 153, 349-62.

Getis, A., and K. Ord. (1992). "The analysis of spatial association by use of distance statistics." *Geographical Analysis*, 24, 189-206.

Fingleton, B. (1983). "Independence, stationarity, categorical spatial data and the chi-squared test." *Environment and Planning A*, 15, 483-500.

Fingleton, B. (1986). "Analyzing cross-classified data with inherent spatial dependence." *Environment and Planning A*, 18, 48-61.

Fotheringham, A.S., and F.B. Zhan. (1996). "A comparison of three exploratory methods for cluster detection in spatial point patterns." *Geographical Analysis*, 28, 200-18.

Griffith, D.A. (1992). "What is spatial autocorrelation? Reflections on the past 25 years of spatial statistics." *L'Espace geographique*, 265-80.

Knudsen, D., and A.S. Fotheringham. (1986). "Matrix comparison, goodness-of-fit, and spatial interaction modelling." *International regional Science Review*, 10, 127-47.

Kulldorf, M.., and N. Nagarwalla. (1994). "Spatial disease clusters: detection and inference." *Statistics in Medicine*, 14, 799-810.

Lawson, A.B. (1993). "On the analysis of mortality events associated with a prespecified fixed point." *Journal of the Royal Statistical Society, Series A*, 156, 363-77.

Oden, N. (1995). "Adjusting Moran's I for population density." *Statistics in Medicine*, 14, 17-26.

Openshaw, S. (1987). "A Mark 1 Geographical Analysis Machine for the automated analysis of point data sets." *International Journal of Geographical Information Systems* ,1, 359-77.

Tango, T. (1995). "A class of tests for detecting 'eneral' and 'focused' clustering of rare diseases." *Statistics in Medicine*, 14, 2323-2334.

CHAPTER 8

SOME EFFECTS OF SPATIAL AGGREGATION ON MULTIVARIATE REGRESSION PARAMETERS

Harold Reynolds and Carl Amrhein

1.0 INTRODUCTION

The Modifiable Area Unit Problem (MAUP), a term introduced in Openshaw and Taylor's (1979) classic paper, has long been recognized as a potentially troublesome feature of spatially aggregated data, such as census data. Aggregation of unit-level (or other high-resolution) data to lower resolution areas is an almost unavoidable feature of large spatial datasets due to the requirements of privacy and/or data manageability. When the original data are aggregated, the values for the various univariate, bivariate, and multivariate parameters will change because of the loss of information. This phenomenon is called the *scale effect*. The N spatial units to which the higher-resolution data are aggregated, such as census enumeration areas or tracts, postal code districts, or political divisions of various levels, are arbitrarily created by some decision-making process and represent only one of an almost infinite number of ways to partition a region into N zones. Each partitioning will result in different values for the aggregated statistics; this variation in values is known as the *zoning effect*. The two effects are not independent, because the lower-resolution spatial structure may be built from contiguous higher-resolution units, such as census tracts from enumeration areas, and the resulting aggregate statistics will be different for each aggregation.

Several studies (for example, Amrhein and Reynolds, 1976, 1997; Fotheringham and Wong, 1991; Amrhein and Flowerdew, 1993; Openshaw and Taylor, 1979) have been published that study the effects of the MAUP on a number of census datasets. Of these, only Fotheringham and Wong (1991) have examined the effects of the MAUP on multiple regression parameters, pessimistically concluding that its effects on multivariate analysis are essentially unpredictable. Amrhein (1993) presents the results of a statistical simulation of the MAUP by aggregating randomly-generated point data into square grids of various sizes, thus avoiding many of the problems associated with the use of census data. This paper expands upon the ideas from both, using statistical simulations to study the effects of the MAUP on multivariate analysis. The fact that Steel and Holt's (1996) analytically derived rules for random aggregation agree with Amrhein's (1993) empirical rules corroborates that simulations are an effective tool for examining the effects of the MAUP.

2.0 THE SYNTHETIC SPATIAL DATASET GENERATOR

The use of census data imposes a serious constraint upon those who seek to understand the mechanics of the MAUP simply because there is no control over: the nature of a region's overall shape; the shapes, sizes and connectivities of its subregions; or the ranges, means, variances and covariances, frequency distributions, and spatial autocorrelations of the variables. The effects of aggregation on a given census variable can be determined readily enough, but few clues to underlying processes can be gleaned because the data cannot be systematically varied to test for the effects of changes. Other weaknesses of census data, such as random rounding and values missing due to the absence or suppression of data, only serve to make the drawing of any conclusions even more difficult.

In order to study the MAUP, it is therefore advantageous to be able to create synthetic spatial datasets over which a researcher can control and systematically vary all of the above features. For this paper, just such a program was created. A region, whose boundaries are defined by the user, is subdivided into a given number of subregions by a Voronoi tessellation (Okabe et al, 1993), the coordinates of the N generator points of which are independently selected from a uniform random distribution. A set of N random numbers, which can be drawn from a uniform or normal distribution, is created and then appropriately scaled and adjusted to have a desired mean and variance. Random permutations of this set are then created, one for each synthetic variable. Depending on the application, the Moran Coefficient (which will frequently be referred to as MC for brevity) of given variables can be set, the Pearson correlation coefficients between an independent variable (with a given MC) and a set of dependent variables can be set, or a dependent variable (with a given MC) and a set of uncorrelated independent variables, can be created. All of these operations are done by rearranging the locations of the variable values. A summary table of means, variances, MCs, and correlations is displayed, so that if two or more variables' correlations are unacceptably high a different random seed can be chosen to generate a more acceptable dataset. This must be done because the MCs and the Pearson's r for two variables are set sequentially. Figure 8.1 illustrates the region used for the experiments discussed in this paper, which is divided into 400 subregions, along with sample aggregations to 180, 100, and 40 zones.

3.0 THE EXPERIMENTS

Spatial autocorrelation is known to play a key role in the MAUP, as is illustrated in the following experiment. Consider a spatial dataset that contains negative spatial autocorrelation; that is, numbers that are dissimilar are located in adjoining subregions. In the aggregation process, contiguous subregions are joined and the individual variable values are (in this case) replaced by their average, hence creating a new dataset with a reduced variance. With some algebra, it is easy to show that the difference between the original variance and the aggregate variance (weighted by the number of units in each zone) is the sum (again weighted by the

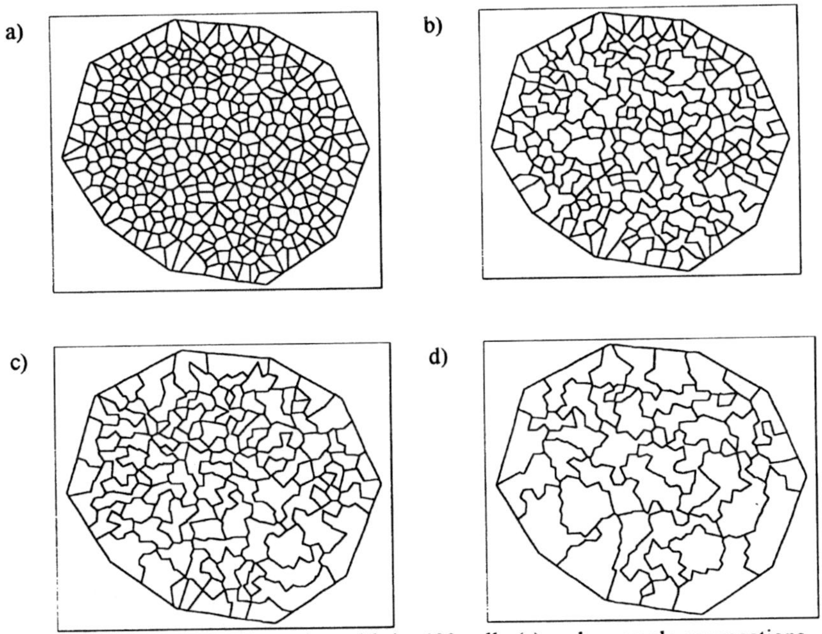

Figure 8. 1. The synthetic region with its 400 cells (a) and a sample aggregations to 180 cells (b), 100 cells (c) and 40 cells (d).

number of units) of the variance of the cells within each zone. For the negatively autocorrelated dataset, it is expected that the values in each cell will have a high variance, and hence the change in variance will be relatively large. As the spatial autocorrelation becomes more positive, the expected internal variance within each cell should decrease, since similar values will tend to become more likely to be adjacent, and hence the change in variance should become less.

The influence of spatial autocorrelation on the behaviour of bivariate and multivariate statistics is more difficult to assess, however. For example, Pearson's correlation coefficient r consists of the covariance between x and y divided by the product of the standard deviations of x and y. Each of these parameters will have a degree of spatial autocorrelation that must be fixed in some way in order to model its effects on the MAUP. It gets even worse for multivariate cases because of the interactions between all the variables.

The experiments explore the effects of aggregation on the various parameters of the linear regression model $y = \beta_0 + \beta_1 x_1 + \beta_2 x_2 + \beta_3 x_3$, as well as other features of interest, with the first two experiments including the effects of spatial autocorrelation. Three independent parameters were considered to be sufficient to capture enough of the complexities involved in multivariate linear regression without creating excessive computational and analytical overhead. Fotheringham and Wong (1991) use a four-variable regression model, in which the variables are all proportions; their results are compared to ours here.

Three different experiments are performed. In the first, y, x_1, x_2, and x_3 are all assigned the same level of spatial autocorrelation (as measured by the MC). Seven datasets are created in which all four variables have MCs of -0.4, -0.2, 0.0, 0.2, 0.4, 0.6, and 0.8 respectively, while keeping them as uncorrelated as possible. This process and others in the subsequent steps of the experiments often require several attempts, since the program is not designed to control both the spatial autocorrelation and the linear correlation at the same time. In the second experiment, x_1, x_2, and x_3 are assigned the same MC, while y is given a different one. Datasets are created with MCs for dependent and independent variables chosen from -0.4, 0.0, 0.4, and 0.8, for a total of twelve combinations, again keeping the correlations as low as possible between variables. Of the 19 sets used in these two experiments, two have a maximum absolute correlation of 0.1169 and two others have one of 0.1032, which are statistically significant (but not markedly so) for a sample size of 400 pairs of normally distributed values. All of these sets have independent variables whose MCs are 0.8. All variables in all data sets are normally distributed and scaled and translated to have a mean of 20.0 and a standard deviation of 4.0. The third experiment involves creating three completely uncorrelated independent variables, whose MCs are close to zero, plus a dependent variable whose MC is set to zero, in order to examine the effects of the MAUP on the collinearity between independent variables. For this dataset, the independent variables are drawn from a N(0,1) distribution and subjected to a varimax rotation to completely remove the correlations between them. Each variable is then scaled and translated to have a mean of 20.0 and a standard deviation of 4.0; these last two operations do not affect the correlations or MCs.

The aggregation algorithm involves the selection of M seed regions at random, then aggregating the other regions to them, with the only constraints being contiguity and attempting to keep the number of regions per zone as uniform as possible. For these experiments, the regions are aggregated to m = 180, 160, 140, 120, 100, 80, 60, and 40 zones, representing from 45% to 10% of the original 400 regions, in order to assess the scale effect of the MAUP. All of these aggregations are performed independently in a run of the model, and each run is independent of the previous runs. To account for the variability of results introduced by the zoning effect, 1000 runs of the model are performed for the first two experiments, and 500 for the third. After each aggregation, the data are fitted by a multiple linear regression model and the resulting parameters, plus the MCs of the residuals, are stored.

Once all aggregations are completed, the maximum, minimum, mean and standard deviation of each parameter for each scale of aggregation are computed and saved for analysis. The analysis plots (see Figure 8.2b as an example) are arranged in groups of eight lines, one line for each scale of aggregation, with the labels for each line being listed in the plot's legend. Each group represents a set of initial conditions for an experiment, and is labeled on the plot. Each line represents the range of values of the parameter that are obtained for the scale over all the runs, and is also marked by the mean value (a heavy dot) and at the mean ± 1 standard deviation (a small horizontal line) to give a rough idea of the distribution of values.

4.0 RESULTS

The results from the first experiment, in which the Moran Coefficients for the dependent and independent variables are the same, show that all of the multivariate regression parameters vary systematically with the change of scale and also with the level of spatial autocorrelation latent in the data. Figures 8.2 to 8.6 illustrate the variations in R^2, the MC of the residuals, and the values for β_0, β_1, β_2, and β_3 and their standard errors. All of the figures show the same pattern, with the ranges for all scales decreasing with increasing spatial autocorrelation. This conforms to expectations, since we expect the scale effect to be less severe with greater positive autocorrelation due to more similar values tending to be aggregated. The figures also show that the variation of all parameter values increases with the magnitude of the scale effect over all levels of spatial autocorrelation. This again agrees with expectations, since more information is lost as the data values are aggregated into fewer zones, and with a larger number of regions going into each zone it is expected that there would be a greater degree of variation in results caused by the choice of partition, even for highly spatially autocorrelated data.

Since all the variables are generated randomly, the values of R^2 for the unaggregated datasets are all close to zero. Figure 8.2a illustrates that aggregation can produce a model that can have, in extreme cases, from 20% to even 80% of the variation explained by the model, depending on the scale of aggregation and the spatial autocorrelation of the data. (Note that the only type of autocorrelation discussed is spatial). The distance of the maximum extreme values from the mean plus one standard deviation mark indicate they are all outliers in the frequency distributions, and as such they will tend to increase the mean value, but even with that in mind it is still apparent that aggregation tends to give models with better fits than the original data, with better fits being associated with greater aggregation. This agrees with expectations, since a reduction in the variability of the data values will tend to produce a better-fitting model.

Figure 8.2b illustrates the change of the spatial autocorrelation of the regression residuals with aggregation. As with the other parameters, the range of variation remains essentially un changed for a given scale over all initial levels of spatial autocorrelation, even though the mean value tends to increase with the spatial autocorrelation of the other variables. There is also a trend, which is more noticeable in the more highly autocorrelated datasets, for the mean value of the distribution to approach zero (random spatial autocorrelation) as the aggregation scale becomes coarser. One of the basic assumptions of a linear regression model is that the residuals are independent, and it is clear that this assumption is being violated since spatially autocorrelated residuals are not independent. The exact reasons behind this behaviour are not obvious, and this remains a matter for further investigation.

a)

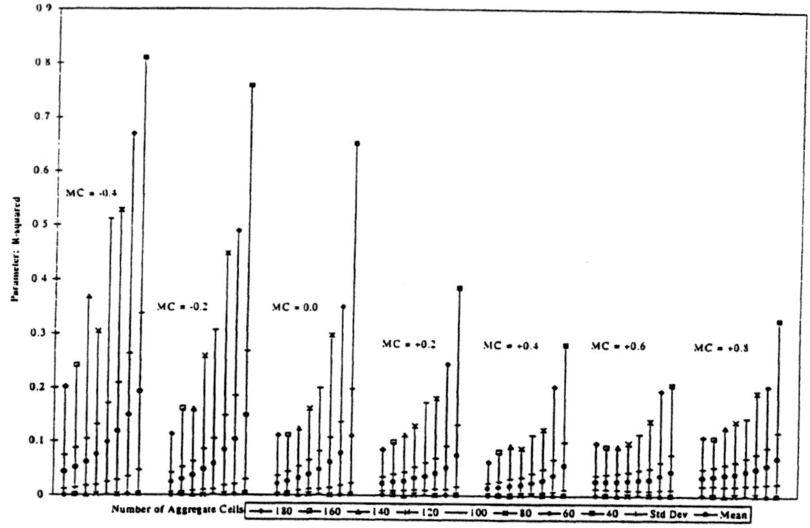

b)

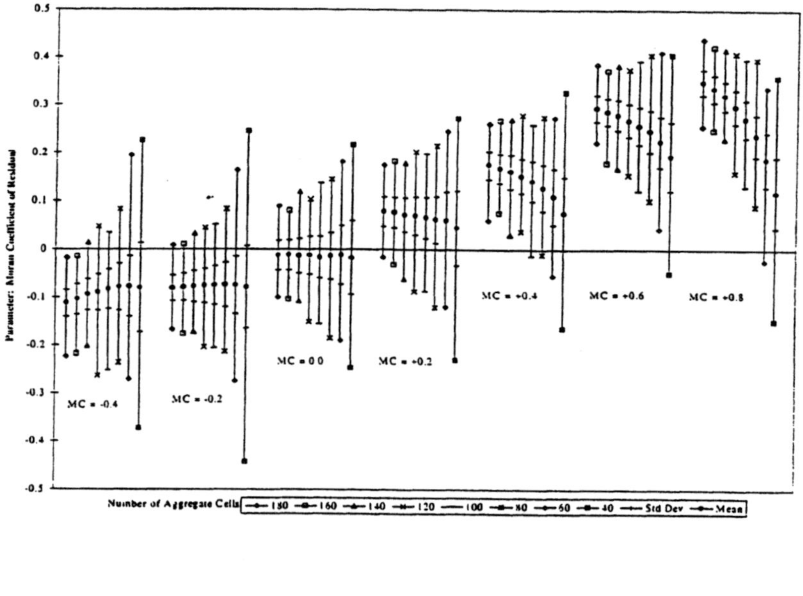

Figure 8.2. Variation of R-squared (top) and the Moran Coefficient of the residual with aggregation over 1000 runs, with all variables (dependent and independent) having the same Moran Coefficients and normal distributions.

a)

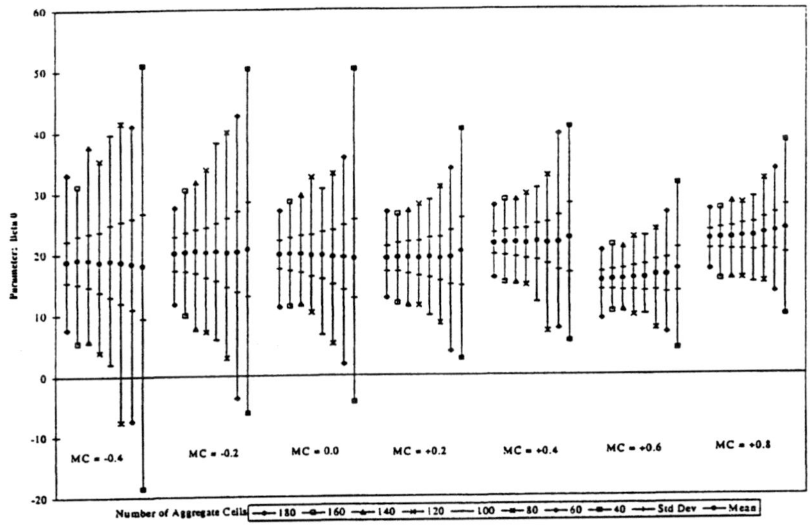

b)

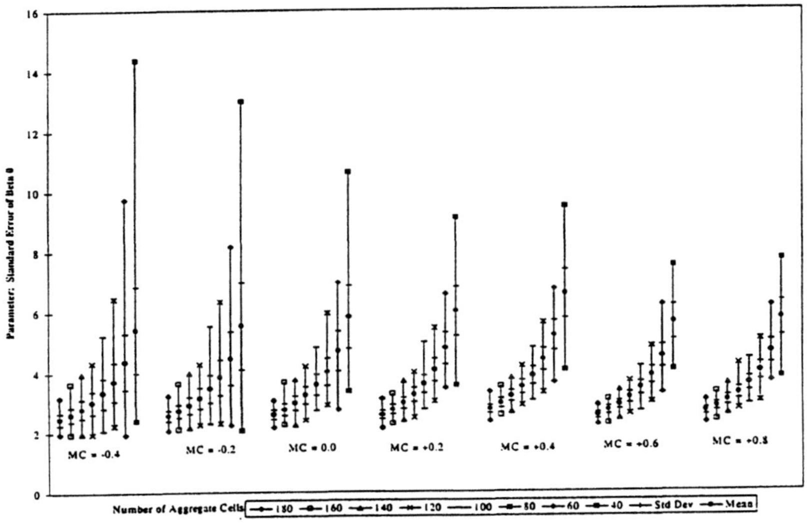

Figure 8.3. Variation of β_0 and its standard error with aggregation over 1000 runs, with all variables (dependent and independent) having the same Moran Coefficients and normal distributions.

a)

b)

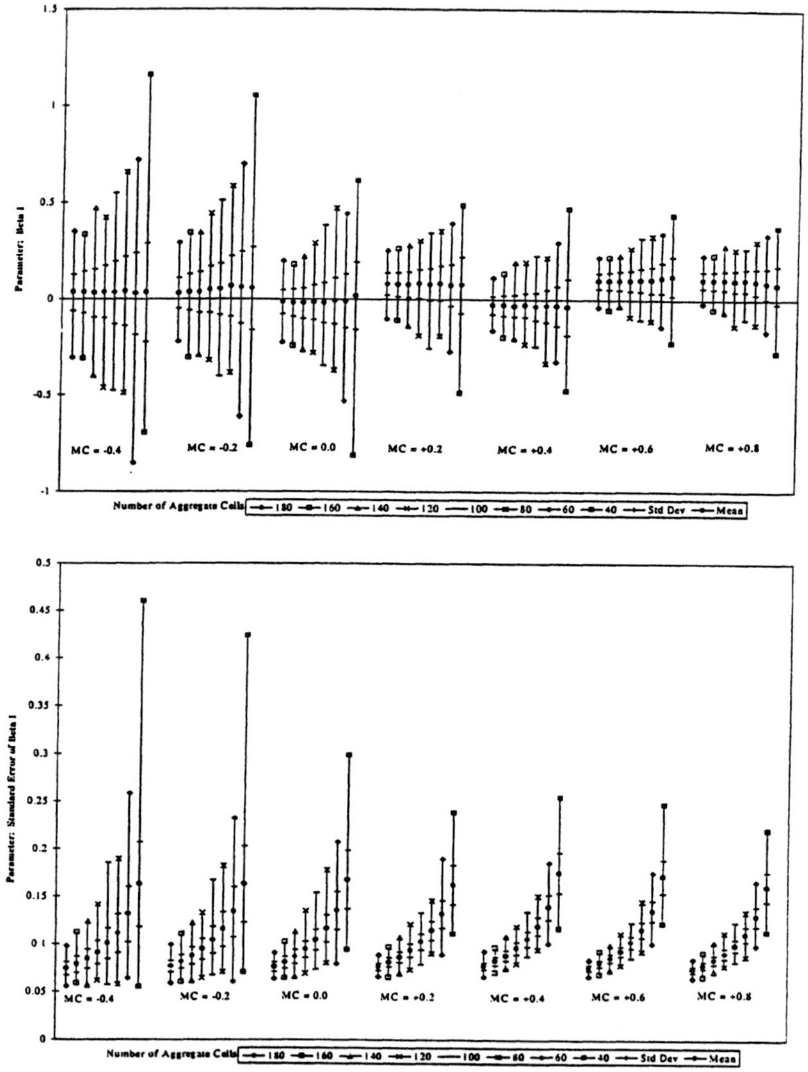

Figure 8.4. Variation of β_1 and its standard error with aggregation over 1000 runs, with all variables (dependent and independent) having the same Moran Coefficients and normal distributions.

a)

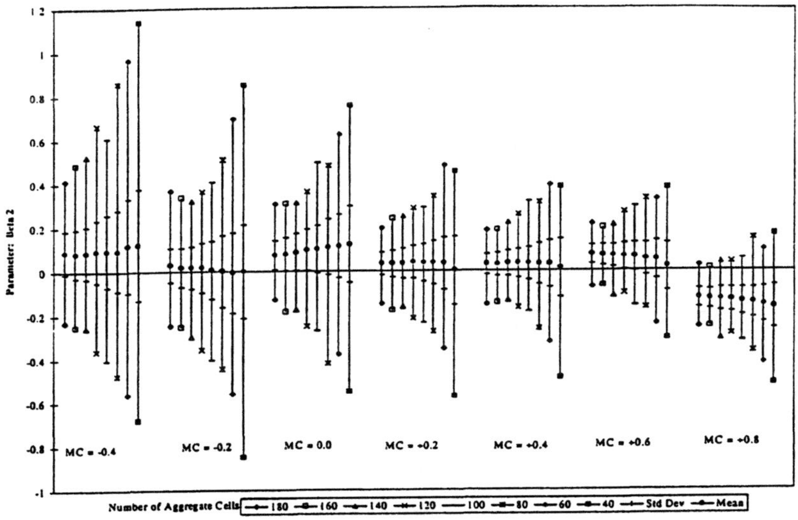

b)

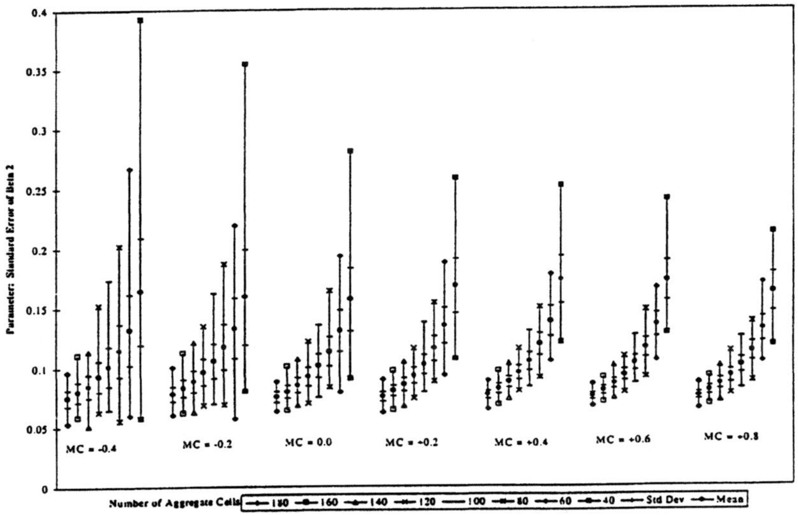

Figure 8.5. Variation of β_2 and its standard error with aggregation over 1000 runs, with all variables (dependent and independent) havng the same Moran Coefficients and normal distributions.

a)

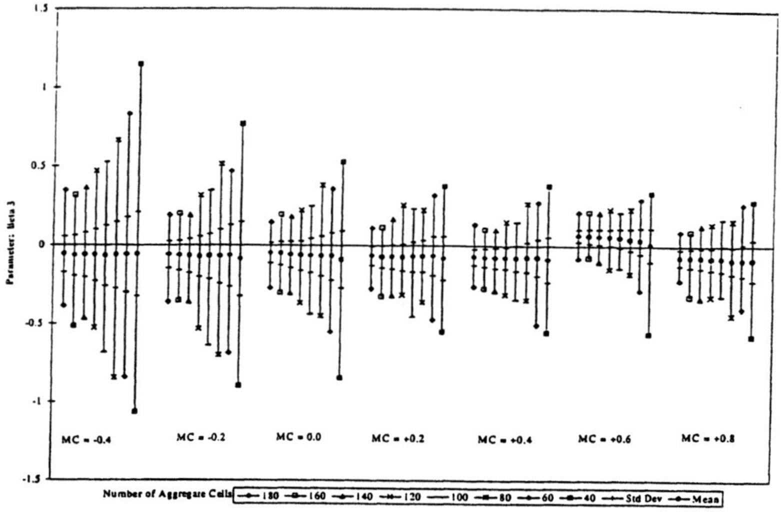

b)

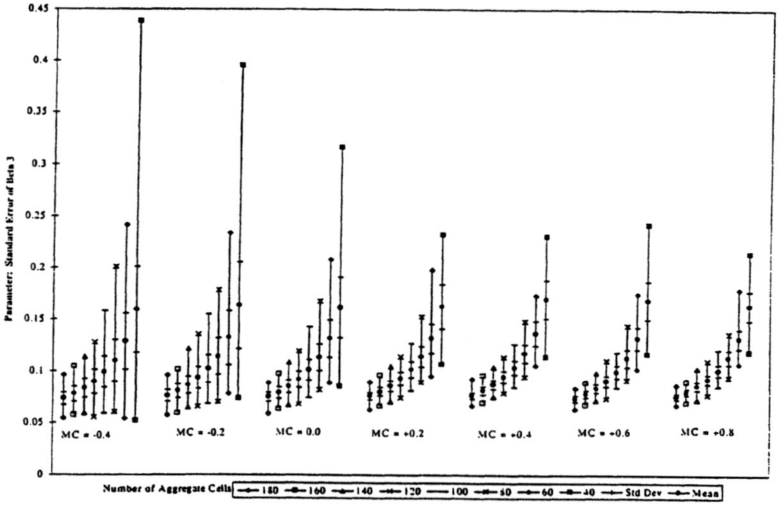

Figure 8.6. Variation of β_3 and its standard error over 1000 runs, with all variables (dependent and independent) having the same Moran Coefficients and normal distributions.

Figures 8.3 to 8.6 show that all of the regression coefficients and their standard errors behave similarly under aggregation. The mean values of β_0, β_1, β_2, and β_3 remain close to their unaggregated values over all levels of spatial autocorrelation and scales, although there are noticeable dips in the β_0 group at an MC of 0.6 and β_2 at the MC of 0.8. In contrast, the average value of the standard error for all coefficients shows a definite increase with the scale effect. This is not unexpected, as Fotheringham and Wong (1991) point out, since the standard error depends partly on the number of aggregated units. Interestingly, even though the range of variation of the standard error due to the zoning effect decreases with increasing spatial autocorrelation, the mean value for a given scale remains essentially constant.

The second experiment, in which the independent variables x_1, x_2 and x_3 contain the same level of spatial autocorrelation, while y has a different one, is not that much more complex than the first experiment. The results are presented in Figures 8.7 to 8.11. Each plot consists of 12 groups of lines, each group representing a combination of MCs for the dependent and independent variables. The groups are organized in four sets of three, with each set's dependent variable having the same Moran Coefficient.

As before, the range of variation of R^2, as well as all the other parameters, increases as the scale decreases. Figure 8.7a shows that when the spatial autocorrelation of the dependent variable is negative or zero, the variation of R^2 decreases with the increasingly positive autocorrelation of the dependent variables. However, when the dependent variable's MC is 0.4 or 0.8, the variability peaks when the autocorrelation of the independent variables is random, and actually decreases when it becomes more positive or more negative. For a given MC of the independent variables, but more pronouncedly so for the lower values, there is a tendency for the range of R^2 values to decrease as the MC of the dependent variable increases. Comparison with Figure 8.2a shows that the range of values is greater for the datasets where all variables have low MCs than for the datasets where only the dependent variable has a low MC. This seems to indicate that some sort of interaction is occurring involving the spatial organization of the variables which is acting to produce a more consistent set of linear fits.

By examining Figure 8.7b and comparing it to Figure 8.2b, it is apparent that the behaviour of the MC of the residuals depends more on the spatial autocorrelation of the dependent variable than that of the independent variables. The patterns are very similar for each MC of the independent variables, and there appears to be no pattern of variation that can be attributed to their spatial organization. The spatial structure of the variables is still not captured by the linear regression model.

As with the first experiment, the regression coefficients and their standard errors each behave in roughly the same way for each combination of spatial autocorrelations. Unlike with R^2, there are three clearly visible patterns, aside from the usual increase in variability with decreasing aggregation scale. First, the mean

a)

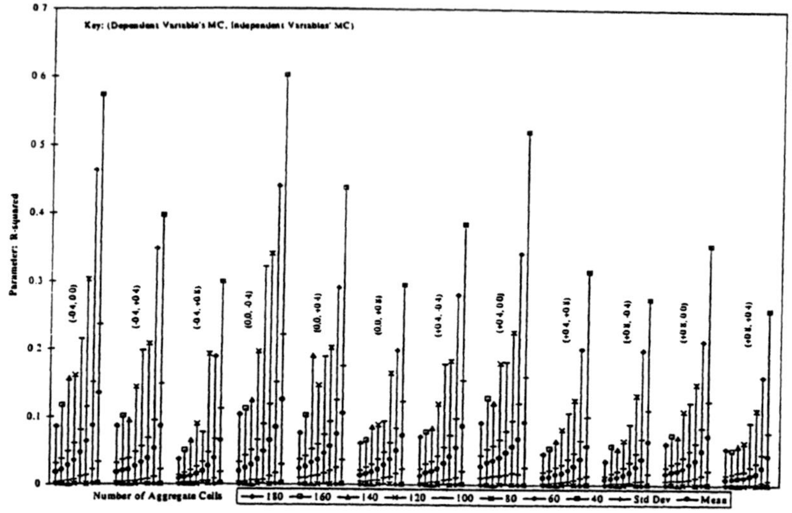

b)

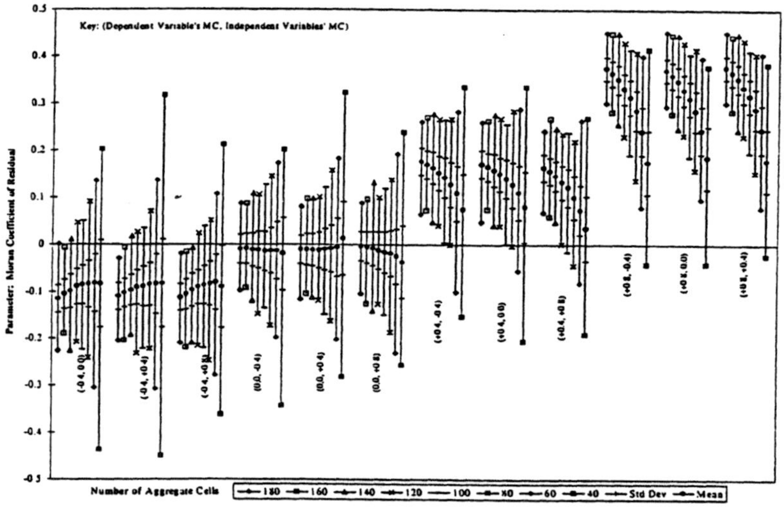

Figure 8.7. Variation of R-squared (top) and the Moran Coefficient of the residual (bottom) for synthetic variables with aggregation over 1000 runs. All variables are normally distributed, with x_1, x_2, x_3 having the same MC and y having a different MC.

a)

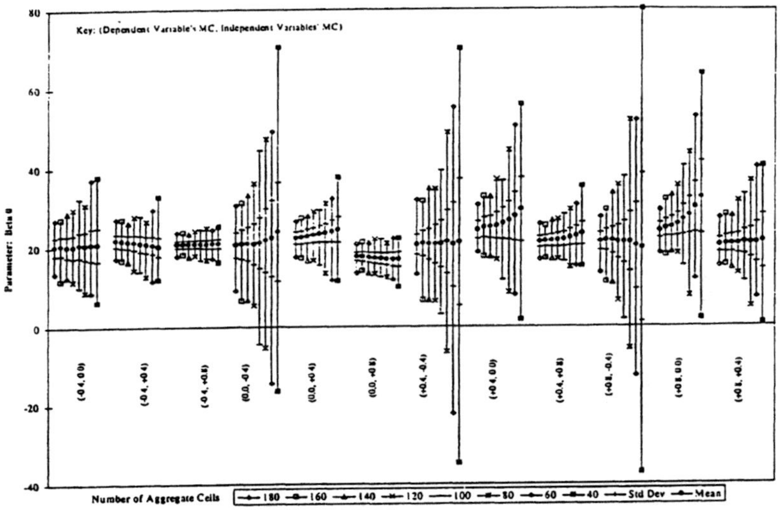

b)

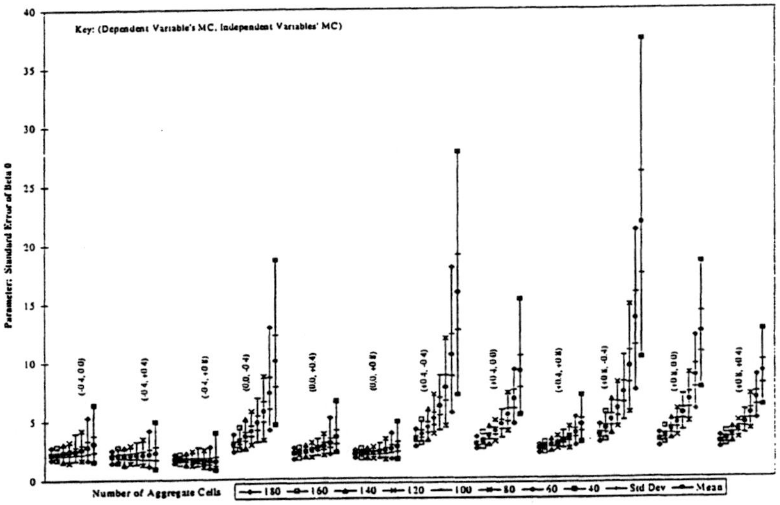

Figure 8.8. Variation of β_0 (top) and its standard error for sythetic variables with aggregation over 1000 runs. All variables are normally distributed, with x_1, x_2, x_3 having the same MC and y having a different MC.

a)

b)

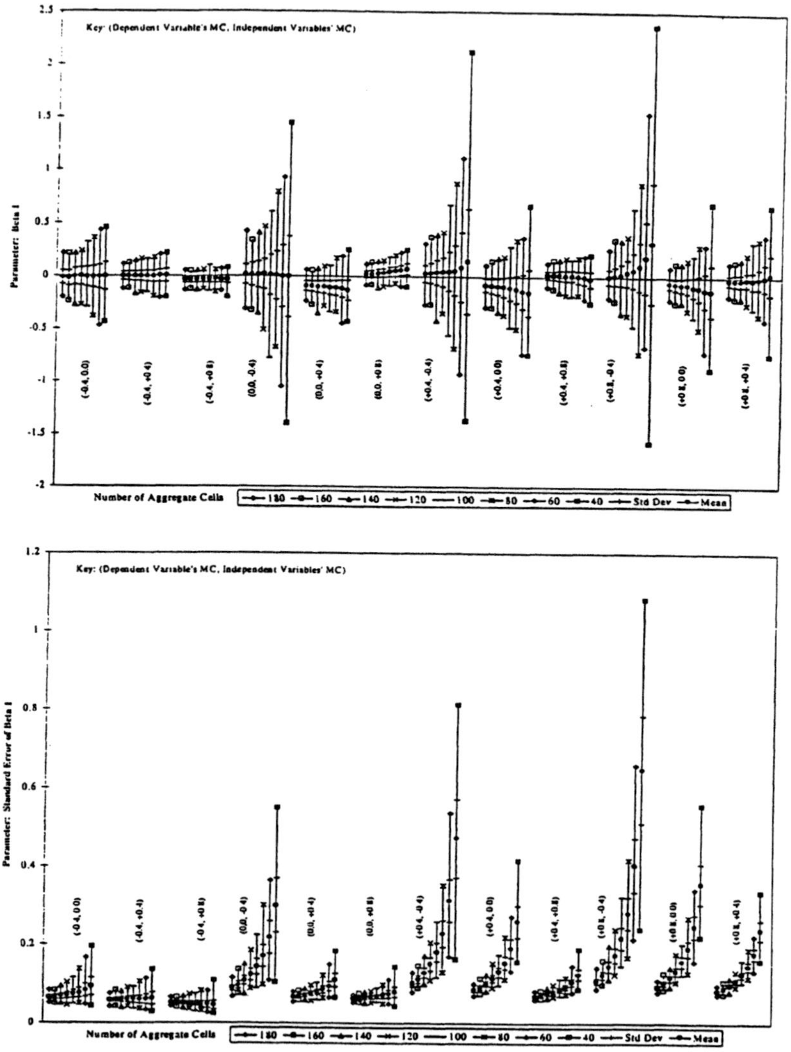

Figure 8.9. Variation of β_1 and its standard error for synthetic variables with aggregation over 1000 runs. All variables are normally distributed, with x_1, x_2, x_3 having the same MC and y having a different MC.

a)

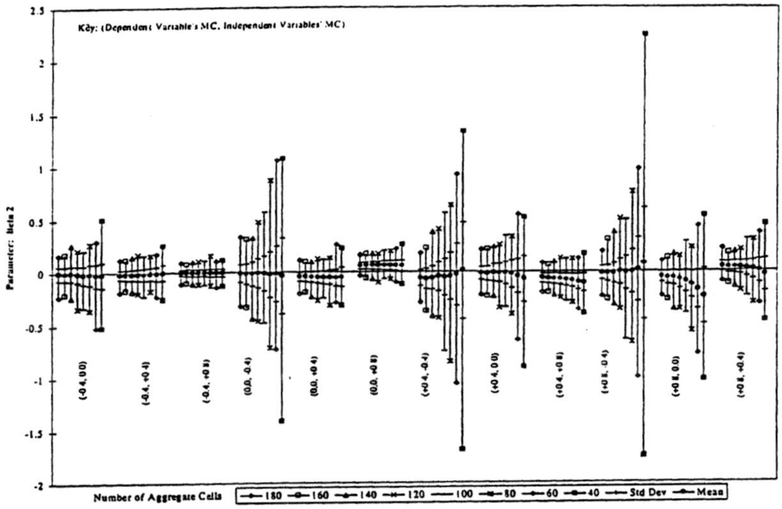

b)

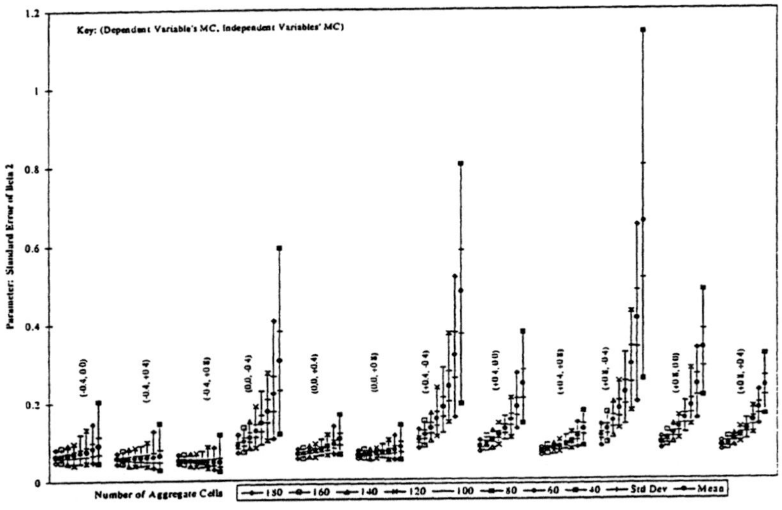

Figure 8.10. Variation of β_2 (top) and its standard error for synthetic variables with aggregation over 1000 runs. All variables are normally distributed, with x_1, x_2, x_3 having the same MC and y having a different MC.

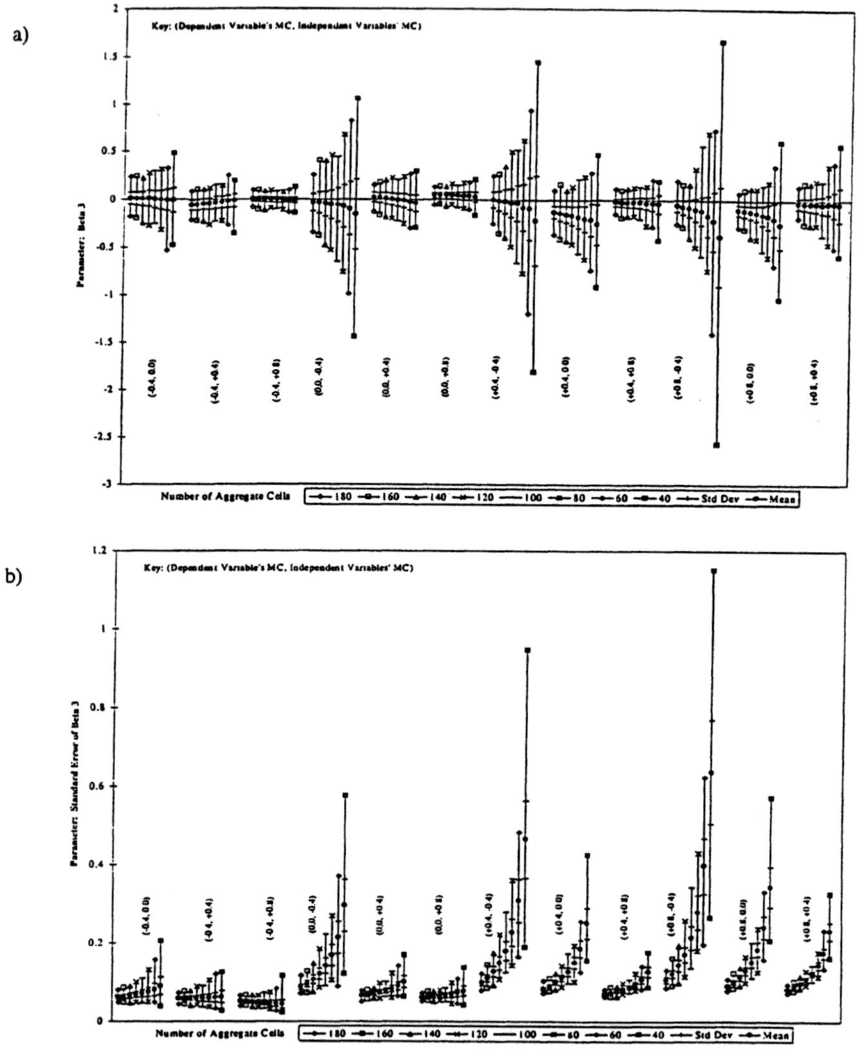

Figure 8.11. Variation of β_3 and its standard error for synthetic variables with aggregation over 1000 runs. All variables are normally distributed, with x_1, x_2, x_3 having the same MC and y having a different MC.

values of the distributions for the regression coefficients, with a few exceptions, tend to remain fairly stable or increase slightly as the number of aggregate cells decreases, while the means of the standard errors tend to increase. Second, for a given MC of the dependent variable, the variability of the ranges increases with increasing MC of the dependent variable. The size of some of the ranges is startling, especially with the intercept parameter β_0 which can be almost 60 above or below the mean of 20 for the 40-cell case in the third from last group in Figure 8.8a. These figures should serve as a clear warning to those who would blindly use multivariate regression methods on aggregated georeferenced data and then expect the results to apply to a higher resolution!

Comparison of these results with those of Fotheringham and Wong (1991) is difficult because the dependent and each of their four independent variables had a different MC, ranging from almost 0.9 for their P^{black} to about 0.25 for P^{eld}. Even from the very simple second experiment, it is clear that having the dependent and independent variables with different MCs increases the complexity of the response of the regression parameters to aggregation. Furthermore, our preliminary work indicates that the frequency distributions of the variables may also play a role in the MAUP for the variables, and hence for the relationships between them. This is to be expected from standard statistical theory.

Fotheringham and Wong's (1991) analysis of the change in Moran Coefficient of the variables can be compared with experimental results, however. A set of eight variables with MCs of -0.4, -0.2, 0.0, ..., 1.0 is created and subjected to 500 runs of the aggregation model; the results are displayed in Figure 8.12. Only 500 runs are used because of little significant change in the results with an increase in the number of runs. The usual pattern of the range of variability increasing as the scale decreases is clearly evident. Except for the smallest of the scales, the size of the range shows a marked tendency to decrease as the spatial autocorrelation increases. It is also clear that spatial organization is lost with aggregation, especially for data whose absolute MC is greater than 0.2, since the original MC value is not even included in the aggregated data's ranges. The loss of organization becomes more pronounced with decreased scale, especially for variables whose MC is 0.4 or greater.

Although Fotheringham and Wong (1991) performed only 20 random aggregations for each spatial scale, had more than twice the number of base units as we used, and used proportional variables (i.e. numerator and denominator are aggregated separately and the results divided) rather than variables which are simply summed or averaged, the patterns exhibited by the changes in MCs in their Figures 8.5 and 8.6, for example, resemble those of our Figure 8.12. The amount of variation in the ranges increases and the mean of the distributions tends to decrease as the scale decreases. The resemblance is most pronounced with P^{black}, whose original MC is about 0.9. The behaviour of the MCs for mean family income, P^{own}, and to a degree P^{blue}, in which the aggregated MC distributions form normal-like curves, do not fit into the pattern of the synthetic data. This could be due to the proportional nature of the variables, since the numerator and denominator of each

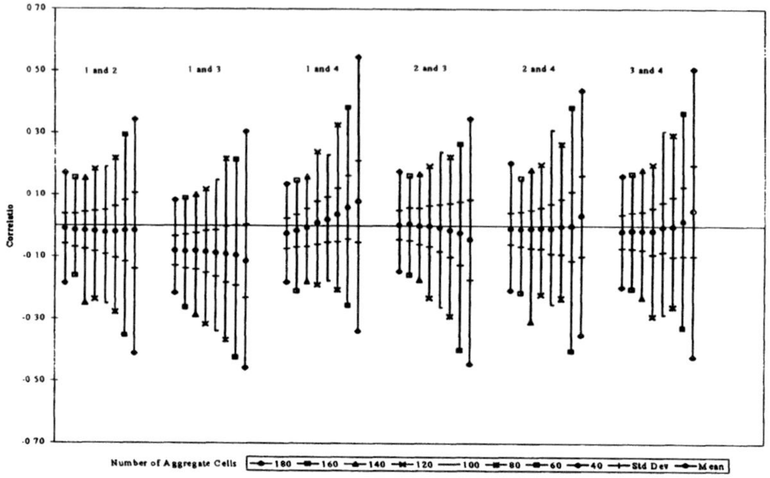

Figure 8.12. The variation of correlation coefficients between the variables of a multivariate linear regression simulation. Here, y is variable 1, x_1 is variable 2, x_2 is variable 3, and x_3 is variable 4. Correlations between the x's were set to zero in the base dataset, and the spatial autocorrelations of all variables were random.

variable are aggregated separately and the new proportion computed from the two new numbers, or perhaps to unknown violations of the regression model assumptions. Further research needs to be done to study the effects of the MAUP on proportion variables.

Also of interest in a study of multivariate linear regression are conditions that violate the assumptions of the model. The easiest one to study is collinearity, the presence of correlation between the independent variables. The results from this experiment, for which 500 runs are performed, are presented in Figure 8.13. The first three groups of lines represent the variations in the correlation between y and x_1, x_2, and x_3 respectively, while the latter three groups show the collinearities introduced by the MAUP.

The ranges of the introduced collinearities are roughly symmetric about zero and increase from close to ±0.2 for the 180-cell scale to approximately ±0.4 at the 40-cell scale. In order to determine if statistically significant correlations are introduced, the formula for the t-test of a correlation being significantly different from zero for a 95% confidence interval is solved for r, and the critical r values are computed for each of the scales of aggregation. The number of correlations for each pair (x_1, x_2), (x_1, x_3), and (x_2, x_3) and each scale which exceeded $\pm r_{crit}$, as well as the number of runs in which any of the three possible correlations is significant, are computed and the results are summarized in Table 8.1. As Figure 8.13 suggests, the number of significant correlations increases as the scale decreases.

Table 8.1. Total number of statistically significant correlations between the independent variables created by the aggregation process. The number of instances when any of the combinations produced a significant correlation is recorded in the column labelled *Any*.

Cells	|r Crit.|	x_1 x_2	x_1 x_3	x_2 x_3	*Any*
180	0.1463	2	3	6	11
160	0.1552	3	4	4	11
140	0.1660	0	7	4	11
120	0.1793	3	4	9	16
100	0.1965	9	8	11	26
80	0.2198	10	2	12	24
60	0.2540	7	11	13	30
40	0.3115	9	10	24	41

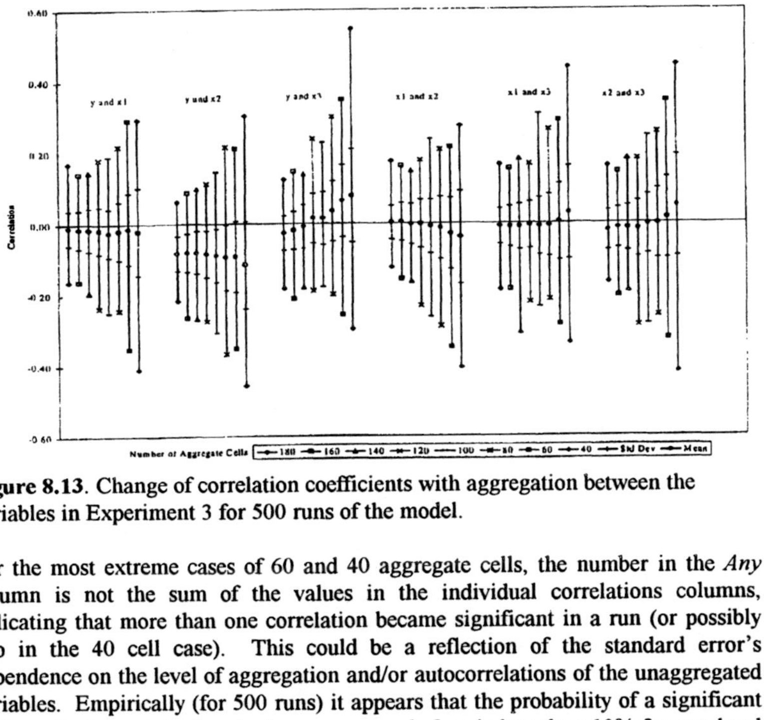

Figure 8.13. Change of correlation coefficients with aggregation between the variables in Experiment 3 for 500 runs of the model.

For the most extreme cases of 60 and 40 aggregate cells, the number in the *Any* column is not the sum of the values in the individual correlations columns, indicating that more than one correlation became significant in a run (or possibly two in the 40 cell case). This could be a reflection of the standard error's dependence on the level of aggregation and/or autocorrelations of the unaggregated variables. Empirically (for 500 runs) it appears that the probability of a significant collinearity being introduced where none was before is less than 10% for any level of aggregation, but this and changes in already present collinearities need to be thoroughly tested. Nevertheless, the fact that there can be a significant change reinforces the need for caution when using multivariate regression techniques on aggregated data.

5.0 CONCLUSIONS

In order to systematically examine the role of the spatial autocorrelation of the data on the response of multivariate regression parameters to aggregation, a spatial dataset generator capable of creating variables with different levels of spatial autocorrelation and aspatial correlation is developed. A multiple linear regression model of the form $y = \beta_0 + \beta_1 x_1 + \beta_2 x_2 + \beta_3 x_3$ has been employed, as three independent variables are sufficient to capture much of the complexity of multivariate regression while minimizing the computational and analytical overhead. The first two of the three experiments performed are designed to test the effect of various spatial autocorrelation levles in the independent and dependent variables on the variation of the regression parameters with aggregation. The third experiment tests to see how much collinearity is introduced between independent variables with increasing aggregatin, when there was none in the unaggregated data.

When all variables have the same spatial autocorrelation, as measured by the Moran Coefficient, the variation of the parameters tended to decrease as the Moran Coefficient increased, as expected, indicating that more positively autocorrelated data are less affected by the MAUP. For all values of MC tested, the mean values of the coefficients β_0, β_1, β_2 and β_3 are found to be essentially constant over all levels of resolution, even when the variation in values increases. Change in the variability is reflected in the standard errors for the coefficients, whose mean values and variabilities tend to increase with decreasing spatial resolution. The mean value of R^2 shows a very large variability for negatively autocorrelated data, which tends to decrease with increasing values of the Moran Coefficient, up to +0.4, folowed by a slight tendency for the variability to increase again beyond this point. The MC of the residuals indicates that spatial organization is not well detected by the linear regression model, since the residuals, primarily for variables whose $|MC| > 0.2$, are much smaller in magnitude than the MCs of the original variables. This effect tends to worsen as the number of regions becomes small, most noticeably at 10% of the original number of regions.

When all of the independent variables have a particular Moran Coefficient, and the dependent variable has a different one, it appears that the MC of the independent variables tends to play a larger factor in the variation of the regression coefficients, R^2, and the MC of the residuals, than does the MC of the dependent variable. For a given MC of the dependent variable, the variability in the coefficients and their standard errors tends to decrease with increasing MC of the independent variables. However, for a given MC of the independent variables, the variability tends to *increase* with increasing MC of the dependent variable. A similar pattern is visible for R^2, but for dependent variables whose MC is positive the range of variability is greater for independent variables whose MC is 0.0 than for those whose $|MC| > 0.0$. It appears that the MC of the residual depends little on the MC of the dependent variable.

Results from the third experiment reveal that collinearities between independent variables are introduced by aggregation. The mean values of the ranges of correlations remain at or very near 0.0 for all save the last two spatial resolutions, even though the ranges show a definite tendency to increase. However, only between 2% (for the 180 aggregate cells) and 8% (for 40 cells) of the aggregations actually produce correlations that are statistically significant.

The results of the experiments in this paper only scratch the surface of the behaviour of multivariate regression parameters when data are aggregated from one level of spatial resolution to another. It is clear that the spatial autocorrelation of each of the variables involved influences the behaviour, and that if each variable has a different autocorrelation it will be difficult to predict ahead of time what the behaviour of the regression parameters will be. Exploration of the effect of the MAUP on multivariate regression using variously autocorrelated variables is a focus for future research.

The variables used in these experiments were all variables that were averaged during the aggregation process. The behaviour of variables that are proportions, in which numerator and denominator are aggregated individually, and variables that are summed in aggregation, also needs to be examined. Comparison of Fotheringham and Wong's (1991) results to ours indicate that multivariate models constructed with other variable types may behave differently under aggregation than the model described here. Models which involve combinations of different variable types may behave even more differently. All of these require further research.

Preliminary results indicate that the frequency distribution of the values in the variables can also influence the MAUP. When a synthetic dataset of normally distributed variables, each of which had the same variance, Moran Coefficient, and (if possible) mean as the original variables, was created for the Lancashire data set described in Amrhein and Reynolds (1996), results are noticeably, albeit not dramatically, different. Attempts to simulate "realistic" datasets by the deliberate inclusion of outliers and zero values to represent suppressed values will also be made as part of future research. Finally, the influence of the initial connectivity matrix on the MAUP also needs to be investigated. The ultimate goal of the research is, of course, to see if it is possible to empirically estimate error in a spatial dataset that has been introduced by aggregation, and the presence of recognizable patterns indicates that the prospects are perhaps not as gloomy as Fotheringham and Wong (1991) first believed.

REFERENCES

Amrhein, C. G. (1993). "Searching for the elusive aggregation effect: Evidence from statistical simulations." *Environment and Planning A*, 27, 105-119.

Amrhein, C. G., and H. Reynolds. (1996). "Using spatial statistics to assess aggregation effects." *Geographical Systems*, 2, 83-101.

Amrhein, C. G., and H. Reynolds. (1997). "Using the Getis statistic to explore aggregation effects in Metropolitan Toronto Census data." *The Canadian Geographer*, (forthcoming).

Amrhein, C. G., and R. Flowerdew. (1993). "Searching for the elusive aggregation effect: Evidence from British census data." Unpublished manuscript available from the authors.

Fotheringham, A. S., and D. W. S. Wong. (1991). "The modifiable area unit problem in multivariate analysis." *Environment and Planning A*, 23, 1025-1044.

Okabe, A., B. Boots, and K. Sugihara. (1992). *Spatial Tessellations: Concepts and Applications of Voronoi Diagrams*. London: Wiley.

Openshaw, S., and P. Taylor. (1979). "A million or so correlation coefficients: Three experiments on the modifiable area unit problem." In *Statistical Applications in the Spatial Sciences*, edited by N. Wrigley, pp. 127-144. London: Pion.

Steel, D. G., and D. Holt. (1996). "Rules for random aggregation." *Environment and Planning A*, 28, 957-978.

ACKNOWLEDGEMENTS

The program which created the Voronoi tessellations was written by Jonathan Richard Shewchuk as part of the Archimedes project (parallel Finite Element Methods) and was made available over the World Wide Web. Primary financial support was obtained from the Canadian Social Sciences and Humanities Research Council (#SSH 410-94-1736) and we are grateful for their continued support.

CHAPTER 9

REEXAMINATION OF THE LIMITED-INFORMATION MAXIMUM LIKELIHOOD ESTIMATION

Yoshio Kimura and Hitoshi Kondo

1.0 INTRODUCTION

With the revision of the Limited-Information Maximum Likelihood (Henceforth, LIML) estimation proposed by Fuller (1977) as a start, the LIML has been reappraised by Fujikoshi et al. (1982) and Morimune (1983), mainly because the modified LIML estimators exhibit fairly well behaved small sample properties. However, the first step of the LIML estimation procedure, a minimisation of a ratio of quadratic forms, has been solved a formula based upon the assumption that the denominator is positive definite, while the positive definiteness is apt to collapse when the sample size is small relative to the number of all predetermined variables included in the model under construction, even if the order condition of the identifiability is fulfilled. On the other hand, we have the canonical corregression proposed by Professor Paelinck (1985; pp.242-47) as an estimation method completely free of the restriction stated above. Therefore, it is of some value to develop a computational procedure which makes the LIML estimation executable without the positive definiteness so far presumed and to synthesise the LIML and the canonical corregression. In addition, it is needless to say that the proposed procedure includes the usual one as a special case and keeps the well behavedness of the LIML estimators aforementioned almost intact.

2.0 REEXAMINATION OF THE LIML

We first consider the system of simultaneous equations consisting of G structural relations with K predetermined variables. In matrix form, the system is written down as;

$$\mathbf{Y}\mathbf{B}' + \mathbf{X}\boldsymbol{\Gamma}' = \mathbf{U},$$

where

$\mathbf{Y}$ is the n by G matrix of observations on the endogenous variables,
$\mathbf{B}$ is a G by G matrix of coefficients of current endogenous variables,
$\mathbf{X}$ is the n by K matrix of observations on all predetermined variables,
$\boldsymbol{\Gamma}$ is a G by K matrix of coefficients of the predetermined variables, and
$\mathbf{U}$ is the n by G matrix of all the sample disturbances.

Let the equation to be estimated be ;

$$\mathbf{y} = \mathbf{Y}_1\beta + \mathbf{X}_1\gamma + \mathbf{u}, \tag{1}$$

where y is an n by 1 vector of observations on the dependent variable of equation (1), $\mathbf{Y}_1[\mathbf{X}_1]$ the n by (g-1)[n by k] matrix of observations on the explanatory endogenous [predetermined] variables appearing in this equation. Moreover, by $\mathbf{Y}_2[\mathbf{X}_2]$ we denote the submatrix obtained from $\mathbf{Y}[\mathbf{X}]$ by deleting $(\mathbf{y}\ \mathbf{Y}_1)[\mathbf{X}_1]$. Thus, $\mathbf{Y} = (\mathbf{y}\ \mathbf{Y}_1\ \mathbf{M}\ \mathbf{Y}_2)$ and $\mathbf{X} = (\mathbf{X}_1\ \mathbf{M}\mathbf{X}_2)$.

In general, econometric models become of larger scale, the more are the number of variables included. On the other hand, it is not easy to increase observations so as to match with the rate of augmentation in the models. Consequently, the matrix $\mathbf{X}'\mathbf{X}$, for example, is likely to be singular. Therefore, we do not specify the rank of matrices to appear and substitute g-inverse for the usual inverse.

Now, to explain the LIML according to Johnston (1983, pp.483-486), we rewrite (1) as follows;

$$\mathbf{Y}_\Delta\beta_\Delta - \mathbf{X}_1\gamma = \mathbf{u} \tag{2}$$

where

$$\beta_\Delta = \begin{pmatrix} 1 \\ -\beta \end{pmatrix} \text{ and } \mathbf{Y}_\Delta = (\mathbf{y}\ \ \mathbf{Y}_1).$$

The usual computational procedure of the LIML is summarized follows;
(i-1) To find the minimum value $\hat{\ell}$ of the ratio

$$\ell = \frac{\beta'_\Delta W^*_{\Delta\Delta}\beta_\Delta}{\beta'_\Delta W_{\Delta\Delta}\beta_\Delta} \tag{3}$$

where $\mathbf{W}^*_{\Delta\Delta} = \mathbf{Y}'_\Delta(\mathbf{I} - \mathbf{X}_1(\mathbf{X}'_1\mathbf{X}_1)^-\mathbf{X}'_1)\mathbf{Y}_\Delta$ and $\mathbf{W}_{\Delta\Delta} = \mathbf{Y}'_\Delta(\mathbf{I} - \mathbf{X}(\mathbf{X}'\mathbf{X})^-\mathbf{X}')\mathbf{Y}_\Delta$ and for later convenience, we define $\mathbf{H}_1[\mathbf{H}] = \mathbf{X}_1(\mathbf{X}'_1\mathbf{X}_1)^-\mathbf{X}'_1[\mathbf{X}(\mathbf{X}'\mathbf{X})^-\mathbf{X}']$. More concretely. $\hat{\ell}$ is determined as the minimum root of the following determinantal equation

$$|\ \mathbf{W}^*_{\Delta\Delta} - \ell\ \mathbf{W}_{\Delta\Delta}| = 0. \tag{4}$$

(i-2) Once $\hat{\ell}$ is known, $\hat{\beta}_\Delta$ can be found as an eigen vector satisfying

$$(\mathbf{W}^*_{\Delta\Delta} - \hat{\ell}\ \mathbf{W}_{\Delta\Delta})\beta_\Delta = 0. \tag{5}$$

(ii) Using $\hat{\beta}_\Delta$ obtained above, we have the estimate $\hat{\gamma}$ of as γ as

$$\hat{\gamma} = (\mathbf{X}_1'\mathbf{X}_1)^{-}\mathbf{X}_1'\mathbf{Y}_\Delta\hat{\beta}_\Delta .$$

Evidently, $\mathbf{W}_{\Delta\Delta}$ is nonnegative definite, but not necessarily positive definite. In fact, (I - **H**) is idempotent by Theorem AP.2(ii-1), and symmetric by Theorem AP.2(ii-2.3). Therefore, assertion (ii-2.2) of Theorem AP.2 guarantees that r(I - **H**) = n−r(**X**). Hence, we have

$$r(\mathbf{W}_{\Delta\Delta}) \le \min\{n - r(\mathbf{X}), r(\mathbf{Y}_\Delta)\}$$

Since the possibility that n is not so large relative to r(**X**), can never be negligibly small, we may well say that the inequalities;

$$r(\mathbf{W}_{\Delta\Delta}) \le (n - r(\mathbf{X})) < r(\mathbf{Y}_\Delta) \le g$$

are apt to hold. In other words, it is likely to occur that $\mathbf{W}_{\Delta\Delta}$ is nonnegative definite, but not positive definite. This means that $\hat{\ell}$ cannot be obtained as the minimum root of (4). Moreover, if there exists a nonzero vector which is not in $N(\mathbf{W}_{\Delta\Delta})$ but in $N(\mathbf{W}^*_{\Delta\Delta})$ then zero is the trivial minimum of (3), since $\mathbf{W}^*_{\Delta\Delta}$ is also nonnegative definite. However, this is contradictory to the well known fact that the ratio of (3) is not less than 1. Therefore, we must ask the relation of set inclusion between $N(\mathbf{W}^*_{\Delta\Delta})$ and $N(\mathbf{W}_{\Delta\Delta})$. To answer this question, it sufficies to clarify the relation between $N((\mathbf{I} - \mathbf{H}_1)\mathbf{Y}_\Delta)$ and $N((\mathbf{I} - \mathbf{H})\mathbf{Y}_\Delta)$, since both $\mathbf{W}^*_{\Delta\Delta}$ and $\mathbf{W}_{\Delta\Delta}$ are known to be nonnegative definite. We can now state and prove;

<u>Theorem 1</u> $N((\mathbf{I} - \mathbf{H}_1)\mathbf{Y}_\Delta) \subseteq N((\mathbf{I} - \mathbf{H})\mathbf{Y}_\Delta)$

<u>Proof</u> Let **q** be any vector in $N((\mathbf{I} - \mathbf{H}_1)\mathbf{Y}_\Delta)$. If $\mathbf{Y}_\Delta\mathbf{q} = \mathbf{0}$ then it is obvious that $\mathbf{q} \in N((\mathbf{I} - \mathbf{H})\mathbf{Y}_\Delta)$. In the remaining case where $\mathbf{Y}_\Delta\mathbf{q} \neq \mathbf{0}$, it holds that

$$\mathbf{0} = ((\mathbf{I} - \mathbf{H}_1)\mathbf{Y}_\Delta)\mathbf{q} = (\mathbf{I} - \mathbf{H}_1)(\mathbf{Y}_\Delta\mathbf{q}) \tag{6}$$

By the definition of $\mathbf{H}_1$, $(\mathbf{I} - \mathbf{H}_1)(\mathbf{Y}_\Delta\mathbf{q}) = \mathbf{e}_1$ is the residual in OLS regression of $\mathbf{Y}_\Delta\mathbf{q}$ on $\mathbf{X}_1$. Therefore (6) implies that $\mathbf{e}_1 = \mathbf{0}$. Similarly, $\mathbf{e} = (\mathbf{I} - \mathbf{H})(\mathbf{Y}_\Delta\mathbf{q})$ is the residual in the regression of $\mathbf{Y}_\Delta\mathbf{q}$ on **X**. On the other hand, the sum of squared residuals of OLS decreases with the number of explanatory variables. This, together with the fact that $\mathbf{e}_1 = \mathbf{0}$, yields $0 \le \mathbf{e}'\mathbf{e} \le \mathbf{e}_1'\mathbf{e}_1 = 0$. Hence $\mathbf{e} = \mathbf{0}$. Thus, $\mathbf{q} \in N((\mathbf{I} - \mathrm{H})\mathbf{Y}_\Delta)$. (Q.E.D.)

By the theorem just verified, it is excluded that zero is the trivial minimum of ratio(3). Thus, applying Theorem AP.1 to (3), we obtain the minimum value of $\hat{\ell}$ ratio (3), provided that a basis of $R(((\mathbf{I} - \mathbf{H})\mathbf{Y}_\Delta)')$ is found. Letting $\tilde{\ell}$ be the modified $\hat{\ell}$ by the formula due to Fuller (1977) and/or Morimune (1983), and solving the equation

$$\Psi\beta = \psi,$$

we surely have the estimate of β, where Ψ is the submatrix obtained from $(\mathbf{W}^{*}_{\Delta\Delta} - \tilde{\ell}\, \mathbf{W}_{\Delta\Delta})$ by deleting its first row and column, ψ the vector consisting of (i, 1) entries (i = 2, ⋯, n) of $(\mathbf{W}^{*}_{\Delta\Delta} - \mathbf{W}_{\Delta\Delta})$, and β of course the same as in (1). The estimates of the other coefficients are given by exerting (ii). It is now certain that the LIML thus obtained exhibits the asymptotic properties shown by Fuller and Morimune, since the very nature of the asymptotic property enables us to consider the sample size so large that the matrix **X** is thought to be of full rank. However, we should notice that there remains a case where the minimisation of (3) requires Theorem AP.1 even if $\mathbf{X}'\mathbf{X}$ is nonsingular. To show this, suppose that $\mathbf{X}'\mathbf{X}$ is nonsingular. Then $(\mathbf{I} - \mathbf{X}(\mathbf{X}'\mathbf{X})^{-1}\mathbf{X}')$ is an idempotent matrix of rank n−K. Moreover, it does not harm the generality to assume that $r(\mathbf{Y}_{\Delta})$ is of full column rank, for otherwise the equation in question would contain at least one redundant explanatory variable which is endogenous. Therefore, if K is so large that n−K is less than the number of all endogenous variables appear in the equation to be estimated, $\mathbf{W}_{\Delta\Delta}$ is by no means positive definite but $N(\mathbf{W}_{\Delta\Delta})$ does contain some nonzero vectors. Consequently, even under the nonsingularity assumption of $\mathbf{X}'\mathbf{X}$, we must resort to Theorem AP.1, the core of the proposed procedure. And this argument leads to an additional result that the LIML estimate obtained by our method is consistent, because as the sample size n tends to infinity, n−K surely exceeds the number of endogenous variables included in the equation to be estimated.

Finally, we turn to Professor Paelinck's canonical corregression method. To summarise the method in our notation, let β_{Δ} be non-normalised. Then the canonical corregression estimates $\ddot{\beta}_{\Delta}$ of β_{Δ} and $\ddot{\gamma}$ of γ are described as the vector which minimises $(\mathbf{Y}_{\Delta}(-\beta_{\Delta}))'\mathbf{H}_1(\mathbf{Y}_{\Delta}(-\beta_{\Delta}))$ subject to $(-\beta_{\Delta})'(-\beta_{\Delta}) = 1$ and as the OLS estimate $\ddot{\gamma}$ of $\mathbf{Y}_{\Delta}\cdot(-\ddot{\beta}_{\Delta}) = \mathbf{X}_1\gamma + \mathbf{u}$. Noticing that the above minimization is equivalent to that of $(\mathbf{Y}_{\Delta}\beta_{\Delta})'\mathbf{H}_1(\mathbf{Y}_{\Delta}\beta_{\Delta})/(\beta'_{\Delta}\mathbf{I}\beta_{\Delta})$ and that the identity matrix is undoubtedly positive definite, we can appraise the canonical corregression as an estimation method which guarantees the consistency of the resultant estimates and, at the same time, ingeniously avoids the difficulty which the usual LIML often encounters.

3.0 CONCLUDING REMARKS

Theoretically speaking, the present paper has developed a generalised formula for the first step of the LIML estimation, which yields the LIML estimate retaining all the asymptotic properties verified so far, and has demonstrate the consistency of Professor Paelinck's canonical corregression estimate by reckoning it as a family of the LIML estimate. On the other hand, to perform the estimation by means of the proposed formula, we must calculate a basis of $R(((\mathbf{I} - \mathbf{H})\mathbf{Y}_{\Delta})')$, as exactly as possible. However, once we encounter the so called ill-conditioned cases caused, in particular, by canceling and/or nonnull but small pivotal elements, it would be very difficult to continue the computation with the desirable accuracy without resorting to the high precision arithmetic. Therefore, we are planning to conduct the computation in arbitrary multiple precision arithmetic.

In another aspect, we further need to scrutinise the statistical properties of approximate distributions of the proposed estimates.

Appendix 1. On the Extrema of the Ratio of Quadratic Forms

In this appendix, we are concerned mainly with the extrema of a real valued function defined by $g(\mathbf{x}) = (\mathbf{x}'\mathbf{A}\mathbf{x}) / (\mathbf{x}'\mathbf{B}\mathbf{x})$, where **A** and **B** are real symmetric matrices of order n and **B** is supposed to be nonnegative definite (or, alternatively, positive semi-definite), that is, $\mathbf{x}'\mathbf{B}\mathbf{x}$ is nonnegative for all $\mathbf{x}$ of the n-dimensional real vector space R^n. If **B** is positive definite, the minimum (maximum) value of $g(\mathbf{x})$ is known to be the smallest (greatest) root of the determinantal equation $|\mathbf{A} - \lambda\mathbf{B}| = 0$ (Henceforth, PD-Theorem). However, we can easily infer if the matrix **B** is singular then PD-Theorem collapses. To see this, let S be an n-dimensional unit circle centered at the orgin and Z be the intersection of $\{R^n \backslash N(\mathbf{B})\}$ and S, where $N(\mathbf{B})$ denotes the set of all $\mathbf{x}$ such that $\mathbf{B}\mathbf{x} = \mathbf{0}$. Then, as is well known, Z can be thought of the domain of $g(\mathbf{x})$. If **B** is singular Z cannot be compact, since Z is by no means closed. On the other hand, the nonsingularity of **B** implies that Z coincides with a compact set S. Therefore, the positive definiteness of **B** does not ensure the compactness of the domain of $g(\mathbf{x})$. This, in conjunction with the famous Weierstrass Theorem, guarantees that $g(\mathbf{x})$ attains its minimum and maximum on the set Z. On the contrary, the singularity of **B** makes Weierstrass Theorem unapplicable. In fact, the following two numerical examples suffice to show that PD-Theorem cannot be true when **B** is nonnegative definite but not positive definite.

<u>Example 1</u> Let a_1, a_2, and b_1 be positive and define

$$\mathbf{A} = \begin{bmatrix} a_1 & 0 & 0 \\ 0 & a_2 & 0 \\ 0 & 0 & 0 \end{bmatrix} \text{ and } \mathbf{B} = \begin{bmatrix} b_1 & 0 & 0 \\ 0 & 0 & 0 \\ 0 & 0 & 0 \end{bmatrix}.$$

Then, $|\mathbf{A} - \lambda\mathbf{B}| = 0$ irrespectively of λ, since the third row of $(\mathbf{A} - \lambda\mathbf{B})$ is a zero vector. In other words, the root of $|\mathbf{A} - \lambda\mathbf{B}| = 0$ can be made arbitrarily small (large). However, $g(\mathbf{x})$ attains its minimum at $\mathbf{x} = (1,0,x_3)'$ with x_3 arbitrary, because $g(\mathbf{x})$ reduces to $(a_1+a_2(x_2/x_1)^2)/b_1$ for all $\mathbf{x} \notin N(\mathbf{B})$.

<u>Example 2</u> $$\mathbf{A} = \begin{bmatrix} a_1 & 0 & 0 \\ 0 & a_2 & 0 \\ 0 & 0 & 0 \end{bmatrix} \text{ and } \mathbf{B} = \begin{bmatrix} b_1 & 0 & 0 \\ 0 & 0 & 0 \\ 0 & 0 & 0 \end{bmatrix},$$ where a_1, a_3, b_1, and b_2 are all positive. Then, $|\mathbf{A} - \lambda\mathbf{B}| = (a_1 - \lambda b_1)\lambda b_2 a_3$. Clearly, $\lambda = 0$ is the smallest root of $|\mathbf{A} - \lambda\mathbf{B}| = 0$. Nevertheless, $g(0,1,1) = -(a_3/b_2) < 0$.

We now turn to our main argument. Since the function under investigation can never be defined for any $\mathbf{x}$ such that $\mathbf{x}'\mathbf{B}\mathbf{x} = \mathbf{0}$, it is reasonable to seek for the extrema of $g(\mathbf{x})$ on a realm where $\mathbf{x}'\mathbf{B}\mathbf{x}$ never vanishes. In view of the assumed nonnegative definiteness of $\mathbf{B}$, it is well known that $\mathbf{x}'\mathbf{B}\mathbf{x} = 0$ if and only if $\mathbf{x} \in N(\mathbf{B})$, and that

$$N(\mathbf{B}) \oplus R(\mathbf{B}') = R^n, \tag{AP.1}$$

where $R(\mathbf{B}') = \{\mathbf{B}'\mathbf{z} | \mathbf{z} \in R^n\}$, the left hand side of (AP.1) is of course the direct sum of $N(\mathbf{B})$ and $R(\mathbf{B}')$. Recalling that $\mathbf{B}$ is assumed to be symmetric, (AP.1) further reduces to

$$N(\mathbf{B}) \oplus R(\mathbf{B}) = R^n \tag{AP.1'}$$

This, in turn, yields the next lemma.

<u>Lemma AP.1</u> By $\mathbf{P}[\mathbf{Q}]$ denote the matrix, all columns of which form a basis of $R(\mathbf{B})[N(\mathbf{B})]$.[1] Then,

(i) $\{R^n \backslash N(\mathbf{B})\} = \{\mathbf{Pu} + \mathbf{Qv} \mid \mathbf{u} \in R_0^r = \{R^r \backslash \{\mathbf{0}\}\}, \mathbf{v} \in R^{n-r}\} = \mathbf{T}$,

(ii) to any $\mathbf{x} \in \{R^n \backslash N(\mathbf{B})\}$, there corresponds a $\mathbf{u} \in R_0^r$ such that $\mathbf{x}'\mathbf{B}\mathbf{x} = \mathbf{u}'(\mathbf{P}'\mathbf{B}\mathbf{P})\mathbf{u}$, and

(iii) $\mathbf{u}'(\mathbf{P}'\mathbf{B}\mathbf{P})\mathbf{u} > 0$ for all $\mathbf{u} \in R_0^r$,

where r of course signifies the rank of $\mathbf{B}$.

<u>Proof</u> (i) Let $\mathbf{x}$ be any vector in $\{R^n \backslash N(\mathbf{B})\}$. Then, the fact that $\{R^n \backslash N(\mathbf{B})\}$ is a subset of R^n, coupled with (AP.1'), implies that there exists $\mathbf{u} \in R^r$ and $\mathbf{v} \in R^{n-r}$ such that $\mathbf{x} = \mathbf{Pu} + \mathbf{Qv}$. Obviously, $\mathbf{u} \neq \mathbf{0}$, for otherwise $\mathbf{x} = \mathbf{Qv} \in N(\mathbf{B})$, violating the hypothesis. Thus $\{R^n \backslash N(\mathbf{B})\} \subseteq \mathbf{T}$.

Conversely, for any $(\mathbf{Pu} + \mathbf{Qv}) \in \mathbf{T}$, we have $\mathbf{B}(\mathbf{Pu} + \mathbf{Qv}) = \mathbf{BPu}$. By definition, all columns of $\mathbf{P}$ are linearly independent and $\mathbf{u} \neq \mathbf{0}$. Hence $\mathbf{Pu} \neq \mathbf{0}$. However, (AP.1') implies that $N(\mathbf{B})$ and $R(\mathbf{B})$ have no nonzero vector in common. Therefore, $\mathbf{Pu}$ which is a nonzero element of $R(\mathbf{B})$ can never be in $N(\mathbf{B})$.

(ii) To any $\mathbf{x}$ of $\{R^n \backslash N(\mathbf{B})\}$, there corresponds a nonzero $\mathbf{u}$ and $\mathbf{v} \in R^{n-r}$ such that $\mathbf{Pu} + \mathbf{Qv} = \mathbf{x}$. If $\mathbf{v} = \mathbf{0}$ no further proof is needed. And if $\mathbf{v} \neq \mathbf{0}$, a direct calculation, with the aid of the assumed symmetry of $\mathbf{B}$, yields

[1] As the matrix $\mathbf{P}$, it suffices to choose an n by r submatrix $\mathbf{B}_1$ of $\mathbf{B}$ with the property that all columns of $\mathbf{B}_1$ are linearly independent.

$$\begin{aligned} \mathbf{x'Bx} &= \mathbf{(Pu + Qv)'B(Pu + Qv)} \\ &= \mathbf{(Pu + Qv)'BPu} && \ll\Lambda\ \mathbf{BQ} = [0] \\ &= \mathbf{u'(P'BP)u+v'((BQ)')Pu} && \ll\Lambda\ \mathbf{B=B'}, \text{ whence } \\ \mathbf{Q'B=Q'B'=(BQ)'=([0])'} \\ &= \mathbf{u'(P'BP)u}. \end{aligned}$$

(iii) Suppose the contrary. Then, there exists a $\mathbf{u} \in R_0^r$ such that $\mathbf{(Pu)'B(Pu)} = 0$, since **B** is assumed to be nonnegative definite. Evidently, $\mathbf{Pu} \neq \mathbf{0}$, for otherwise all columns of **P** would be linearly dependent, contradicting the definition of **P**. Again by the nonnegative definiteness of **B**, **Pu** belongs to N(**B**). However, this is absurd, because N(**B**) and R(**B**), which is an orthogonal component of N(**B**), can have no nonzero vector in common. (Q.E.D.)

We can now turn to the extremisation of g(**x**). Since the maximisation of g(**x**) is nothing else than the minimisation of -g(**x**), we henceforth confine ourselves to the problem of minimising g(**x**). With the aid of the lemma just established, we can state and verify;

Theorem AP.1 Suppose that **A** is, in addition to **B**, nonnegative definite. Then it holds true that if there exists an $\tilde{\mathbf{x}}$ N(**A**), which is not in N(**B**) then

$$0 = g(\tilde{\mathbf{x}}) \leq g(\mathbf{x}) \quad \text{for all } \mathbf{x} \in \{R^n \backslash N(\mathbf{B})\}, \tag{AP.2}$$

otherwise (ie, $N(\mathbf{A}) \subseteq N(\mathbf{B})$), g(**x**) attains the minimum on $\{R^n \backslash N(\mathbf{B})\}$ and the minimum value is given by the smallest root of

$$|\mathbf{P'(A - AQ(Q'AQ)^{-}(Q'A))P} - \ell\mathbf{(P'BP)}| = 0, \tag{AP.3}$$

where **P** and **Q** are the same as in Lemma AP.1.

Proof In view of the assumed nonnegative definiteness of **A** and **B** and the definition of $\tilde{\mathbf{x}}$, (AP.2) is rather trivial.

Turning to the proof of the second half of the theorem. Lemma AP.1 implies that the minimisation under investigation can be divided into the following two steps;

(i) to find $\mathbf{v_u}$ of R^{n-r} such that $\mathbf{v_u}$ minimises the numerator **G**(·) of **g**(·) for any given **u** of R_0^r, and

(ii) to determine **u** of R_0^r which minimizes $g(\mathbf{Pu + Qv_u}) = g(\mathbf{u}, \mathbf{v_n})$ on R_0^r.

(i) Let **u** be any given vector of R_0^r. Then, Lemma AP.1 guarantees that $(\mathbf{Pu + Qv})$ is in $\{R^n \backslash N(\mathbf{B})\}$ for all **v** of R^{n-r}, and a direct calculation yields

$$G(\mathbf{Pu + Qv}) = \mathbf{u'(P'AP)u} + 2(\mathbf{v'Q'APu}) + \mathbf{v'(Q'AQ)v}.$$

Since **A** is nonnegative definite, so is **Q′AQ**. Hence, as is well known, G(**Pu** + **Qv**) attains the minimum at a vector **v** satisfying

$$(\mathbf{Q'AQ})\mathbf{v} = -(\mathbf{Q'APu}) \tag{AP.4}$$

and vice versa. Taking into account of the nonnegative definiteness of **A**, (AP.4) is surely consistent. Let **y** be any solution of (AP.4). Then, it is obvious that

$$G(\mathbf{Pu} + \mathbf{Qy}) = \mathbf{u'(P'AP)u} - \mathbf{y'Q'APu}. \tag{AP.5}$$

Moreover, **y** is expressed as the sum of $(\mathbf{Q'AQ})^-(-\mathbf{Q'APu})$ and the linear combination of vectors in N(**Q′AQ**) which is a subset of N(**Q′A**), where $(\mathbf{Q'AQ})^-$ is a g-inverse of (**Q′AQ**). Therefore, our objective function reduces to

$$g(\mathbf{u}, (\mathbf{Q'AQ})^-(-\mathbf{Q'APu})) = \{\mathbf{u'(P'(A - AQ(Q'AQ)^-(Q'A))P)u}\} / (\mathbf{u'(P'BP)u}) \tag{AP.6}$$

(ii) Recalling Lemma AP.1, **u′(P′BP)u** is positive definite on R^r. Thus, the assertion follows directly from PD-Theorem. (Q.E.D.)

Appendix 2. On the Generalized Inverse of a matrix

Here, we state and prove some fundamental properties of the generalised inverse of a given matrix (abbreviated as g-inverse, for short) and refer to the implication of g-inverse to the least squares method, so long as the implication is relevant to the limited-information maximum likelihood estimation.

Lemma AP.2 Let **A** be an m by n complex matrix. Then the following two statements are mutually equivalent.

(i) There exists an n by m matrix $\mathbf{A}^-$ such that

$$\mathbf{A}(\mathbf{A}^-\mathbf{y}) = \mathbf{y} \quad \text{for all } \mathbf{y} \in R(\mathbf{A}), \text{ and}$$

(ii) there exists an n by m matrix $\mathbf{A}^-$ for which

$$\mathbf{AA}^-\mathbf{A} = \mathbf{A}.$$

Proof (i) ⇒ (ii) By $\mathbf{a}^j$ denote the j-th column of **A**. Since $\mathbf{a}^j$ (j = 1, ⋯, n) are in R(**A**), we have

$$\mathbf{A}(\mathbf{A}^-\mathbf{a}^j) = \mathbf{a}^j \quad j = 1, \Lambda, n,$$

or equivalently,

$$\mathbf{AA}^-\mathbf{A} = \mathbf{A}.$$

(ii) ⇒ (i) With any **y** ∈ R(**A**), there is associated an **x** satisfying that **Ax** = **y**.

Hence,

$$AA^{-}y = AA^{-}Ax = Ax = y. \qquad \text{(Q.E.D.)}$$

The lemma just shown implies that it makes no difference whether we choose (i) or (ii) to define the g-inverse. Since we prefer (ii) to (i), we arrive at the following definition.

Definition AP.1 For any m by n matrix **A**, an n by m matrix $\mathbf{A}^{-}$ such that $\mathbf{AA^{-}A} = \mathbf{A}$ is said to be the g-inverse of **A**.

Remark concerning Definition AP.1 The usual elimination method guarantees that for any **A**, there exists $\mathbf{A}^{-}$ such that

$$\mathbf{AA^{-}A} = \mathbf{A} \quad \text{and } \mathbf{A^{-}AA^{-}} = \mathbf{A}^{-}.$$

For the detail, see Rao (1973, pp.26-27).

Lemma AP.3 Let $L_i(i=1, 2)$ be two linear subspaces with the properties that $L_2 \subseteq L_1$ and that $\dim L_1 = \dim L_2 = d$. Then $L_1 = L_2$, where by $\dim L_i$ we mean the number of vectors forming a basis of L_i.

Proof Suppose the contrary. Then there exists an **x** of L_1 which does not belong to L_2. Let $\{\mathbf{y}^1, \mathbf{y}^2, \Lambda, \mathbf{y}^d\}$ be a basis of L_2. Since **x** is not in L_2, the vectors $\mathbf{x}, \mathbf{y}^1, \mathbf{y}^2, \Lambda, \mathbf{y}^d$ are linearly independent, for otherwise there exists a nonzero vector $(c_0, c_1, c_2, \Lambda, c_d)$ such that

$$c_0\mathbf{x} + c_1\mathbf{y}^1 + \cdots + c_d\mathbf{y}^d = \mathbf{0}$$

If $c_0 = 0$, $c_i = 0$ $(i = 1, \cdots, d)$, for $\mathbf{y}^1, \mathbf{y}^2, \cdots, \mathbf{y}^d$ are linearly independent by definition. Thus, $c_0 \neq 0$, whence **x** is expressed as a linear combination of $\mathbf{y}^j$ $(j = 1, \cdots, d)$. Consequently, **x** should be in L_2, which violates the hypothesis that **x** is not in L_2. Hence, $\mathbf{x}, \mathbf{y}^1, \mathbf{y}^2, \cdots, \mathbf{y}^d$ are linearly independent and in L_1, because $\mathbf{y}^j \in L_2 \subseteq L_1$ $(j = 1, \Lambda, d)$. Therefore, $d = \dim L_1 \geq d+1$, a self-contradiction.

Theorem AP.2 Let **A** be an m by n complex matrix. Then $\mathbf{A}^{-}$ possesses the properties stated below (Assertions (i) through (iii) are due to Rao & Mitra (1971; Lemma 2.2.6)).

(i) $(\mathbf{A^{-}A}) = (\mathbf{A^{-}A})^2$, that is, $\mathbf{A^{-}A}$ is idempotent,
(ii) if **V** is a matrix such that $r(\mathbf{A^*VA}) = r(\mathbf{A})$ then
  (ii-1) $\mathbf{A}(\mathbf{A^*VA})^{-}(\mathbf{A^*VA}) = \mathbf{A}$ and $(\mathbf{A^*VA})(\mathbf{A^*VA})^{-}\mathbf{A^*} = \mathbf{A^*}$,
  (ii-2) $\mathbf{A}(\mathbf{A^*VA})^{-}\mathbf{A^*}$ has the properties;
    (ii-2.1) $\mathbf{A}(\mathbf{A^*VA})^{-}\mathbf{A^*}$ is invariant for any choice of $(\mathbf{A^*VA})^{-}$,
    (ii-2.2) $r(\mathbf{A}(\mathbf{A^*VA})^{-}\mathbf{A^*}) = r(\mathbf{A})$, and
    (ii-2.3) if $\mathbf{A^*VA}$ is hermitian, so is $\mathbf{A}(\mathbf{A^*VA})^{-}\mathbf{A^*}$,
and finally
(iii) for any $\mathbf{y} \in R(\mathbf{A})$, the general solution of $\mathbf{Ax} = \mathbf{y}$ is given by

$$\mathbf{A}^{-}\mathbf{y} + (\mathbf{I} - \mathbf{A}^{-}\mathbf{A})\mathbf{v},$$

where **v** is an arbitrary vector.

Proof (i) $(\mathbf{A}^{-}\mathbf{A})(\mathbf{A}^{-}\mathbf{A}) = \mathbf{A}^{-}(\mathbf{A}\mathbf{A}^{-}\mathbf{A}) = \mathbf{A}^{-}\mathbf{A}$.

(ii-1) The definition of g-inverse yields

$$(\mathbf{A}^*\mathbf{V}\mathbf{A})(\mathbf{A}^*\mathbf{V}\mathbf{A})^{-}(\mathbf{A}^*\mathbf{V}\mathbf{A}) = \mathbf{A}^*\mathbf{V}\mathbf{A}. \quad \text{(AP.7)}$$

Rearranging the terms of (AP.7), we have

$$(\mathbf{A}^*\mathbf{V}\mathbf{A})((\mathbf{A}^*\mathbf{V}\mathbf{A})^{-}(\mathbf{A}^*\mathbf{V}\mathbf{A}) - \mathbf{I}) = [\mathbf{0}].$$

In other words, every column of $((\mathbf{A}^*\mathbf{V}\mathbf{A})^{-}(\mathbf{A}^*\mathbf{V}\mathbf{A})) - \mathbf{I})$ is in $N(\mathbf{A}^*\mathbf{V}\mathbf{A})$ which equals $N(\mathbf{A})$ by Lemma AP.3. This verifies the first half of assertion (ii-1).

From (AP.7) it follows that $((\mathbf{A}^*\mathbf{V}\mathbf{A})(\mathbf{A}^*\mathbf{V}\mathbf{A})^{-} - \mathbf{I})(\mathbf{A}^*\mathbf{V}\mathbf{A}) = [\mathbf{0}]$.

To prove the second half, it suffices to notice that the first matrix of the left hand side of the above matrix equation lies in $N_L(\mathbf{A}^*\mathbf{V}\mathbf{A}) = N_L(\mathbf{A}^*)$.

(ii-2.1) By $\mathbf{D}_1$ and $\mathbf{D}_2$ denote any two g-inverses of $(\mathbf{A}^*\mathbf{V}\mathbf{A})$. Applying the second half of (ii-1), we obtain

$$((\mathbf{A}^*\mathbf{V}\mathbf{A})\mathbf{D}_i - \mathbf{I})\mathbf{A}^* = [\mathbf{0}] \;\; ; \;\; i = 1, 2.$$

This further reduces to

$$(\mathbf{A}^*\mathbf{V}\mathbf{A})(\mathbf{D}_1 - \mathbf{D}_2)\mathbf{A}^* = [\mathbf{0}]. \quad \text{(AP.8)}$$

Employing Lemma AP.3 as in the proof of the first half of assertion (ii-1), (AP.8) implies that $\mathbf{A}(\mathbf{D}_1\mathbf{A}^* - \mathbf{D}_2\mathbf{A}^*) = [\mathbf{0}]$, from which it immediately follows that

$$\mathbf{A}\mathbf{D}_1\mathbf{A}^* = \mathbf{A}\mathbf{D}_2\mathbf{A}^* \qquad \text{for any g-inverse of } (\mathbf{A}^*\mathbf{V}\mathbf{A}).$$

(ii-2.2) $r(\mathbf{A}) \geq r(\mathbf{A}(\mathbf{A}^*\mathbf{V}\mathbf{A})^{-}\mathbf{A}^*) \geq r(\mathbf{A}(\mathbf{A}^*\mathbf{V}\mathbf{A})^{-}\mathbf{A}^*\mathbf{V}\mathbf{A}) = r(\mathbf{A})$

(ii-2.3) Let **H** be an hermitian matrix. Then, as is well known, there exists a unitary matrix **Q** such that $\mathbf{Q}^*\mathbf{H}\mathbf{Q} = \begin{pmatrix} \Xi & 0 \\ 0 & 0 \end{pmatrix}$ where Ξ is a real diagonal matrix, the diagonal elements of which are real nonzero eigen values of **H**. Furth ermore, a direct calculation yields

$$\mathbf{H}\left(\mathbf{Q}\begin{pmatrix} \Xi^{-1} & \mathbf{0} \\ \mathbf{0} & \mathbf{0} \end{pmatrix}\mathbf{Q}^*\right)\mathbf{H} = \mathbf{Q}\begin{pmatrix} \Xi, & \mathbf{0} \\ \mathbf{0} & \mathbf{0} \end{pmatrix}\mathbf{Q}^* = \mathbf{H} \quad \textit{and} \quad \mathbf{Q}\begin{pmatrix} \Xi^{-1} & \mathbf{0} \\ \mathbf{0} & \mathbf{0} \end{pmatrix}\mathbf{Q}^*.$$

Consequently, $Q\begin{pmatrix} \Xi^{-1} & 0 \\ 0 & 0 \end{pmatrix}Q^* = D$ is an hermitian g-inverse of **H** and **A*DA** = **A(A*VA)⁻A*** is hermitian for any g-inverse **(A*VA)⁻** of **(A*VA)**.

(iii) A direct computation, with Lemma AP.2 and Definition AP.1 in mind, assures that

$$\mathbf{A}(\mathbf{A}^{-}\mathbf{y} + (\mathbf{I} - \mathbf{A}^{-}\mathbf{A})\mathbf{v}) = \mathbf{A}\mathbf{A}^{-}\mathbf{y} = \mathbf{y} \qquad \text{(Q.E.D.)}$$

Consider now estimate β of the model

$$\mathbf{Y} = \mathbf{X}\beta + \mathbf{u},$$

Where **X(y)** is an n by K matrix (n by 1 vector) of observations, **u** the vector of disturbances, and n of course the sample size.

The least squares estimates $\hat{\beta}$ of β is known to be the solution of the form;

$$\hat{\beta} = (\mathbf{X}'\mathbf{X})^{-}\mathbf{X}'\mathbf{y} + (\mathbf{I} - (\mathbf{X}'\mathbf{X})^{-}(\mathbf{X}'\mathbf{X}))\mathbf{v}, \qquad \text{(AP.9)}$$

where **v** can be any vector of K-dimensional real vector space.

Define the estimate $\hat{\mathbf{y}}$ of y by $\mathbf{X}\hat{\beta}$ and the residual e by $\mathbf{y} - \hat{\mathbf{y}}$. Then in view of Theorem AP.2(ii-1: the first half), we have

$$\mathbf{e} = (\mathbf{I} - \mathbf{X}(\mathbf{X}'\mathbf{X})^{-}\mathbf{X}')\mathbf{y}. \qquad \text{(AP.10)}$$

Therefore, Theorem AP.2(ii-2.1) asserts that e is independent of the g-inverse used but dependent solely on the data observed. And (AP.10) affords a basis for interpreting the denominator [numerator] of (3) in the text as the sum of squared residuals obtained from regressing $\mathbf{z} = \mathbf{Y}_\Delta\beta_\Delta$ on $\mathbf{X}[\mathbf{X}_1]$.

List of Notation and/or Symbols[2]

{a}	: a singlton consisting of a vector **a**.
$\tilde{R}$ **(B)**	: a complement of **{0}** with respect to R(**B**), in symbol $\tilde{R}$ (**B**) = **{R(B)\\{0}}**.
[0]	: a zero matrix.
$L_1 \oplus L_2$	: the set consisting of all **x** + **y** (**x** ∈ L_1 & **y** ∈ L_2), where L_i (i = 1, 2) are linear subspaces of a vector space, say R^n, such that $L_1 \cap L_2$ = **{0}**.
{X\\Y}	: the complementary set of **Y** with respect to a set **X** containing **Y**.
N_L**(A)**	: a set of row vectors **y** such that **yA** = **0** and it is clear that N_L(**A**) is a linear subspace of dimension m-r(**A**), where m is the number of rows of **A** and r(**A**) denotes the rank of the matrix **A**.

[2] The notation and/or symbols collected here are confined to those which are not defined explicitly either in the text or in appendices.

ACKNOWLEDGMENTS

This is a revised version of the paper presented at a session in honour of Professor Jean Paelinck of the Thirty-Sixth European Congress of RSA held in ETH, Zürich, from August 26 to August 30, 1996. Meanwhile, the paper presented at the Thirty-Sixth European Congress is a revision of our paper read at a session in honour of Professor Paelinck of the Fifth World Congress of RSAI held in Rissho University, Tokyo, from May 3 to May 6, 1996. Authors are particularly grateful to Professor Paelinck for his comments at the above sessions and his suggestion on the relationship between the canonical corregression and the LIML. We express our gratitute to Professor Otani of Kobe University for his comments at the World Congress. Moreover, authors also owe Professors Antonie Bailey and Lay James Gibson thanks for their having an opportunity to present the earlier version at the Paelinck session.

REFERENCES

Fujikoshi, Y., K. Morimune, N. Kunitomo, and M. Taniguchi. (1982). "Asymptotic Expansions of the Distributions of the Estimates of Coefficients in a Simultaneous Equation System", *Journal of Econometrics*,18, 191-205.

Fuller, W.A. (1977). "Some Properties of a Modification of the Limited Information Estimator", *Econometrica*, 45, 939-953.

Johnston, J. (1984). *Econometric Methods* (Third Edition). New York, McGraw-Hill.

Morimune, K. (1983). "Approximate Distributions of the *k*-class Estimators When the Degree of Overidentifiability is Large Compared to the Sample Size", *Econometrica*, 51, 821-841.

Paelink, J.H.P. (avec la collabolation de J.P. Ancot, H. Gravesteijn, J.H. Kuiper et Th. Ten Raa) (1985). *Elements D'analyse Economique Spatiale* (*Elements of Spatial Economic Analysis*), Geneve, Editions Regionales Europeennes.

Rao, C.R. and S.K. Mitra. (1971). *Generalized Inverse of Matrices and Its Applications*. New York, John Wiley & Sons.

Rao, C.R. (1973). *Linear Statistical Inference and Its Applications* (Second edition). New York, John Wiley & Sons.

CHAPTER 10

DEVELOPMENTS IN FLOW-BASED LOCATION-ALLOCATION MODELS

M. John Hodgson

1.0 INTRODUCTION

Location-allocation (LA) models optimally locate service facilities and allocate demand to them. They have been used to locate many types of facility and service (Hodgson et al., 1993). Many different objectives have been optimized in the literature, the most popular being of distance-minimizing or demand-covering types. Whatever the objective, almost without exception, demand is conceived of as occurring in points from which patrons travel to facilities, or from which services are delivered to patrons. There is a growing recognition that not all demands are *point-based* (expressed by patrons at points), but that demands may be *flow-based* (expressed by flows, by patrons who are traveling on a pre-determined journey). In this paper, I consider several models which locate facilities to serve flow-based demands.

2.0 ANALYSIS

2.1 The Location Of Public Facilities Intermediate To The Journey To Work

While applying LA models to locating child care facilities in Edmonton, Canada, (Hodgson and Doyle, 1978), we became increasingly dissatisfied with the assumption that daycare centers should be located to minimize the travel from the child's residence, or from a parent's workplace. Interviews with users of publicly funded daycare told us that most trips were by public transit, and that children were usually dropped off at a facility during a parent's journey to work. Parents would make this journey whether or not a child were involved; the "daycare" travel costs of parents were those *in excess of the normal journey to work.* I derived a model which minimized these travel costs (Hodgson, 1981). The model was based on the familiar, point-based, p-median model. Demand was estimated for a number of traffic zones, for which interzonal transit travel times were available.

The p-median model has the objective:

$$\text{MIN:} \quad Z = \sum_{i=1}^{n} W_i \sum_{j=1}^{n} t_{ij} \lambda_{ij} \qquad (1)$$

where n is the number of traffic zones; W_i, is the demand for the service in zone i; t_{ij} is the transit travel time between demand zone i and a potential facility in zone j; and λ_{ij} is a binary variable taking the value of 1 if zone i is allocated to a facility in zone j and 0 if not. Constraints upon the problem (ReVelle and Swain, 1970) ensure that each demand point is allocated to one and only one facility and that exactly p facilities are located. The model minimizes the aggregate demand-weighted travel time between residential and facility zones.

The journey to work model minimizes the aggregate travel time *in excess* of the normal journey to work:

$$\text{MIN:} \quad Z' = \sum_{i=1}^{n} \sum_{j=1}^{n} J_{ij} \sum_{k=1}^{n} T_{ijk} \lambda_{ijk} \qquad (2)$$

Where J_{ij} is the number of work journeys between i and j; T_{ijk} *is* the excess travel time incurred in diverting a work trip between i and j to employ a facility at k, defined as: $T_{ij} = t_{ik} + t_{kj} - t_{ij}$ and λ_{ijk} is a binary variable taking the value of 1 if a work trip from i to j is allocated to a facility at k, 0 if not.

This expression can be reduced, because the basic unit underlying it is the origin-destination work journey: the number of journeys, J_{ij} ; excess travel time, T_{ijk} ; and the allocation variable λ_{ijk} ; are each defined in terms of the OD pair, ij. We can redefine this basic unit as origin-destination pair, q, and rewrite (2) as:

$$\text{MIN:} \quad Z' = \sum_{q=1}^{n^2} J_q \sum_{k}^{n} T_{qk} \lambda_{qk} \qquad (3)$$

This reduction underlies the notation of all of the flow-based models in this paper.

The journey to work model is structurally identical to the p-median model, and can besolved using the same techniques. Moreover, the combinatorial dimensions of the problem are the same as in the node-based model: $_nC_p$. The model is sized as one with n^2 demand points and n potential facilities, it is only linearly more costly to solve than the simple node-based model.

I applied the model to the location of daycare facilities in Edmonton, and compared the results with point-based models minimizing aggregate weighted travel times from residences and to workplaces. The persons catered to by this model, those who did drop children off *en route* to work would be much better served by this model. Moreover, persons who delivered their children to daycare from their residence would be much better served than they would be from a workplace-oriented model. Persons seeking accessibility to the workplace would be much better served by the journey to work model than they would be from a residence-oriented model. In short, as well as optimizing for parents who drop their children off on the way to work, the journey to work model emerged as an excellent compromise for the two node-based groups of patrons.

2.2 The Flow Capturing Location-Allocation Model (FCLM)

Network location-allocation models treat demand as being exerted at the nodes of the network. The marketing literature is replete, however, with examples of businesses (convenience stores, gasoline stations, banking machines, billboards, for instance), for which traffic flows exert demand. The marketing literature does not consider the systematic nature of multiple facility location, however, suggesting only that a location's desirability is proportional to the amount of traffic passing it. The strategy of choosing high-traffic locations is unsuited to locating multiple facilities, however, because it ignores self-competition. On its journey between origin and destination, traffic passing along links and through nodes has passed, and will pass, along other links and through other nodes. Two adjacent nodes may have a large amount of *common* traffic passing through them. If one node is selected for a facility, it is essential to account for the traffic captured there before assessing the desirability of the other node. One of these facilities might be better located elsewhere in the network, capturing traffic that might otherwise go unserved. Otherwise, traffic is double-counted, and two such facilities compete for their common traffic. This self-competition is given the colorful name *cannibalization.*

The location community was schizophrenic. On one hand were operations researchers with LA models, well suited to locating *systems* of facilities optimally, ignoring flow based demands. On the other, were marketing analysts, stressing the importance of flow-based demand (Davies and Rogers, 1984), ignoring the systematic nature of facility location. The FCLM (Hodgson, 1990) reconciled these two approaches. This reconciliation was timely, the same model was developed by Berman *et al* (1992) around the same time. The FCLM is formulated as:

$$\text{MAX: } Z = \sum_{q \in Q} f_q y_q \tag{4}$$

Subject to:

$$\sum_{k \in K} x_k = y_q, \forall q \in Q \tag{5}$$

$$\sum_{k \in K} x_k = p \tag{6}$$

where:

Z is the objective function, total flows captured at least once.
Q indicates a particular OD pair.
Q is the set of all OD pairs.
f_q is the exogenously-provided flow between OD pair Q.

Y_q	is a binary variable, = 1 if f_q is captured, 0 if not.
k	is a node, a potential facility location.
K	is the set of all nodes that are potential facility locations.
x_k	is a binary variable, = 1 if there is a facility at node k, 0 if not.
N_q	is the set of nodes capable of capturing fq.
p	is the number of facilities to be located.

Flows are captured if they pass through a node at which a facility is located. The objective (4) is to capture as much flow as possible, subject to the restrictions that flow on path q cannot be captured unless there is at least one facility on path q (5), and that exactly p facilities be located (6).

This formulation is structurally identical to the maximum covering location problem (MCLM, Church and ReVelle, 1974). The difference lies in the definition of N_q, which in the MCLM, is the set of nodes within the covering distance of demand node q, and in the FCLM, is the set of nodes on the path taken by the flow f_q. In either case, it is the set of nodes capable of providing the service; of covering a point or capturing a flow. As discussed with the journey to work model, the FCLM has many more demands than the node-based covering model, the number of flow pairs being of the order of n^2. My interest in flow capturing was to bring the systematic optimization tools of LA to bear upon location in reference to traffic flow. I stressed system-wide optimization; much of this paper was devoted to a discussion of the flow cannibalization problem. Berman et al. (1992), in an operations research orientation, concentrated on developing solution techniques. Both papers indicated that a simple greedy heuristic is very robust for this model. I, and Berman and his colleagues, have continued to develop flow-based LA modeling; their developments have gone in quite different directions. In the remainder of this paper, I shall concentrate on applications and developments in my own work and leave the interested reader to pursue other developments in a recent review chapter by Berman et al. (1995), which suggests that the term *flow intercepting* models be adopted, in deference to the probabilistic nature of some of their work.

Hodgson (1990) demonstrated the FCLM with a small random test problem. We have recently tested the model with data for Edmonton, Canada, a city of over 600,000 (Hodgson et al., 1996a). The network, based on 177 traffic zones, comprised 703 nodes and 2198 links, and gave rise to 23,350 OD flows. We solved the problem using binary linear programming (BLP) and substantiated earlier findings that the simple greedy heuristic model is extremely robust for this model. We also produced a real-world assessment of the FCLM's ability to combat the flow cannibalization problem. Flow cannibalization arises from the bundling of flows at strategic places in the network. Locating at nodes with high flows may result in a bunching of facilities at these strategic nodes, resulting in some flows being captured more than once. Where resources (facilities) are limited, redundant flow capturing is likely to leave other flows in the network uncaptured. *Cannibalization* is the effect of capturing flow more than once at the expense of flows elsewhere in the network not being captured at all.

We investigate cannibalization by comparing the results of a solution in which cannibalization is minimized and one in which it is not considered. The first solution is the *optimal* solution, found by solving the BLP in statements (4) - (6). The second solution, termed the *naïve* solution, simply locates facilities at the p nodes with the highest flows. We compare the results of the optimal and naïve $p =$ 15 solutions. The naïve approach locates two tight facility clusters, one in the central business district and the other along a major freeway (Figure 10.1). We demonstrate cannibalization by comparing the flows that the model naïvely expects to capture (Figure 10.1) and what it actually would capture after double-counting is eliminated (Figure 10.2). The optimal set of facilities is more widely distributed, avoiding, as much as possible, redundant capturing (Figure 10.3). The naïve strategy's objective function rises strongly, based strongly on double-counting, with 50 facilities, it appears to have captured more than three times the total flows in the system (Figure 10.4). In reality, it performs more poorly than the greedy algorithm which rises to capture over 80 percent of the system's flows with 50 facilities. This discrepancy between apparent and actual performance of the naïve approach, resulting in sub-FCLM performance, arises from the cannibalization process.

We have argued that cannibalization results from capturing some flows redundantly at the cost of others. We observe evidence of this redundancy mechanism in Figure 10.5. The graph compares three solution approaches, the *optimal,* the *greedy* (solved using the simple add and adjust strategy of Kuehn and Hamburger, 1963), and the *naïve* strategy implied by locating at the 15 nodes of largest flow. The *naïve* strategy is highly redundant, capturing almost two percent of flows nine times, and failing to capture 53.8 percent of flows at all. No solution can capture flows only once, but the greedy and optimal procedures capture 45.8 percent of network flows only once, and none more than four times. The resources so released allow much more flow to be captured at least once. The redundancy data are strongly consistent with the postulated flow cannibalization process, and they also corroborate the greedy heuristic's robustness.

2.3 A Billboard Location Model

The FCLM is strongly dedicated to the notion that redundant flow capturing results in flow cannibalization and must be avoided. In some situations, however, redundant capturing may be advantageous. The advertising literature indicates that multiple exposure to the same message can be important in getting that message across. Multiple exposure usually means several exposures over a period of time on an electronic medium such as television. Outdoor advertising, in the form of billboards, is an example of a medium in which multiple exposure can be spatial. For example, a person who drives along a route will be exposed to several billboards giving the same, or closely related, messages.

We have done some research aiming modifications of the FCLM to billboard advertising (Hodgson and Berman, 1997). The essential differences in this work are:

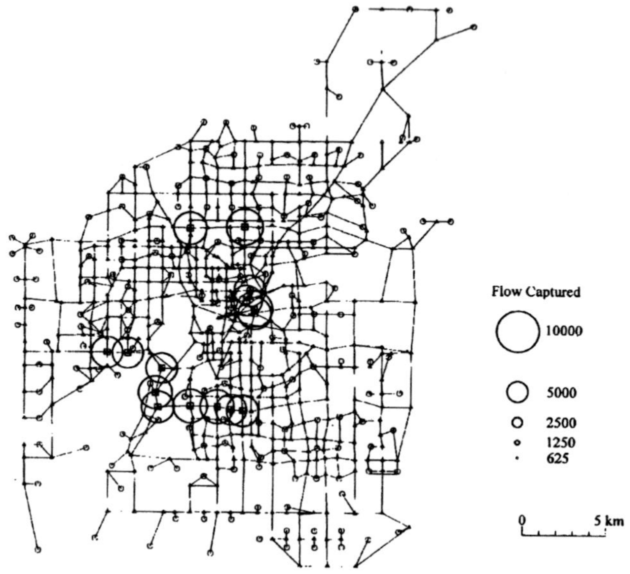

Figure 10.1. Naïve model, expected flows captured.

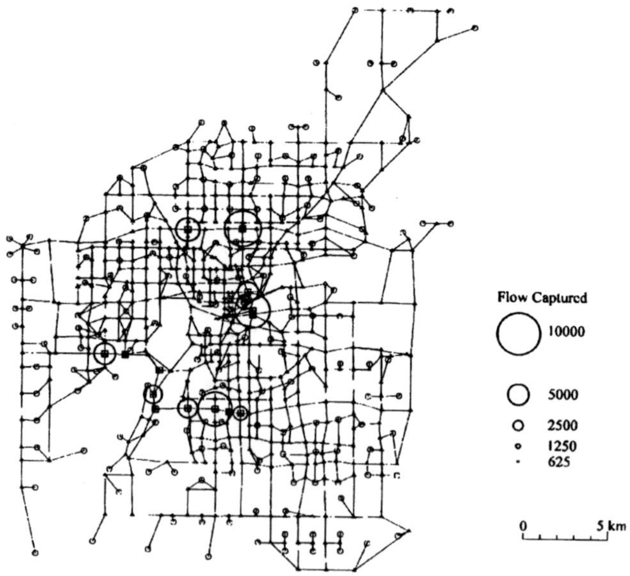

Figure 10.2. Naïve model, actual flows captured.

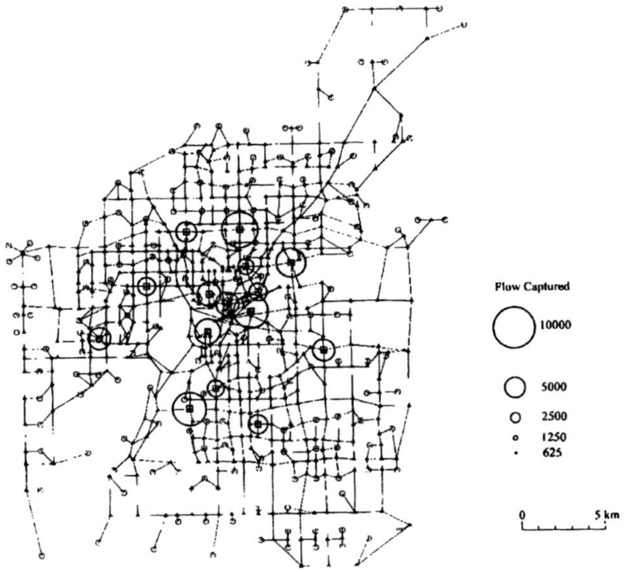

Figure 10.3. FCLM, flows captured.

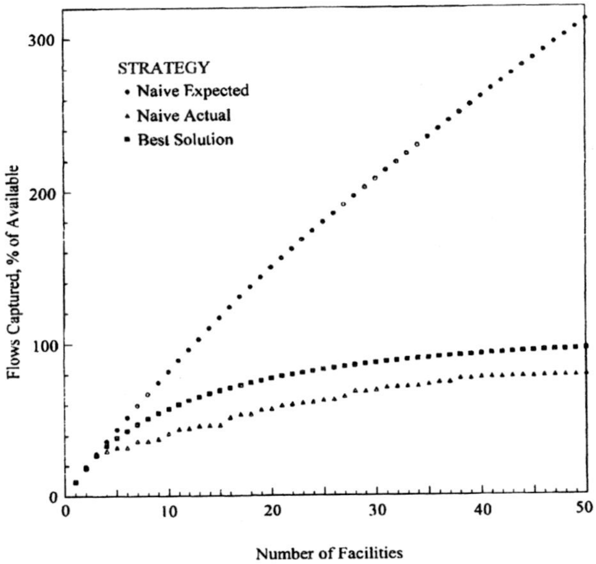

Figure 10.4. Flows captured by each model.

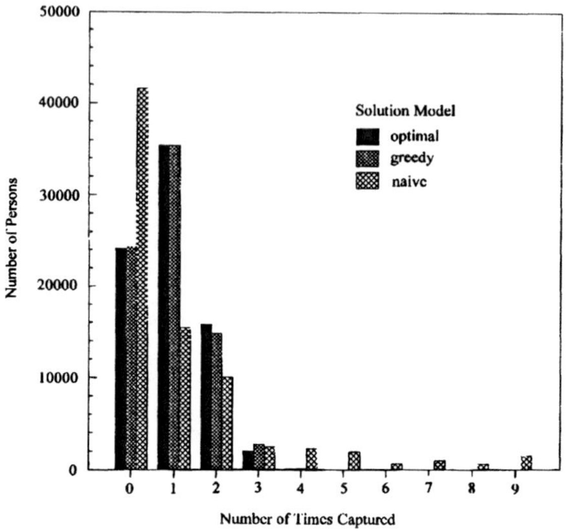

Figure 10.5. Redundancy characteristics.

1. Facilities are located within links, rather than at nodes, of the network.
2. Facilities may be located on either side of the link to accommodate one-way and two way streets.
3. Rather than ignore cannibalization, or conversely, to give no credit to multiple capturing, a functional relationship describing the advantages of second, third, ... exposures to the message is incorporated into the objective function.

We formulate and test an IP formulation of the model and an heuristic solution method. We applied the model to Edmonton road traffic. This research continues. It will lead the way in bridging the gap between traditional retail location schemes which do not discount multiple capturing, and the FCLM which gives no credit to beneficial redundant capturing.

2.4 Bicriterion Location-Allocation Model: Flow-Capturing and *p*-Median

The *p*-median, and other traditional network LA models, treat demand expressed at nodes. The FCLM was developed in the realization that traffic flows also exert demand for many goods and services. Neither extreme is perfectly correct; there is almost certainly, within urban areas at least, a mix of behavior for any type of business. Gasoline stations are more highly flow oriented, small supermarkets are more oriented to residences, but there is a mix. Most retail businesses cater to both types of demand; they serve persons who travel specifically to the outlet from their homes *and* they serve passing traffic. Hodgson and Rosing

(1992) presented a bicriterion LA model based on the trade-off between serving demands arising in nodes and demands arising from flows. Hodgson et al. (1995) tested this model with traffic in the road network of Edmonton, Canada.

The model trades off the objectives of the flow-capturing location-allocation model and the *p*-median model. It is a straight-forward hybrid of the flow capturing and the traditional *p*-median models, in which we applied weights totaling 1.0 to the separate objectives. Thus we could vary weights from the situation in which all demand arises from residential locations (*p*-median), through to that in which all demand arises from passing traffic (FCLM).

Our analysis focused on the consequences upon each type of demand behavior of locating for the other. The FCLM solution, illustrated above in Figure 10.3, locates facilities at strategic flow bundling points on the transportation network. Because morning peak traffic is modeled, it tends to focus on central locations, resulting in bundling of traffic at relatively central intersections of major arterials and expressways. This tendency to central locations results in imbalanced *p*-median service areas, some are quite small, others overly large (Figure 10.6). The *p*-median solution presents a looser cluster of facilities reacting to the higher population densities in the center (Figure 10.7), but it also exhibits a greater spread of facilities throughout the city and a better balanced set of service areas (Figure 10.8). None of the *p*-median locations capture large flows and many capture very little flow at all; being located to minimize average distance, they are located on major flow paths only by chance, if at all.

We determined that, in Edmonton, with morning traffic, residence-based demand will tolerate flow-capturing optimality better than would flow-based demand tolerate residence oriented optimality (Figure 10.9). We use the term *damage* to describe how much worse the solution of one model is when evaluated against the objective of the other. With *p* between five and 15, the FCLM locations are about 1.5 times as poor as *p*-median ones; *p*-median solutions are consistently more than 2.1 times as bad as FCLM ones. This is basically because the *p*-median model is quite tolerant of minor locational shifts; a location at a major nearby intersection will not damage severely its effectiveness. On the other hand, flow-capturing decrees locations on the major routes of a network. Moving facilities even slightly from these major routes impairs seriously their ability to serve traffic. The analysis highlighted the importance of knowing to what extent a facility's custom is derived from passing traffic and from local residence-based sources, and of adopting a multiobjective approach.

2.5 A Model For Inspecting Hazardous Vehicles

Vehicle inspection programs are designed to protect networks from risks such as hazardous cargoes and drunk drivers. Locating inspection stations is an important element of such programs. These types of risks are clearly flow-based and the FCLM could be used to optimally intercept offenders. The FCLM enacts a *punitive* approach, however, the inspector's goal would be to intercept and inspect

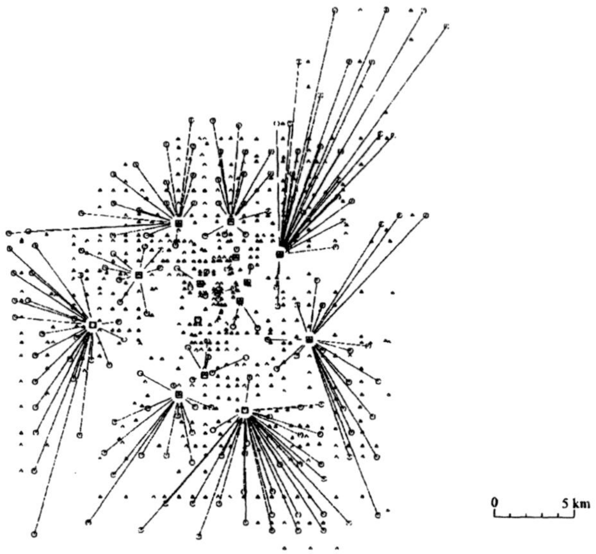

Figure 10.6. FCLM: *p*-median allocations.

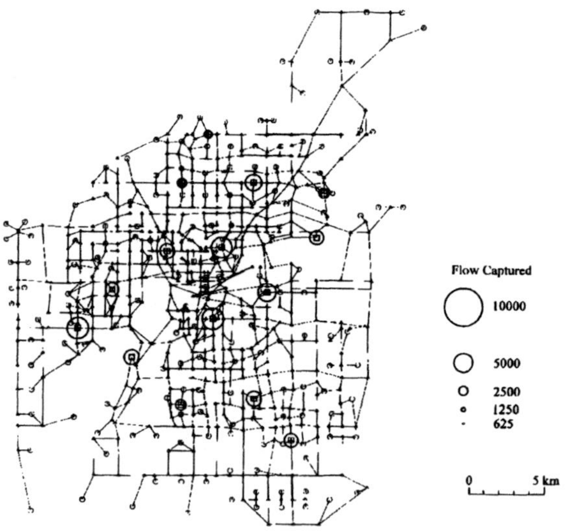

Figure 10.7. *p*- median: flows captured.

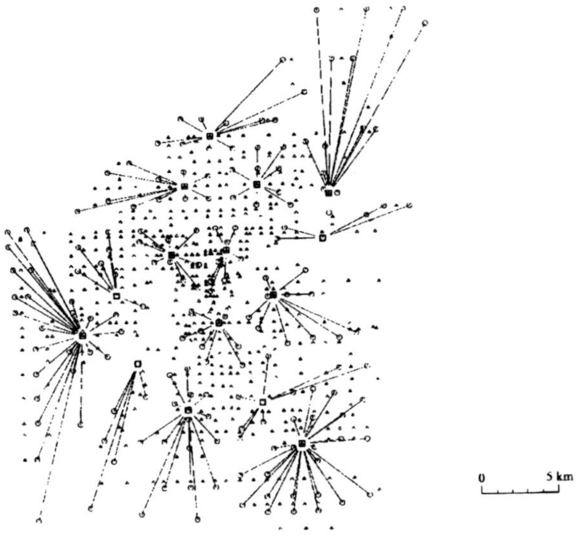

Figure 10.8. *p*-median: *p*-median allocations.

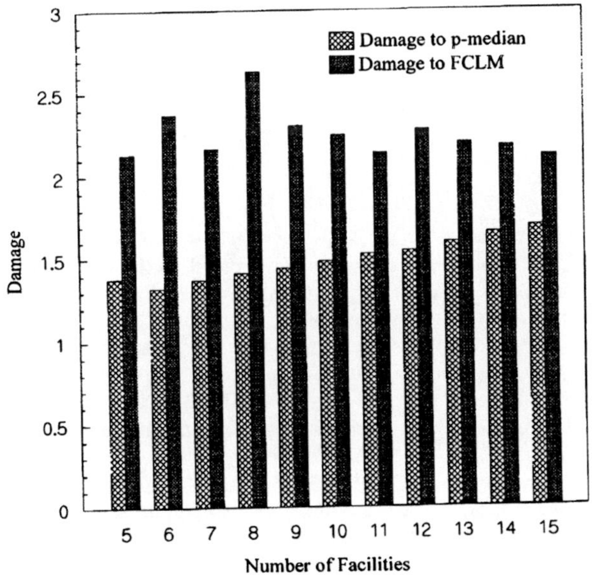

Figure 10.9. Damage statistics.

as many vehicles as possible, regardless of where in their journeys. We proposed a model espousing a new philosophy for inspecting traffic in networks (Hodgson et al., 1996b). Rather than *a punitive approach*, we proposed *a preventative* approach which locates inspectors to protect network occupants as much as possible. We model the public's potential exposure to risk as the product of the number of persons occupying (traveling, living, working, shopping, and visiting on or within a critical distance of) the link and the link's length. Traffic flows from *sources to sinks.* Links are protected by inspecting vehicles above (sourceward) them; when this has occurred, we say that *the link has been protected*, or that *the link's risk has been eliminated.*

We formulated the network inspection problem as a mixed integer program which locates inspection stations to maximize protection against risk. It is formulated as:

$$\text{MAX:} \quad Z'' = \sum_{q=1}^{n_q} \sum_{i \in \Lambda_q} R_{qi} X_{qi} \tag{7}$$

SUBJECT TO:

$$\sum_{i \in \Lambda q} X_{qi} \leq 1.0, \forall q \tag{8}$$

$$Y_i - X_{qi} \geq 0 \; \forall q, i \in \Lambda_q \tag{9}$$

$$\sum_{i=1}^{n} Y_i = p \tag{10}$$

where: variables are defined as above, or:

Λ_q is the set of nodes which can eliminate some or all of the risk posed by a particular source-sink pair q's flow: i.e.: the set of all nodes on path q between and including that source and sink.

R_{qi} is the protection available to path q at node i. It is calculated as the product of the source sink flow on path q and the persons at risk on path q between node i and the sink.

X_{qi} is the proportion of the total protection available at node i to path q which is used.

The objective function, (7), maximizes the amount of protection the network receives. Constraint (8) ensures that each path receives no more than 100 per cent of the protection that one inspection station can provide. Constraint (9) ensures that a node cannot provide protection to a path unless it has an inspection station. Constraint (10) specifies that p inspection stations will be located.

We tested the model with several problems simulating hazardous waste disposal, hazardous material interactions, and general network interaction problems. The solution times for even reasonably sized networks were high. Moreover, the simple greedy heuristic, robust for related flow intercepting problems, is not robust for this model. A major concern of future research must be to find solution methods which are more efficient than MIP and more robust than our greedy heuristic. Another arises from conversations I enjoyed with Jean Paelink when I was Visiting Tinbergen Professor of Economics and Erasmus University in 1994. That concerns the likelihood that drivers may try to avoid inspection by altering their routes. We are, at this time, experimenting with inspection/avoidance games.

3.0 SUMMARY AND CONCLUSIONS

Network location-allocation problems have traditionally been oriented toward node-based demand. Many location problems, however, are driven by flow-based demands. The FCLM, introduced in 1990, was the first model to reconcile the systematic power of LA modeling with the need to serve flow-based demands. I have discussed several of my applications and extensions of this simple model, and the reader is encouraged to review others in Berman et al., (1995). I hope that as the flow-based LA model becomes more ingrained on the consciousness of location analysts, its underlying principles will be used by others to adapt and extend the model to other problems facing flow-based demands.

REFERENCES

Berman, O., M. J. Hodgson, and D. Krass. (1995). "Flow intercepting models." In *Facility Location: A Survey of Applications and Methods*, edited by Z. Drezner, 427-52. New York: Springer-Verlag.

Berman, O., R.C. Larson, and N. Fouska. (1992). "Optimal location of discretionary service *facilities.*" *Transportation Science*, 26, 201-1 1.

Davies, R. L. and D. S. Rogers, eds. (1984). *Store Location and Store Assessment Research.* NewYork: John Wiley and Sons.

Church, R. L. and C. S. ReVelle. (1974). "The maximal covering location problem." *Papers of the Regional Science Association*, 32, 101-18.

Hodgson, M.J. (1990). "A flow-capturing location-allocation model." *Geographical Analysis*, 22, 270-279.

Hodgson, M.J. (1981). "The location of public facilities intermediate to the journey to work." *European Journal of Operational Research*, 6, 199-204.

Hodgson, M.J. and O. Berman. (1997). "A billboard location model." *Geographical and Environmental Modelling*, 1, 25-45.

Hodgson, M.J. and P. Doyle. (1978). "The location of public services considering the mode of travel." *Socio-Economic Planning Sciences*, 12, 25-39.

Hodgson, M.J. and K.E. Rosing. (1992). "A network location-allocation model trading off flow capturing and *p*-median objectives." *Annals of Operations Research*, 40, 247-60.

Hodgson, M.J., K.E. Rosing, and A.L.G. Storrier. (1996a). "Applying the flow capturing location-allocation model to an authentic network: Edmonton, Canada." *European Journal of Operational Research*, 90, 427-43.

Hodgson, M. J., K.E. Rosing, and A.L.G. Storrier. (1997). "Testing a bicriterion location-allocation model with real-world network traffic: the case of Edmonton, Canada." In *Multicriteria Analysis*, edited by J. Clímaco, 484-95. New York: Springer-Verlag.

Hodgson, M.J., K.E. Rosing, and J. Zhang. (1996b). "Locating vehicle inspection stations to protect a transportation network." *Geographical Analysis*, 28, 299-314.

Hodgson, M.J., K.E. Rosing, and F. Shmulevitz. (1993). "A review of location-allocation applications literature." *Studies in Locational Analysis*, 5, 3 -29.

ReVelle, C. S. and R. Swain. (1970). "Central facilities location." *Geographical Analysis*, 2, 30-42.

Kuehn, A.A. and O. Hamburger. (1963). "A heuristic program for locating warehouses." *Management Science*, 9, 643-66.

Teitz, M.B. and P. Bart. (1968). "Heuristic methods for estimating the generalized vertex median of a weighted graph." *Operations Research*, 16, 955 -61.

CHAPTER 11

HEURISTIC CONCENTRATION: ITS CARE AND FEEDING

K.E. Rosing

1.0 INTRODUCTION

Rosing (1997) has demonstrated, specifically in the case of the Teitz and Bart (1968) heuristic applied to the *p*-median problem, that the quality of the solution provided by an interchange heuristic deteriorates as either the number of basic individuals (termed demand nodes and symbolised as n) and/or the number of medians to be located (termed facilities and symbolised by *p*) increases. The deterioration is shown to involve both the probability of finding the optimal solution and, judged by functional value, the closeness of a typical solution to the optimal. Applications of combinatorial analysis in GIS, in facility location, in studies of aggregation error and in many other fields involve extremely large values for the number of basic individuals, n, and the number of medians to be chosen from the basic individuals or the number of groups, *p*. If the trends identified by Rosing (1997) are indeed general to interchange heuristics and if they hold for problems outside the domain studied (n # 300, *p* # 50) it is an extremely serious situation since optimal methods are unavailable for these larger problems.

Heuristic Concentration (Rosing and ReVelle, 1996a, 1996b) is being developed specifically to deal with these larger problems. HC is a two stage process. Stage one involves doing some number (q) of random-start runs of an interchange heuristic in order to develop a data base. Some number (m) of these solutions are then subjected to a simple analysis in order to develop the Concentration Set (CS). Stage two is the selection of a good solution (heuristically derived) or the best solution (by an exact method) from the CS. If the optimal solution to the original problem is contained within the CS then the result of the application of an exact method to the CS will be the optimal solution to the original problem. The likelihood of optimality is then a function of the quality of the CS. The parameters q and m are obviously of extreme importance to the CS. This paper attempts to specify good values for these two parameters.

2.0 THE EXAMPLE STUDY

Since HC is intended to be used in cases where, because of problem size, the optimal solution is difficult to obtain or unobtainable it is important to establish the general characteristics of its behaviour in situations where the optimal solution is known. For this reason the present study is again based upon the data sets used to investigate the characteristics of behaviour with increasing n and p by Rosing (1997) and are described there. The combinations of nine values of n = 100, 125, 150, ..., 300 and nine values of p = 10, 15, 20, ..., 50 produce 81 instances. Of these three instances, as indicated in Table 11.1, were unusable for technical reasons leaving 78 valid instances.

2.1 Stage one, making the CS

An interchange heuristic stops when no one-at-a-time change can improve the objective function. This is termed an SPP since it is stable. Such stable solutions may be optimal but usually the vast majority are sub-optimal. While different starting points can arrive at the same solution a range of different solutions will generally be found. Multiple random starts of an interchange heuristic, declaring the best found to be either "optimal or close to the optimal," have been used for over a generation. Each solution has a functional value and a list of the nodes which are selected to be facilities. Generally many of the nodes in the sub-optimal SPP will be identical to the list in the optimal solution. Each sub-optimal SPP, however must differ from the optimal in having at least two nodes which are not in the selected node list of the optimal solution. If these are ordered best to worst by functional value the better SPPs will be found to have node lists that are more similar to the optimal solution than the worst. Figure 11.1, based on 200 random starts for each instance shown in Tables 11.1 and 11.2, shows the percent of nodes which are identical to those in the optimal solution. To construct this figure first any optimal solutions found were discarded. Second, the range from best sub-optimal to worst sub-optimal, for each instance, was divided into six classes and number of identical nodes recorded. Third, the total over all instances summed, class by class, and percents calculated. Note that for the best one-sixth over 80% of the nodes are identical and even for the worst one-sixth over 50% are identical.

For this experiment the heuristic was run a sufficient number of times to find 15 different sub-optimal SPPs (q). These were ordered best to worst and the CS made as the union of the solution set lists of nodes. This was done for three values of m, the best 5, the best 10 and for all 15. The hope is that different solutions represent errors occurring in different parts of the network and the CS will as a result contain all correct nodes (plus a small selection of incorrect nodes) composing the optimal solution. This experiment is to see how limited the information to build the CS can be.

2.2 Stage two, selecting the solution

The one best solution can be extracted from the CS by using an optimal procedure to extract the optimal solution to this sub-problem or a good solution (possibly optimal) by a heuristic. For this demonstration we choose to use an integer linear programme (ILP).

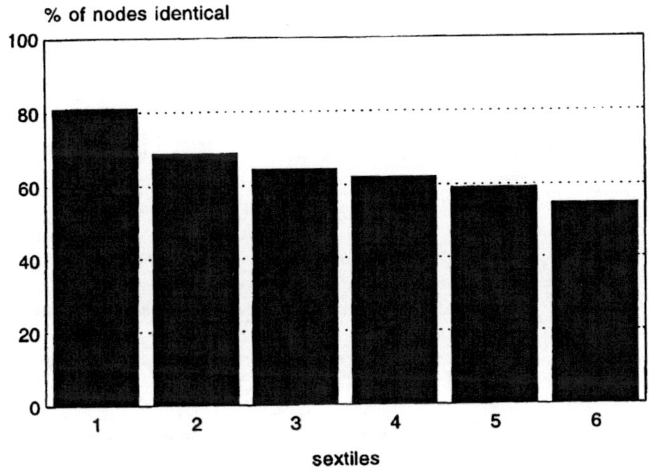

Figure 11.1. Percent sub-optimal nodes matching optimal nodes.

The programme is:

ILP-1

Minimise $$Z = \sum_{i=1}^{n} \sum_{j \varepsilon CS} a_i d_{ij} X_{ij} \quad (1)$$

Subject to: $$\sum_{j \varepsilon CS} X_{ij} = 1 \qquad \text{for all i} \quad (2)$$

$$X_{jj} - X_{ij} \geq 0 \qquad \text{for all i, for all } j \in CS, i \neq j \quad (3)$$

$$\sum_{j \varepsilon CS} X_{jj} = p \quad (4)$$

$$X_{jj} = 0,1 \qquad \text{for all } j \in CS \quad (5)$$

Where: d_{ij} = the distance i to j;
a_i = the weight associated with demand node i;
i = the index of demand nodes;
j = the index of potential facility sites;
X_{ij} = 1 if the ith demand node assigns to the jth facility and 0 otherwise;
CS = the concentration set.

Table 11.1. Results of Stage 2.

m = 5

p/n	100	125	150	175	200	225	250	275	300
50	■■■	■■■	■■■	■■■	■■■		■■■	82 82	
45	■■■	■■■	■■■	■■■	■■■	3 3	982982	70 70	4 4
40	■■■	■■■	■■■	79 79	948948	954954	■■■	■■■	899899
35	■■■	■■■	■■■	4 4	4 4	■■■	5 5	■■■	824824
30	■■■	======	71 71	■■■	■■■	■■■	0 0	979979	6 6
25	■■■	■■■	■■■	■■■	6 70	■■■	■■■	■■■	72 72
20	■■■		■■■	■■■	■■■	■■■	■■■	■■■	■■■
15	======	■■■	■■■			■■■		■■■	■■■
10	■■■	======	■■■	0 0	985985	■■■	■■■		■■■

m = 10

p/n	100	125	150	175	200	225	250	275	300
50	■■■	■■■	■■■	■■■	■■■	■■■	■■■	82 82	
45	■■■	■■■	■■■	■■■	■■■	■■■	■■■	70 70	834834
40	■■■	■■■	■■■	■■■	948948	■■■	■■■	■■■	■■■
35	■■■	■■■	■■■	■■■	■■■	■■■	■■■	■■■	■■■
30	■■■	======	■■■	■■■	■■■	■■■	■■■	■■■	6 6
25	■■■	■■■	■■■	■■■	■■■	■■■	■■■	■■■	908908
20	■■■	■■■	■■■	■■■	■■■	■■■	■■■	■■■	■■■
15	======	■■■	■■■			■■■	■■■	■■■	■■■
10	■■■	======	■■■	0 0	985985	■■■	■■■		■■■

m = 15

p/n	100	125	150	175	200	225	250	275	300
50	■■■	■■■	■■■	■■■	■■■	■■■	■■■	■■■	
45	■■■	■■■	■■■	■■■	■■■	■■■	■■■	■■■	834834
40	■■■	■■■	■■■	■■■	■■■	■■■	■■■	■■■	■■■
35	■■■	■■■	■■■	■■■	■■■	■■■	■■■	■■■	■■■
30	■■■	======	■■■	■■■	■■■	■■■	■■■	■■■	■■■
25	■■■	■■■	■■■	■■■	■■■	■■■	■■■	■■■	■■■
20	■■■	■■■	■■■	■■■	■■■	■■■	■■■	■■■	■■■
15	======	■■■	■■■			■■■	■■■	■■■	■■■
10	■■■	======	■■■	0 0	■■■	■■■	■■■	2 2	■■■

KEY:

	ILP-2	ILP-1
m= 5	---	
m=10	X	X
m=15	XXX	**XXX**

====== not valid for the analysis, < 15 non-optimal SPPs
, three blanks, no improvement
X , one digit, > 0.0% to < 70%
XX, two digits, 70% to < 80%
XXX, three digits, 80% to < 90%
XXX, three bold digits, 90% to < 100%
■■■, three black squares, optimal solution found

Percentages are percent of the range, best non-optimal SPP to optimal.

Table 11.2. Results of Stage 2, after Interchange Heuristic.

m = 5

p/n	100	125	150	175	200	225	250	275	300
50	█████	█████	█████	█████	█████		█████	82 82	
45	█████	█████	█████	█████	█████	3 3	982982	70 70	4 4
40	█████	█████	█████	79 79	948948	█████	█████	█████	899899
35	█████	█████	█████	976976	4 4	█████	5 5	█████	█████
30	█████	======	71 71	█████	█████	█████	0 0	979979	█████
25	█████	█████	█████	█████	6 █████	█████	█████	█████	72 72
20	█████		█████	█████	█████	█████	█████	█████	█████
15	======	█████	█████			█████		█████	█████
10	█████	======	█████	0 0	█████	█████	█████		█████

m = 10

p/n	100	125	150	175	200	225	250	275	300
50	█████	█████	█████	█████	█████	█████	█████	82 82	
45	█████	█████	█████	█████	█████	█████	█████	70 70	834834
40	█████	█████	█████	█████	948948	█████	█████	█████	█████
35	█████	█████	█████	█████	█████	█████	█████	█████	█████
30	█████	======	█████	█████	█████	█████	█████	█████	6 6
25	█████	█████	█████	█████	█████	█████	█████	█████	█████
20	█████	█████	█████	█████	█████	█████	█████	█████	█████
15	======	█████	█████			█████	█████	█████	█████
10	█████	======	█████	0 0	█████	█████	█████		█████

m = 15

p/n	100	125	150	175	200	225	250	275	300
50	█████	█████	█████	█████	█████	█████	█████	█████	
45	█████	█████	█████	█████	█████	█████	█████	█████	834834
40	█████	█████	█████	█████	█████	█████	█████	█████	█████
35	█████	█████	█████	█████	█████	█████	█████	█████	█████
30	█████	======	█████	█████	█████	█████	█████	█████	█████
25	█████	█████	█████	█████	█████	█████	█████	█████	█████
20	█████	█████	█████	█████	█████	█████	█████	█████	█████
15	======	█████	█████			█████	█████	█████	█████
10	█████	======	█████	0 0	█████	█████	█████	2 2	█████

See Table 1 for Key

In order to solve this as a linear programme constraint (5) must be relaxed to

$$X_{ij} \geq 0 \qquad \text{for all } i, j. \tag{6}$$

This (1-6) is the "normal" ILP formulation for the *p*-median problem from ReVelle and Swain (1970) with the modification of only considering as potential facilities those nodes in the CS. Consideration of the nodes in the individual solutions whose union forms the CS reveals however that a large proportion of the nodes appear in all the individual solutions. These conform to portions of the network were there are few or no sub-optimal traps which would require two at a time (or more than two at a time) interchanges. The interchange algorithm is able to quickly and easily move to the optimal position in these areas. Where nodes appear only in a small number of the solutions we are dealing with local traps and alternative nodes have been identified as alternative elements of the solution. If we consider those nodes which appear in all the solutions to actually be the optimal locations for that set of facilities we can fix open facilities there and further reduce the problem by only solving the ILP for those nodes which appear in at least one but not all solutions. This programme is formulated as follows:

ILP-2

Minimise $$Z = \sum_{i=1}^{n} \sum_{j \in R_i} a_i d_{ij} X_{ij} \tag{7}$$

Subject to: $$\sum_{j \in R_i} X_{ij} = 1 \qquad \text{for all } i \neq j \in CS_o \tag{8}$$

$$X_{jj} = 1 \qquad \text{for all } j \in CS_o \tag{9}$$

$$X_{jj} - X_{ij} \geq 0 \qquad \text{for all } i, \text{ for all } j \in R_i,\ i \neq j \tag{10}$$

$$\sum_{j \in CS} X_{jj} = p \tag{11}$$

$$X_{jj} = 0,1 \qquad \text{for all } j \in CS_f \tag{12}$$

Where: variables are as defined above and

$$r_i = \{ j \mid \min (d_{ij,\, j \in CS_o}) \} \qquad \text{for all } i \neq j \in CS_o \tag{13}$$

$$R_i = \{ j \in r_i \} \cup \{ j \in CS_f \mid d_{ij} < d_{ir_i} \} \qquad \text{for all } i \neq j \in CS_o \tag{14}$$

As is shown the CS is now divided into two sets, CS_o is the set of nodes which appear in all trials. We make the assumption that they really are facilities and open them with constraint (8). Since, in the p-median, all demand node must assign to their closest facility we now define two new sets. The set r_i has one member for each demand node. It is the one member of set CS_o which is closest (13). Set R_i then contains that one closest fixed open facility and any members of set CS_f which are closer (14). The set R_i, for each i therefore contains the potential facility sites to which it could assign. The sets R_i, CS_o and CS_f are then used to modify ILP-1 and creating ILP-2.

3.0 RESULTS

Table 11.1 shows the results of applying ILP-1 (right-hand side of each cell) and ILP-2 (left-hand side of each cell) to each of the 78 valid instances.

The table has three sections arranged one above the other each corresponding to a value of m. Within each section there are nine columns each corresponding to particular number of observations. In each cell the information reported is the percent of the range from the best sub-optimal (minimum functional value) to the optimal solution closed by using HC. Since this is an extremely complex table (78 valid cells each with two values repeated three times) We attempt to give a visual impression of the results as well as the information. Wherever the optimal solution was found this is shown by a black bar three character positions wide. No improvement over the best non-optimal solution are shown by three blanks. Solutions which close the gap from > 0.0% to < 70.0% are reported by a single digit with a leading and a trailing blank, for example as " 2 ". Cells where the improvement was between 70.0 and < 80.0% are reported by two digits with either a leading or trailing blank, "79 " or " 79". Values of 80.0% to < 90.0% are given by three digits; improvement of 90.0% to less than the optimal solution are again reported by three digits but now printed in bold characters.

The increase in the amount of black in the table as m increases is obvious. There also appear to be diminish returns moving from m = 5 to m = 15. This is, however, not strictly the case 54% of the non-optimal values when m = 5 become optimal when m = 10. When we compare m = 10 with m = 15 then 50% of the remaining non-optimal cells now have become optimal. In various non-optimal cells there is also improvement in the percentages between the three sections of the table.

The results of HC in stage 2 were extracted by an optimal method. It is quite possible that, when the solution is not the optimal solution to the full problem it is also not a stable solution in the sense of an interchange heuristic. We can submit the solution to an interchange heuristic as a fixed starting point and see if the interchange heuristic can improve upon it. Table 11.2 show the results of this exercise. In the cases m = 5 and m = 10 the interchange heuristic is able to improve upon the straight forward result from the ILP. These results are given numerically in Table 11.3. A total of 96.2% of the cells reporting improvement and a figure of 92.3% for optimality are impressive. It is also worth pointing out that in 41 cases (52.6%) the optimal solution had not been found after 15 runs of the heuristic. For these 41 cases 1,000 runs of the interchange heuristic was insufficient to find the optimal solution in three cases. HC provided the optimal solution in 97.6% (40) of the 41 cases and in all of the sub-set of three cases.

Table 11.3. Summary Statistics of Improvement and Optimality

		Stage 2			Through Interchange		Final
Model	m=	improve	optimal	valid	improve	optimal	optimal
ILP-2	5	91.0%	64.1% (50)	21	23.8% (5)	19.0% (4)	69.0% (54)
ILP-1	5	91.0%	64.1% (50)	21	28.6% (6)	23.8% (5)	70.5% (55)
ILP-2	10	94.9%	84.6% (66)	8	25.0% (2)	25.2% (2)	87.2% (68)
ILP-1	10	94.9%	84.6% (66)	8	25.0% (2)	25.2% (2)	87.2% (68)
ILP-2	15	96.2%	92.3% (72)	3	0.0% (0)	0.0% (0)	92.3% (72)
ILP-1	15	96.2%	92.3% (72)	3	0.0% (0)	0.0% (0)	92.3% (72)

Numbers in parenthesis are absolute counts

4.0 CONCLUSION

HC appears to be a more than adequate method. The quality of the solution is heavily dependent upon the values of q and m. It would seem appropriate to run the base interchange heuristic as many times as economically feasible to insure the quality of the results from the base heuristic and then to use as many of these results as are technically feasible. The occurrence of many cases which can be improved by re-application of the interchange heuristic would appear to symptomatic of insufficient information in the data base -- too small a value of q and/or m.

REFERENCES

ReVelle, C.S. and R. Swain. (1970). "Central Facility Location." *Geographical Analysis*, 2, 30-42.

Rosing, K.E. (1997). "An Empirical Investigation of the Effectiveness of a Vertex Substitution Heuristic." *Environment and Planning: Series B*, (forthcoming).

Rosing, K.E. and C.S. ReVelle. (1996a). "Heuristic Concentration: A Metaheuristic for Combinatorial Location Problems." *Studies in Locational Analysis*, 9, 109-12.

Rosing, K.E. and C.S. ReVelle. (1996b). "Heuristic Concentration: Two Stage Solution Construction." *European Journal of Operations Research*, (forthcoming).

Teitz, M.B. and P. Bart. (1968). "Heuristic Methods for Estimating the Generalized Vertex Median of a Weighted Graph." *Operations Research*, 16, 955-61.

PART THREE

APPLICATIONS

CHAPTER 12

SPATIAL MODELLING OF DISEASE DISPERSION USING A LOCAL STATISTIC: THE CASE OF AIDS

Arthur Getis and J. Keith Ord

"...randomization tests appear to be superior or equal to their parametric counterparts in most cases."

Jean H.P. Paelinck, Leo H. Klassen, *Spatial Econometric*, 1979, p. 87

1.0 INTRODUCTION

In this paper, a statistical test based on a randomization procedure is discussed with regard to the hypothesis that a spatial cluster or hot spot exists. Clusters or "hot spots" represent a greater degree of a specified activity in a region than one would expect by chance. The test can be practically applied in a number of areas where the identification of a cluster may lead to a further understanding of the phenomena's behavior. In particular, the procedure is well-suited for the identification of disease clusters where sample data may be very large and deviate appreciably from normal form. Paelinck, in his pioneering work on spatial econometrics, made clear that randomization tests possess properties of great power, consistency, and unbiasedness when normal-theory assumptions are true and are statistically efficient for distribution-free situations.

Recently, a number of statistics have been developed that measure spatial dependence in a sub-region of a larger study area (Getis and Ord, 1992; Anselin, 1995). They identify the association between a single value at a particular site, say the incidence of a disease in a given county, and its neighbors up to a specified distance from the site in question. These statistics, called local statistics, are well suited to identify the existence of pockets or hot spots, such as regions in which the incidence of a disease is greater than elsewhere. In addition, they can be used to identify distances beyond which no discernible spatial association obtains, that is, they may indicate the general boundaries of a disease cluster, subject to the granularity of the regions for which data are recorded. Just as spectral analysis cannot determine the contributions of frequencies higher than the Nyquist level, so these methods cannot hope to make distance determinations finer than half the width of a typical areal unit.

An extensive related set of tests is available in the epidemiology literature, with the primary aim of cluster identification; for an extensive recent review, see Marshall (1991). Many of these tests, such as the uniformly most powerful test developed in Waller et al. (1992) are focussed; that is, they are designed to test for clusters about a pre-specified focus, such as a toxic waste site. The test considered in this paper is designed for use without such an a priori specification, although it is arguable that such a focus exists in the particular application we describe. Both focussed and general tests seek to identify the extent of a cluster, but the difference between them is that a focussed test operates from a specific source, whereas a general test allows all sites to be possible sources.

This paper uses a local statistic, G_i, developed by Getis and Ord (1992) and Ord and Getis (1995), to focus on the clustering of AIDS in the area surrounding San Francisco for the period 1989 to the end of 1994. The statistic allows us to identify any clustering of the disease, at the county level, as distance increases from San Francisco. The focus is on how northern California counties relate to San Francisco over time. In section two of this paper, we explain Getis and Ord's local statistic, G_i, in the context of the empirical work that is to follow. In section three, we briefly review the relevant epidemiological literature where space or distance is considered explicitly. Section four discusses the data and the necessary data transformations. In section five, we formulate our expectations, and in section six, present results. Finally, the empirical work is discussed in section seven.

2.0 THE G_i STATISTIC

In this section, we show the way the statistic is formulated and briefly give several examples of its uses.

2.1 The structure of the statistic

Consider an area, such as a state, subdivided into n counties, where each county is identified with a geo-referenced point, $i = 1,2,...,n$. In this study, the geo-referenced points are the coordinates that represent the centers of population of each county in northern California (see Figure 12.1). Each of these points has associated with it a value x_i that represents an observation, say, the AIDS rate in county i as one realization of a variable X, called AIDS rates. When we focus on a particular x_i, the remaining observations are denoted as x_j. In northern California there are $n = 48$ counties. For example, San Francisco County (whose boundaries correspond to the city of San Francisco), is represented by $i = 31$ (31st in alphabetical order) and the surrounding counties (Alameda, Contra Costa, Marin, and San Mateo) are denoted as $j = 1, 7, 18$, and 33.

Let us begin by specifying a null hypothesis that there is no association between the value of X at site i and its neighbors, the j's, up to and including a distance called d, measured from i in all directions. On a planar map, this distance is often expressed as a circle of radius d from i but the meaning of d can be specified as something besides Euclidian distance, such as the number of regions separating i and j, when taking the shortest path (fewest boundary crossings) from i to j. The null hypothesis is that the sum of values at all the j sites within d of i is not more (or less) than one would expect by chance given all the values in the entire study area

Figure 12.1. Centers of population for northern California counties.

(both within and beyond d). Note that the null hypothesis appropriate for the G_i statistic requires that x_i be the focus of study but the X value at i does not itself enter into any calculations. (Another statistic, G_i^*, not discussed here, includes the i site in all calculations.) If spatial association exists between i and the j, there is a clustering of high or low values of X at the j within d of i. When there is a preponderance of high values among the j, the resulting G_i will be positive. Low values yield negative Gi.

The statistic is written as follows

$$G(d) = \frac{\sum_j w_{ij}(d)x_j - W\overline{x}}{s_i\left\{\left[\left((n-1)S_{ii}\right) - W_i^2\right]/(n-2)\right\}^{.5}}, \; j\neq 1 \tag{1}$$

where $\{w_{ij}(d)\}$ is a spatial weights vector. If d_{ij} denotes the distance between i and j, we assume that: $w_{ij}(d) = 0$ for $d_{ij} > d$. Further, in this paper, we shall use $w_{ij}(d) = 1$ for $d_{ij} < d$, although such a restriction is clearly not necessary. Finally in equation (1) the weight for the link of i to itself (w_{ii}) is zero. We define

$$W_i = \Sigma_j \, w_{ij}(d) \;, \qquad j \neq i,$$

$$S_{1i} = \Sigma_j \, w_{ij} 2, \qquad j \neq i,$$

and the mean

$$\overline{x} = \frac{\sum_j x_j}{(n-1)}, \qquad j \neq 1$$

and variance

$$s_i^2 = \frac{\sum_j x_j^2}{(n-1)} - \left[\overline{x}_i\right]^2, \qquad j \neq 1$$

In Getis and Ord (1992), we show that G_i is asymptotically normally distributed. The expectation under the null hypothesis is 0; the variance is 1. Therefore, in order to evaluate the G_i statistic, one need only consider the distribution of a standard variate. For testing purposes, the conservative approach is to apply a Bonferroni-type adjustment (see Ord and Getis, 1995) recognizing that San Francisco was selected on the basis of prior knowledge. If we assume that the $\{G_i\}$ follow a multivariate normal distribution, the upper percentage points for G_i, based on a Bonferroni-type test, for n-1=47 are 2.85 at the .90 level and 3.07 at the 95 level.

2.2 Uses For The Statistic

2.2.1 Finding clusters

Suppose that a disease strikes the population of a region in a random manner; that is, the incidence will tend to be normally distributed for the given spatially demarcated subsets of the population since typical administrative regions vary in population size. Thus, we will often use standard scores to allow comparisons across regions; see (2) below. It may be, however, that within the overall spatial distribution of the subsets, pockets of hot spots of high incidence clusters exist. For example, in the case of sudden infant death syndrome (SIDS), the expectation in the

United States is for about 3 deaths for every 1000 live births and for a small variance from place to place. A study of SIDS in North Carolina counties for the period 1979-84 (Getis and Ord, 1992) identified a hot spot in the south central portion of the state that may be related to a paucity of health care facilities in the area.

2.2.2 Cluster identification

Local statistics can help identify the magnitude of a hot spot about a core location by computing G_i for each of a series of increasing distances from that location. An intuitively appealing definition of the boundaries of the hot spot is Given by selecting the critical distance (d_c) for which $G_i(d)$ is maximized with respect to d. That is, for distances beyond dc, the "new" x_j values that contribute to the numerator of G_i are less in sum than that expected under the null hypothesis of no clustering. Multiple maxima for $G_i(d)$ are certainly possible, but were not observed in our study. Either the first local maximum or the global maximum might be selected in such cases, depending on the scale of the data. Such cluster identifications are intended only as a guide.

2.2.3 Tracing clustering over time

Tracing local G_i statistics over time allows us to identify possible increases or decreases in cluster size. If a cluster increases in size, diffusion is most likely the responsible agent. If the disease intensifies but the cluster does not expand, spatial diffusion may be operating but only at a smaller scale than that of the reporting units.

3.0 SPATIAL EPIDEMIOLOGICAL LITERATURE ON AIDS

Researchers in many different disciplines have studied the epidemiological characteristics of AIDS, but only a handful of these studies have explicitly considered the spatial progression of the disease. Of these, only Aldrich et al. (1990) and Smallman-Raynor et al. (1992) studied the spatial distribution of AIDS within San Francisco. They found that the vast majority of cases (87 percent) are among homosexuals and that the cases cluster to a very high degree in central San Francisco, especially the Castro district. Their studies, however, do not consider the region outside of San Francisco.

Among those who have theorized about the spread of the disease are Gould (1993) and Golub et al. (1993), who present evidence of a spatial hierarchical and expansionary trend since the onset of the disease in Ohio in 1981 to 1990. That is, the disease began by diffusing through the major metropolitan areas and from there to the major urban areas and so on. However, once established in a region, subsequent cases are largely generated internally (cf Cliff et al., 1981 for similar arguments on measles). Our study focuses on the spread of AIDS from 1989 to 1994, so, in a sense, our study is a continuation of theirs, considering AIDS at a more mature period of its evolution.

Thomas (1994) provides a modeling framework for the space-time structure of AIDS based on similar successful modeling efforts for influenza. While recognizing that the degree of infectiousness in a Given area for influenza is hundreds of times greater than that for AIDS, he concludes that the mixing factor is about the same. After identifying the structural differences between the diseases, he suggests that a successful multiregion model of AIDS would profitably depend on variables representing high and low risk groups. Since the number of homosexuals or intravenous drug users in the San Francisco area is not precisely known, we are not in a position to divide the population by degree of risk.

A number of studies like Gould's (1993) trace the spread of the disease in the United States from its beginnings in the early 1980's core locations of New York-Philadelphia, southeast Florida, Denver, and coastal California regions. For example, Shannon et al. (1990) show an expansionary diffusion to much of the coastal areas and inland areas of Colorado and Illinois by the mid-1980's. Gardner et al. et al. (1989), in their study of military applicants, Give evidence, like that of Gould, that supports a mixed hierarchical and expansion diffusion from the core areas of northern California (San Francisco area), Florida, and Texas. The New York core area is less a center for outward spread, perhaps a function of the higher proportion of intravenous as opposed to homosexual cases. A useful description of these trends is found in Smallman-Raynor et al. (1992).

4.0 THE DATA AND NECESSARY TRANSFORMATIONS

San Francisco County, an urban hot spot, has perhaps the highest cumulative incidence of AIDS, defined as the total number of cases per 100,000 population. By March 1995, 18,803 cases had been reported since the disease was first identified in 1981, and 12,597 people had died from the disease. The cumulative incidence in San Francisco in March 1995 was 2,500 cases per 100,000 population (Department of Health Services, 1995).

Data on the cumulative incidence of the AIDS disease are available by county, by month or quarter for the state of California for the period January 1989 to the present from the Department of Health Services, Office of AIDS, California HIV/AIDS Update, Volumes 4 to 8 (Table: AIDS Cases and Cumulative Incidence 1981 through 1994 in California). All data reflect the place of residence at the time of diagnosis. There are two major problems with the data. The first is that AIDS is not reported to the Department of Health at the time of diagnosis. Officials at the Office of AIDS estimate that the lag is anywhere from a few days to six months; the lag rarely is greater than nine months. These delays cause some uncontrollable variation in the data; however, by analyzing both new cases and cumulative incidence, we hope to minimize the impact of such lags.

Another data problem relates to the change in definition of what constitutes AIDS. All data from January 1993 to the present use a wider definition that is more inclusive than before. The new definition includes cases of HIV-infected people in whom severe immunosuppression has been diagnosed (which typically occurs before the onset of AIDS-defining opportunistic illnesses), as well as cases of pulmonary tuberculosis, recurrent pneumonia and invasive cervical cancer. These greatly increase the number of AIDS cases. Fortunately, the G_i statistic is not affected by the magnitude of the data, only by the relative differences among the data. In the long run, this characteristic will make it possible to identify the effect of the new definition on the spatial and temporal patterns of reported AIDS cases. The exact interpretation of such changes is open to question; they may reflect differences either in the spatial patterns of residence of newly diagnosed patients, or in diagnostic practice. It is probably worth waiting to see whether systematic effects show up in the data before devising methods to distinguish these two mechanisms.

Our goal in this paper is to test the notion that AIDS spread spatially from San Francisco to nearby counties during the period of our data, 1989 to the end of 1994. We chart the cumulative number of cases per 100,000 population at the end of June and December for each year for the counties of northern California (see Table 12.1). A spatial pattern of the incidence of AIDS had been established by 1989 (see Figure 12.2). The question here is simply: Have there been recognizable changes in the pattern since that time?

In order to identify significant changes in pattern, our hypothesis requires that we randomly permute the rates of the 47 counties of Northern California (48 less the rate in San Francisco). If the pattern in the region surrounding San Francisco is rare among the random permutations, we consider the pattern statistically significant. Repeating this process for different time periods allows us to identify changes in patterns of clustering. The random permutations approach requires that, under the null hypothesis Ho, all possible assignments of the county values to the counties are equally likely. Besag and Newell (1991) point out, however, that when county i has r_i cases of a disease in a population of ti, the random permutations distribution for a spatial statistic may not be an appropriate frame of reference. To illustrate this, suppose that a heavily populated urban area and a sparsely populated rural area have the same proportions of cases. In the permutation process, rather than score the two areas equally, we may prefer to Give a higher 'score' to the far higher number of cases in the heavily populated area. In northern California, county populations and rates vary greatly (see Table 12.1), and, in addition, counties with high or low population tend to cluster. Further, county sizes range widely. These difficulties may be resolved by finding the mean study area rate, $p = \text{ä}r_i/\text{ä}t_i$, and then computing the standard score for each county as:

$$
\begin{aligned}
z_i &= (r_i - pt_i)/[t_i p(1-p)]^{.5} \\
&= \{(r_i/t_i) - p\}/[p(1-p)/t_i]^{.5} \qquad (2)
\end{aligned}
$$

Thus, we use z_i in (2) to 'stabilize' rates for counties with small populations. The z_i values for each of 12 time periods, one for each June and December from 1989 to 1994, become the data from which the local statistics are calculated for San Francisco.

Table 12.1. Cumulative incidence of AIDS per 100,000 population by counties of Northern California for December of 1989 to 1994.

County	Coordinates	Population 1990	1989	1990	1991	1992	1993	1994
Alameda	195 500	1279182	86.79	129.16	144.70	173.90	207.48	290.11
Alpine	318 560	1113	0	0	0	0	0	0
Amador	265 550	30039	6.97	19.17	19.97	39.95	53.27	55.05
Butte	220 630	82120	20.62	27.46	35.14	47.22	54.91	54.79
Calaveras	280 530	31998	3.21	2.91	6.25	12.5	12.50	10.90
Colusa	195 598	16275	12.45	12.38	30.72	36.87	43.02	51.87
Contra Costa	192 515	803732	46.84	68.38	87.22	104.10	121.81	176.59
Del Norte	100 790	23460	0	0	4.26	8.53	17.05	39.43
El Dorado	260 580	125995	20.09	24.85	31.75	44.45	54.77	66.05
Fresno	320 425	667490	22.79	30.77	41.8	54.83	66.37	86.73
Glenn	180 630	24798	20.36	24.54	28.23	28.23	28.23	26.62
Humbolt	90 705	119118	17.68	28.06	47.85	58.77	67.17	109.88
Inyo	450 403	18281	16.14	21.68	21.88	21.88	21.88	31.91
Kings	315 380	101469	9.05	13.77	24.64	32.52	42.37	60.25
Lake	155 597	50631	26.17	46.13	65.18	73.08	88.88	124.10
Lassen	270 710	27598	3.84	7.27	21.74	18.12	18.12	34.60
Madera	315 455	88090	4.62	10.10	19.30	23.84	35.19	50.53
Marin	175 510	230096	117.30	151.05	215.60	269.90	309.44	420.22
Mariposa	305 485	14302	0	0	6.99	6.99	20.97	31.65
Mendocino	125 602	80345	60.76	75.85	80.90	97.08	105.79	148.33
Merced	285 470	178403	9.38	15.06	19.62	23.54	29.14	37.23
Modoc	265 765	9678	10.08	10.34	10.33	10.33	10.33	9.71
Mono	380 515	9956	0	0	0	0	0	9.66
Monterey	212 415	355660	38.94	45.53	66.36	68.89	92.51	124.87
Napa	185 545	110765	38.63	45.17	64.10	71.32	90.28	110.35
Nevada	255 610	78510	17.46	16.87	25.47	29.30	63.70	77.19
Placer	270 595	172796	12.24	14.88	16.78	20.26	22.00	29.88
Plumas	272 660	19739	4.90	4.85	5.07	5.07	5.07	4.77
Sacramento	235 548	1041219	45.62	56.00	75.97	101.20	125.72	163.57
San Benito	220 430	36697	5.62	5.43	13.63	16.35	21.80	37.36
San Francisco*	185 503	723959	900.29	1212.10	1434.10	1664.50	1907.57	2405.85
San Joaquin	236 520	480628	22.36	31.43	40.99	47.23	61.79	87.85
San Mateo	190 490	649623	57.21	84.56	106.60	128.80	148.85	201.06
Santa Clara	202 475	1497577	38.29	51.32	61.03	73.39	88.28	131.67
Santa Cruz	200 450	229734	44.31	53.12	72.26	87.49	96.63	132.97
Shasta	197 712	147036	17.94	21.67	25.84	36.05	42.85	47.83
Sierra	275 630	3318	27.13	55.25	60.28	90.42	90.42	89.02
Siskiyou	180 782	43531	13.59	13.30	13.78	13.78	13.78	15.50
Solano	192 540	340421	37.89	67.10	78.43	96.65	126.32	184.03
Sonoma	170 535	388222	105.20	133.90	155.80	185.20	213.28	285.61
Stanislaus	265 491	370522	22.73	28.46	33.20	39.40	63.96	84.57
Sutter	210 590	64415	14.38	17.00	18.63	20.18	27.94	41.37
Tehama	193 680	49625	4.11	8.16	12.09	12.09	18.14	31.48
Trinity	140 702	13063	6.88	7.02	22.97	22.97	30.63	59.26
Tulare	365 385	311921	15.86	16.21	19.56	24.37	33.35	43.77
Tuolumne	303 515	48456	16.76	20.39	39.21	45.40	53.65	62.74
Yolo	205 570	141092	15.13	22.27	33.31	35.44	45.36	69.22
Yuba	228 604	58228	15.78	18.68	25.76	34.35	48.09	54.31

As explained in the text, the data for San Francisco do not enter directly into the analysis. Also, occasionally, there is a downward movement in the cumulative incidence for an individual county. This may be due to the effect on counties having few cases when there is either the use of new population figures from the 1990 US Census or an official revision in the number of cases. Source: California Department of Health Services, Office of AIDS, *California HIV/AIDS Update*, 1989-1994, Sacramento, CA.

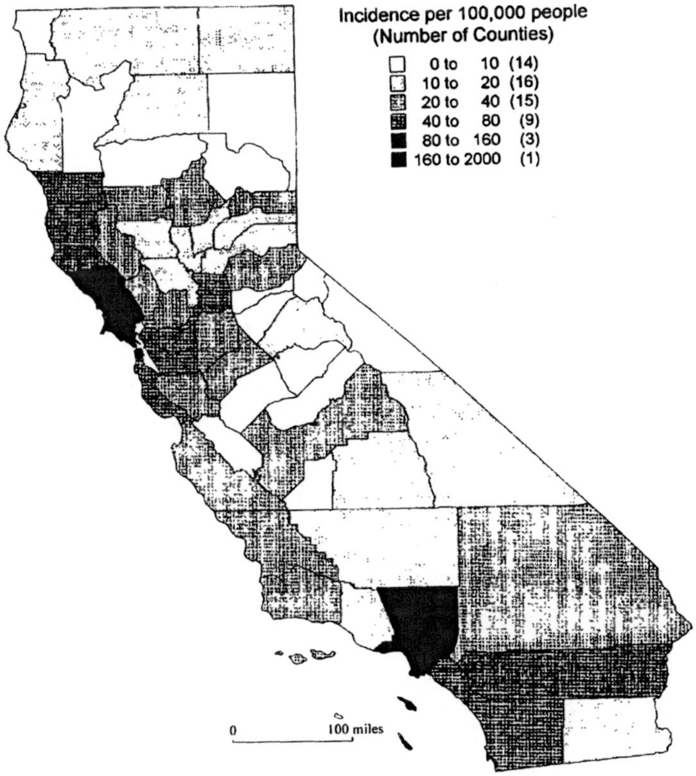

Figure 12.2. Cumulative incidence of AIDS in California, 1981 through Dec. 1989.

5. 0 STUDY EXPECTATIONS

In our application of the G_i statistic, we use a number of different distances from San Francisco for different time periods. In principle, it is possible to choose that value of d for which the standardized statistic is maximized, somewhat in the spirit of the analysis in Stone (1988) and Getis (1995). For the spatial (non-temporal) case, we want to know the shape of a distance decline curve of G_i values outward from San Francisco. For the expected case that the incidence decreases monotonically with distance from San Francisco, the implication is that the rate, $x_i = (r_i/t_i)$, in region i is of the form:

$$x_i = \alpha - \beta(d_i - D) + \varepsilon \qquad (3)$$

where d_i denotes the distance from the source, D is the mean distance from the source and ε_i denotes an error term with mean zero and variance σ^2 for all i. If we use binary weights, we obtain from (1),

$$G_i(d) \propto \Sigma_j x_j \ , \qquad \{_j : d_j \leq d\}. \qquad (4)$$

When (3) holds and the number of counties within d of county i is J (J much less than n), the expected value for (4) is, approximately,

$$-\beta \, \Sigma \, (d_j - D) / \sigma\sqrt{J} \ . \qquad (5)$$

Examination of (5) indicates that the expectation will increase initially, identifying the tendency for clustering, and then decline beyond the critical distance, d_c (see Section 3.2.2 and Figure 12.3).

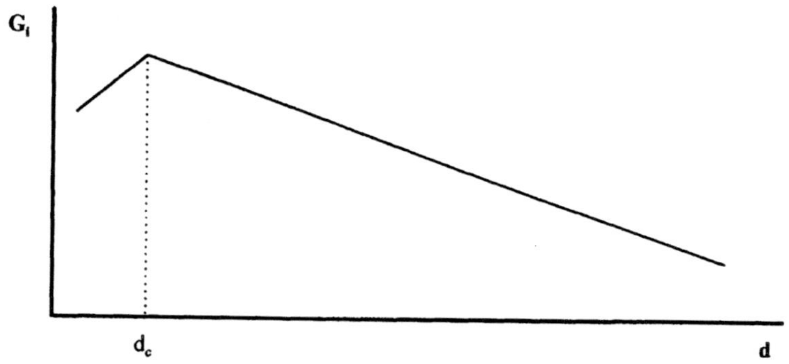

Figure 12.3. The critical distance dc. An increase in d_c along the distance axis, d, over time, represents disease diffusion.

Any increase in G_i over time for distances up to d_c represents an intensification of the disease and a faster growth of the disease than in the study area as a whole. Diffusion is represented by increases in dc. Decreases in G_i up to d_c imply that the incidence of the disease has increased more slowly than the mean increase. Increases beyond d_c are only indicative, but are not unequivocal, that some diffusion exists. Only if the decreases up to d_c are considerably greater than the increases beyond d_c would an hypothesis of diffusion likely hold.

It is interesting to note that if the distance curves are higher for succeeding time periods and are roughly parallel to each other, an allometric-type growth is in evidence, that is, total numbers in high incidence areas are increasing proportionately faster than in low incidence areas. No change in G_i values indicates that there is a spatial equilibrium, that is, there is no change in the pattern of clustering or diffusion.

6.0 THE PATTERN OF AIDS IN THE SAN FRANCISCO AREA 1989-1994

Figure 12.4 and Table 12.2 summarize the main results of the study. For each of six distances, from 20 to 120 miles from San Francisco, Figure 12.4 shows the G_i values for the z_i for the cumulative number of cases per 100,000 population for each of the 12 time periods (Table 12.2 is shortened to 6 time periods). The dashed lines connect the G_i values for each distance at the beginning, middle, and end of the study period. Figure 12.5 and Table 12.3 show the G_i values for the z_i for the (newly) reported cases per 100,000 population in each of the years 1990 to 1994.

Table 12.2. G_i Values of the z_i for the Cumulative Number of AIDS Cases per 100,000 Population by County in Northern California from 1981 to December of 1989-1994 at 20 Mile Increments From San Francisco.

Distance	1989	1990	1991	1992	1993	1994
20	4.491	4.780	5.003	4.993	4.923	5.010
40	4.723	4.933	4.909	4.857	4.929	5.035
60	3.920	4.003	4.058	3.955	3.912	4.075
80	3.613	3.585	3.747	3.742	3.749	3.847
100	2.568	2.513	2.681	2.608	2.731	2.794
120	2.200	2.114	2.232	2.181	2.258	2.269
140	1.548	1.456	1.540	1.492	1.603	1.535
160	1.382	1.362	1.403	1.406	1.496	1.387
180	1.067	1.085	1.124	1.130	1.218	1.124
200	1.074	1.097	1.127	1.134	1.221	1.136

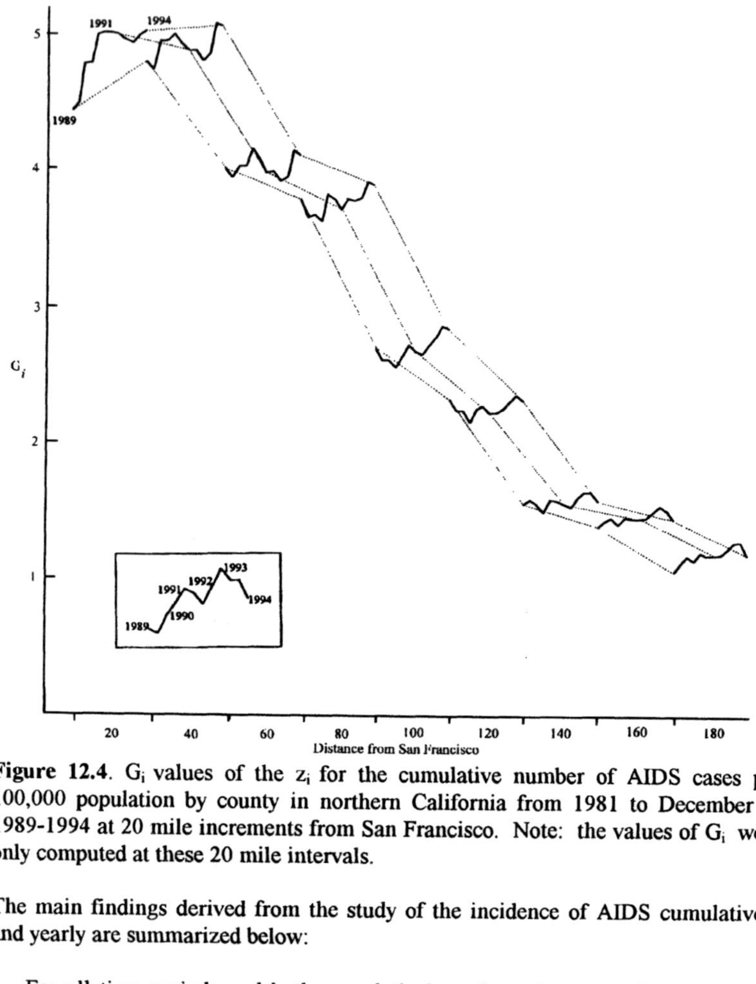

Figure 12.4. G_i values of the z_i for the cumulative number of AIDS cases per 100,000 population by county in northern California from 1981 to December of 1989-1994 at 20 mile increments from San Francisco. Note: the values of G_i were only computed at these 20 mile intervals.

The main findings derived from the study of the incidence of AIDS cumulatively and yearly are summarized below:

a. For all time periods and both cumulatively and yearly counts there is a peak close to San Francisco and a steady decline outward, indicating that the basic AIDS pattern of rapidly declining intensity with distance has not changed appreciably from the beginning of the study period.

b. The critical distance d_c is 40 miles (includes seven counties) from June 1989 to December 1990. At that time, d_c shortens to 20 miles (includes only the four nearest neighboring counties) but reverts to dc=40 miles in 1993. However, the absolute differences in the G_i values are relatively slight. The implication here is that a strong tendency for clustering includes the 7 counties within 40 miles of San Francisco. Cumulative and year curves are similar.

c. For the cumulative G_i values, the areas beyond d_c show steady but modest increases in the later part of the study period. This implies that there was a small tendency for diffusion during 1993. This result is particularly clear at 80 miles for the yearly values. Since the large city of Sacramento is at that distance from San Francisco, most likely we are seeing an element of hierarchical diffusion.

d. The pattern over distance by time indicates rather small changes from period to period. The point made above about allometric growth appears to hold to a great extent.

e. Some of the variation in the results for 1993 and 1994 must be a function of the changed definition of AIDS. In 1994, the region surrounding San Francisco probably had proportionately more of the new definition cases than did the northern California study region as a whole.

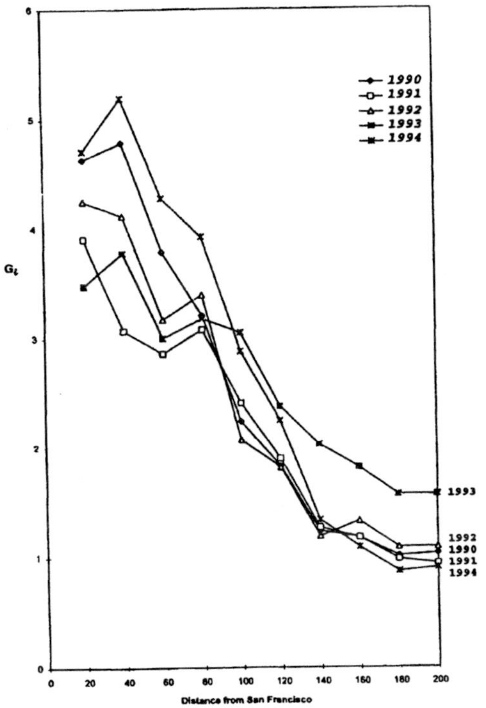

Figure 12.5. G_i values of the z_i for period-to-period AIDS cases per 100,000 population by county in northern California for years 1990, 1991, 1992, 1993, and 1994 by 20 mile increments from San Francisco.

Table 12.3. G_i Values of the z_i for the Number of Cases of AIDS per 100,000 Population by County in Northern California in Each of the Years, 1990 to 1994, at 20 Mile Increments From San Francisco.

Distance	1990	1991	1992	1993	1994
20	4.63	3.91	4.25	3.48	4.71
40	4.79	3.07	4.12	3.78	5.20
60	3.79	2.86	3.17	3.00	4.28
80	3.21	3.08	3.40	3.18	3.93
100	2.24	2.41	2.11	3.05	2.88
120	1.83	1.90	1.82	2.38	2.25
140	1.24	1.27	1.19	2.03	1.34
160	1.18	1.18	1.33	1.82	1.09
180	1.01	0.98	1.09	1.57	0.87
200	1.03	0.94	1.09	1.57	0.90

Recent reports indicate that the number of new cases of AIDS as defined before January 1993 is beginning to decrease in most parts of the country. The disease may have peaked as a result of changes in human behavior. In addition, new theories in cell biology concerning the immune system and the internal spread of the virus are beginning to help in the treatment of HIV in its early stages.

Our spatial analysis allows us to answer the question posed earlier, that is, has there been a change in pattern during the study period? Our analysis focused on whether incidence of the disease displayed greater concentration or increased diffusion. The G_i values peak at distances of 20 and 40 miles and decline thereafter. Indeed, closer inspection of the data pinpoints Sonoma County as the major contributor in the 20 to 40 mile wide band to the cluster composed of Alameda, Contra Costa, Marin, and San Mateo Counties (see Figure 12.6). Any diffusion beyond these five counties appears to be minimal.

The most notable characteristic of the pattern over time is that of an apparent allometric growth phenomenon. Cases of AIDS were being reported in counties at about the same relative rate in 1992 as in 1989. As the new definition of AIDS began to play a role, more cases were reported in 1993 and 1994, but the increases appear to remain consistent with the allometric growth hypothesis. Whatever diffusive tendencies exist, they are barely discernible outside the core counties surrounding San Francisco. Over the period 1989 to 1994, the disease presents a pattern of within-county intensification, and the diffusion beyond the metropolitan district surrounding San Francisco appears to be relatively unimportant.

The G_i statistic used in this study is a sensitive indicator of pattern and pattern change. It was able to identify the extent of the hot spot in the San Francisco area. The statistic appears to be well suited to study AIDS in different circumstances, especially where the number of people susceptible to infection varies greatly from place to place. It would be of considerable interest and value to explore such patterns at a finer level of spatial aggregation such as census tracts, as in Waller et al. (1992). In addition, it would be useful to trace the spatial trends in other diseases. Perhaps a better understanding of the mechanisms of disease transmission and diffusion will result.

Figure 12.6. The counties surrounding San Francisco containing statistically significantly high values of G_i and a location within the critical distance d_c in 1994.

REFERENCES

Aldrich, M.R., S.F. Payne, S.M. Little, J. Mandel, and H.W. Feldman. (1990). "Classic epidemiological mapping of AIDS among San Francisco drug injectors, 1987-1989." VI International Conference on AIDS, San Francisco, 20-24 June, Abstract Th.C. 705.

Anselin, L. (1995). "Local indicators of spatial association - LISA." *Geographical Analysis*, 27, 93-115.

Besag, J. and J. Newell. (1991). "The detection of clusters in rare diseases." *Journal of the Royal Statistical Society, Series A*, 154, 143-55.

California Department of Health Services, Office of AIDS. California AIDS Update, 1988-1990, *California HIV/AIDS Update*, 1990-1994.

Cliff, A.D., P. Haggett, J.K. Ord, and G.R. Versey. (1981). *Spatial Diffusion*. London: Cambridge University Press.

Department of Health Services, Office of AIDS, *California HIV/AIDS Update*, Vol. 8, No. 2, April 1995.

Gardner, Jr., L.I, J.F. Brundage, D.S. Burke, J.G. McNeil, R. Visintine, and R.N. Miller. (1989). "Spatial diffusion of the human immunodeficiency virus infection epidemic in the United States, 1985-87." *Annals of the Association of American Geographers*, 79, 1, 25-43.

Getis, A. (1995). "Spatial filtering in a regression framework: experiments on regional inequality, government expendititures, and urban crime." In *New Directions in Spatial Econometrics*, edited by L. Anselin and R. Florax, pp. 172-185. Amsterdam: North Holland.

Getis, A. and J.K. Ord. (1992). "The analysis of spatial association by use of distance statistics." *Geographical Analysis*, 24, 189-206.

Golub, A., W.L. Gorr, and P.R. Gould. (1993). "Spatial diffusion of the HIV/AIDS epidemic: modeling implications and case study of AIDS incidence in Ohio." *Geographical Analysis*, 25, 85-100.

Gould, P.R. (1993). *The Slow Plague: A Geography of the AIDS Pandemic*. Oxford: Blackwell.

Marshall, R.J. (1991). "A review of methods for the statistical analysis of spatial patterns of disease." *Journal of the Royal Statistical Society, Series A*, 154, Part 3, 421-41.

Ord, J.K. and A. Getis. (1995). "Local spatial autocorrelation statistics: distributional issues and an application." *Geographical Analysis*, 27, 286-306.

Paelinck J.H.P. and L.H. Klassen. (1979). *Spatial Econometrics*. Westmead, England: Saxon House.

Shannon, G., G. Pyle, and R. Bashshur. (1990). *The Geography of AIDS*. New York: Guilford Press.

Smallman-Raynor, M., A.D. Cliff, and P. Haggett. (1992). *Atlas of AIDS*. Oxford: Basil Blackwell International.

Stone, R.A. (1988). "Investigations of excess environmental risks around putative sources: statistical problems and a proposed test." *Statistics in Medicine*, 7, 649-60.

Thomas, R.W. (1994). "Forecasting global HIV-AIDS dynamics: modelling strategies and preliminary simulations." *Environment and Planning A*, 26, 1147-66.

Waller, L.A., B.W. Turnbull, L.C. Clark, and P. Nasca. (1992). "Chronic disease surveillance and testing of clustering of disease and exposure: application to leukemia incidence and TCE-contaminated dumpsites in upstate New York." *Environmetrics*, 3, 281-300.

ACKNOWLEDGEMENTS

This research was supported by the National Science Foundation, Grant No. SES-9123832. The authors appreciate the cooperation of employees of the Office of AIDS (Department of Health Services, State of California) and the assistance of Scott Munroe, who drafted the figures.

CHAPTER 13

REGIONAL DISPARITY IN THE EUROPEAN COMMUNITY 1950 - 1990

Hans Kuiper

1.0 INTRODUCTION

Economic development in a country (or group of countries) can be analyzed by looking at the development of separate regions located in the country. The principle of an asymmetric development always can be observed; sectors are flourishing in some regions and lacking behind in others. In some regions activities seem to concentrate and other regions are specialized in just one particular sector.

The picture one observes is not static. Continuously activity levels are changing and a process of adaptation is going on. Sometimes inequalities between regions are diminishing and another moment they seem to enlarge. The output levels in the system of regions never reaches an equilibrium.

It is interesting to know more about the regional factors that are determining the output levels. Regional factors effect each sector represented in the region in a different way. For each sector one can wonder if there is a tendency to more equality between the regions. How fast are sector output levels changing and what causes the change? How close are "optimum" levels approximated and what is the influence of political measures on output levels of neighbour regions? Do regions have characteristics properties concerning the adaptation process, or are they changing in an unpredictable way; is it possible to forecast regional output?

In order to find answers it is useful to describe the system of regions and the distribution of sectors over regions in models. These models should not be too complicated and they have to describe the dynamic interregional structure. Relations should be defined between regional output and the output level of the country, or between sectoral output in a region and the total sectoral output level.

In this paper regional development in the European Union is described over a period of 1950-1990. For a number of sectors regional disparities are measured. Europe is decided into groups of regions depending on the location of these regions. The paper starts with the presentation of two models explaining regional development; a static model explaining location patterns for different economic sectors and a dynamic model explaining changes in regional output levels.

Output levels for a number of sectors concerning European regions are measured for 1950, 1960, 1970, 1980 and 1990. Economic developments are presented and explained.

2.0 MODELS EXPLAINING REGIONAL DEVELOPMENT

In this section models will be mentioned, a static and a dynamic model, explaining regional development. Location theory is fundamental for the development of regional science. Location theory explains the spatial distribution of production activities in an economy.

2.1 A Static Model

The theory of optimal location for a firm (partial location analysis) is in general based on the assumption that the markets for the firms outputs and inputs are given and located at vertices of a network. The quantities of outputs sold and of inputs purchased by the firm are known. The transport rates of the outputs and inputs are given. Mostly the location is chosen that minimizes total transportation costs.

In Kuiper et al. (1993) a general location analysis is presented explaining a spatial economic equilibrium in which each market shows an equilibrium and the location of *all* produces is determined in an optimal way, using the hypothesis of Tinbergen and Bos.

The system is optimised minimising total transportation costs. Many optimal solutions are shown for different number of firms per sector. The region described in the model is a Manhattan circle (Figure 13.1).

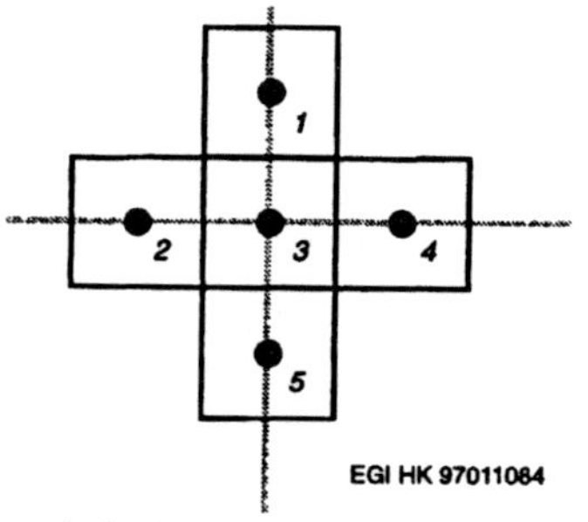

Figure 13.1. A Manhattan circle, $R = 1$.

It appears that the optimal location for a sector containing a limited number of firms will be found in the centre of the region (circle); if the number of firms is increasing, optimal locations will be found in a circle close to the centre of the area. As the number of firms is increasing further, firms start locating at more different locations at bigger distances from the centre of the area. If more sectors have to be located a comparable development can be observed. If the number of firms is limited, sectors tend to locate at the same location close to the centre. So these central locations show big concentrations. If the number of firms of different sectors increases, more firms will locate outside the big central locations, so the area will be more equally filled with locations for sectors, as this reduces total transportation costs. This tendency is demonstrated in Figure 13.2, where total transportation costs are shown for different numbers of firms of two different sectors in a Manhattan circle ($R = 2$). Also an optimal location pattern is showed for an economy with two sectors, sector one contains nine firms, sector two contains four firms.

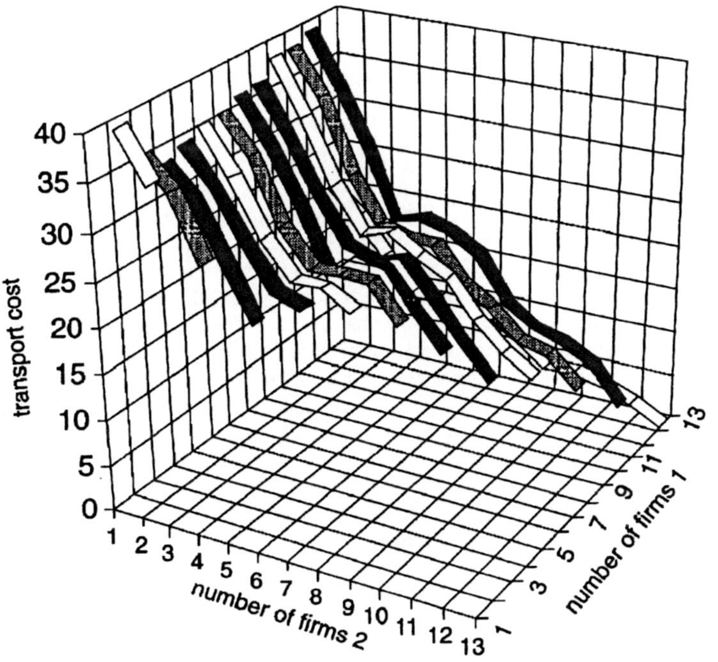

Figure 13.2. Transportation costs for two sectors in a Manhattan circle, $R = 2$.

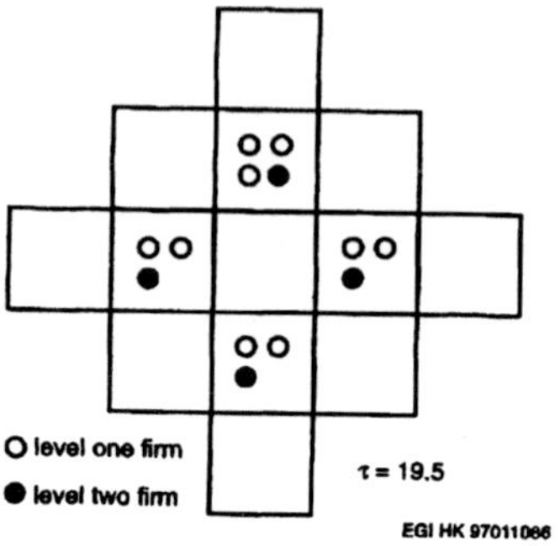

Figure 13.3. Optimal location pattern for nine firms of level one (x) and four firms of level two (0).

2.2 A Dynamic Model

The development of output levels of sectors in regions is determined by a number of variables; the general economic development of the country, specific political measures (sectoral of regional), changes within regions concerning for instance the infrastructure, changes in neighbour regions, changes within sectors concerning production methods, innovations, price levels and consumers preferences, all are influencing regional sector outputs in a different way and all are hard to predict. That means it is very risky to predict output levels of sectors in regions. The best thing to do is try to find general trends in the sectoral development of regions. If stable trends in the past can be found, it could be possible to indicate futural development for a relative short period.

A way of modelling the regional development of sectors in time, is to use the adaptation model Fleur (Ancot and Paelinck, 1983):

$$Y_{rt} - Y_{rt-1} = a\left\{Y^{o}_{rt-1} - Y_{rt-1}\right\} + \frac{a}{2}\left\{Y^{o}_{rt} - Y^{o}_{rt-1} - Y_{rt} + Y_{rt-1}\right\}$$

where Y_{rt} is the output of region r at time t, and

Y^{o}_{rt} is the equilibrium value of output of region r at time t

The share of region r in the total sector output time t is:

$$S_{rt} \triangleq \frac{Y_{rt}}{Y_t} \text{ and } \Delta S_{rt} = S_{rt} - S_{rt-1}$$

The change of the output share of region r is:

$$\Delta S_{rt} = \frac{Y_{rt}}{Y_t} - \frac{Y_{rt-1}}{Y_{t-1}} - \frac{Y_{rt} - Y_{rt-1}}{\frac{1}{2}(Y_t + Y_{t-1})}$$

This model explains how sector outputs change in time according to their reached output level in the previous period and the equilibrium output levels in the present and previous period. Using this model it is possible to show in what direction outputs are moving, and simulate a possible development over a number of years (Paelinck, 1985). Note that the only thing that is to be explained here, is the distribution of the sector outputs over the regions. The way total sector output of the country is developing in time will be considered as known. From the adaption model next result can be found:

$$\Delta S_{rt} = \alpha\left(S^o_{rt} - S_{rt}\right)$$

where S^o_{rt} is the equilibrium output share of region r and time t.

From this model one can conclude:
Suppose $\alpha > 0$: then the share of region r is increasing

if $S_{rt} < S^o_{rt}$, and this share is decreasing

if $S_{rt} > S^o_{rt}$; so there is a tendency towards egalisation.

Supposing $\alpha < 0$, the share of region r is decreasing if $S_{rt} < S^o_{rt}$ and increasing

if $S_{rt} > S^o_{rt}$ so there is a tendency towards growing apart; the big ones become bigger and the small ones disappear. These results are simulated and presented in Paelinck (1985).

3.0 REGIONAL DISPARITIES IN EUROPE

3.1 Introduction

According to the Tinbergen Bos model on economy showing a limited number of sectors, will concentrate in just a few regions (close to the centre). A limited number of regions will grow if the economy is growing, so regional differences will increase. If the economy becomes stronger showing more growing sectors, there will be a tendency to locate in more regions (away from the centre); so in that case more regions will grow. Still regional differences will be observed but the growth will be spread over more regions.

According to the adaption model one can expect convergence tendencies if sectors are growing. If a sector is declining regional differences will grow and these sectors will be produced in a limited number of regions. In order to study regional development in Europe, containing many regions and also many different sectors, one needs to observe a long time period.

3.2 The Development Of Sectors In Europe

The industrial structure of the European Union is well known. Looking at the broad sectors, the trends over the whole period are shown in Table 13.1 and Table 13.2.

The decline in agriculture, the rise and fall of the manufacturing sector and the remarkable rise of service sectors are very clear. In Table 13.2 the development of total employment for a number of branches is presented. In the manufacturing sector two branches are declining during the whole observation period, fuel and power products and also textile and clothing, leather and footwear. Another extreme branch is paper and printing products; this sector has been growing during the period.

3.3 Regional Distribution Of Sectors

Knowing the development of sectors in the whole area, it is interesting to measure how these sectors are distributed over the regions. The change in the spatial structure of sector development can be described using location coefficients. The location coefficient lc_i, is defined as:

$$lc_i = \frac{\sum_{r=1}^{R} |S_{ir} - S_2|}{2}$$

where $S_{ir} = \frac{W_{ir}}{W_i}$, the share of region r is employment of sector I, and

$S_r = \frac{W_r}{W}$, the share of region r is total employment.

So these coefficients indicate the concentration of a sector by the degree to which the sector distribution diverges from the distribution of total employment across all regions. A value of 0 implies a perfectly spread sector; a high value implies concentration in one region. Table 13.3 shows the location coefficients for a number of economic branches.

Table 13.3 shows a trend towards less concentration for the majority of branches. Only agriculture (B01) and also food leverages and tobacco (B36), textile and clothing, leather and footwear (B42) show opposite tendencies. The tertiary sector shows a very clear pattern; all branches have spread over Europe during the whole period.

Table 13.1. Development of total employment of four branches (millions).

Branch	1950	1960	1970	1980	1990
Agriculture, forestry and fishery products	32.4	24.7	15.4	12.3	8.5
Industries	34.1	40.1	41.0	36.6	33.4
Building and construction	7.4	9.7	11.2	10.3	10.2
Services	35.0	43.9	54.3	72.8	87.6
Total	108.9	118.9	121.9	132.0	139.7

Table 13.2. Development of total employment by branch 1950-1990 (millions).

Branch	NACE Code	1950	1960	1970	1980	1990
Agriculture, forestry and fishery products	B01	32.4	24.7	15.4	12.3	8.5
Fuel and power products	B06	3.0	3.3	2.6	2.1	1.7
Ferrous and non-ferrous ores and metals, other than radioactive	B13	1.5	1.9	1.9	1.4	1.0
Non metallic minerals and mineral products	B15	1.9	2.3	2.2	1.9	1.6
Chemical products	B17	1.4	1.9	2.3	2.1	2.0
Metal products, machinery, equipment and electrical goods	B24	6.6	9.4	11.0	10.6	10.6
Transport equipment	B28	2.9	3.6	4.1	3.5	3.0
Food, beverages and tobacco	B36	3.6	4.2	4.1	3.7	3.5
Textiles and clothing, leather and footwear	B42	8.3	7.8	6.6	5.0	3.6
Paper and printing products	B47	1.7	2.2	2.5	2.5	2.5
Products of various industries	B50	3.2	3.5	3.7	3.8	3.9
Building and construction	B53	7.4	9.7	11.2	10.3	10.2
Recovery, repair, trade, lodging and catering services	B58	14.7	18.5	20.9	24.9	26.8
Transport and communication services	B60	6.4	7.1	7.4	8.2	8.1
Services of credit and insurance institutions	B69	1.3	1.9	2.8	3.5	4.1
Other market services	B74	4.2	5.9	8.2	15.9	24.4
Non market services	B86	8.4	10.5	15.0	20.3	24.2
Total		109.1	118.4	121.9	131.9	139.8

Table 13.3. Location coefficients for economic branches.

	B01	B06	B13	B15	B17	B24	B28	B36	B42
1950	0.29	0.44	0.38	0.17	0.26	0.24	0.32	0.13	0.20
1960	0.33	0.40	0.37	0.15	0.24	0.23	0.26	0.12	0.19
1970	0.38	0.28	0.36	0.15	0.23	0.20	0.24	0.11	0.21
1980	0.37	0.26	0.36	0.17	0.23	0.19	0.24	0.14	0.24
1990	0.36	0.19	0.35	0.20	0.21	0.21	0.24	0.14	0.33

	B47	B50	B53	B58	B60	B69	B74	B86
1950	0.25	0.14	0.10	0.14	0.16	0.23	0.15	0.12
1960	0.22	0.12	0.08	0.09	0.13	0.19	0.12	0.11
1970	0.19	0.13	0.08	0.06	0.10	0.17	0.11	0.10
1980	0.18	0.14	0.08	0.06	0.09	0.15	0.11	0.10
1990	0.17	0.15	0.07	0.06	0.08	0.15	0.13	0.09

3.4 Regional Specialisation

When there is a trend towards lower concentration of branches, the degree to which regions are specialised in certain branches is likely to show a decreasing trend too. The specialisation coefficient is used to measure this; SC_{r} is defined as:

$$SC_{r} = \frac{\sum_{i=1}^{I} |\sigma_{ir} - \sigma_{i}|}{2} \text{, where}$$

$\sigma_{ir} = \frac{W_{ir}}{W_{.r}}$, the share of sector i in the employment of region r

$\sigma_{i.} = \frac{W_{i.}}{W_{..}}$, the share of sector i in total employment.

High values of $SC_{..r}$ correspond with strong specialisation; the value 0 means an average regional structure. Core regions with strong employment structures and lagging regions can deviate from the average region in the same way and therefore generate identical specialisation coefficients.

Table 13.4 shows in many cases de-specialisation trends although some countries like the Netherlands, Germany, Luxembourg and Denmark generate increasing values. It is interesting to study this figures more detailed by looking at smaller regions in Europe. It appears important to distinguish between the location of the regions. Table B1 shows detailed figures of all European regions and one can conclude that the low-specialized regions are mostly located in the heartland of North-Western Europe. The high specialized region can be found in the periphery of the EU. These regions are often specialized in the more traditional industries.

Table 13.4. Specialisation coefficients of European Countries.

		$SC_{,r}$ 50	$SC_{,r}$ 60	$SC_{,r}$ 70	$SC_{,r}$ 80	$SC_{,r}$ 91
Deutschland	R1	0.05	0.07	0.07	0.07	0.08
France	R2	0.08	0.07	0.06	0.05	0.06
Italia	R3	0.19	0.18	0.13	0.1	0.1
the Netherlands	R4	0.12	0.1	0.11	0.13	0.15
Belgium	R5	0.15	0.12	0.08	0.09	0.07
Luxembourg	R6	0.16	0.2	0.22	0.24	0.2
United Kingdom	R7	0.2	0.15	0.1	0.07	0.08
Ireland	R8	0.19	0.23	0.19	0.15	0.12
Denmark	R9	0.1	0.11	0.1	0.12	0.15
Europe (9) R	0	0	0	0	0	

Looking at the figures for the four regions of the Netherlands next specialization coefficients can be observed:

Table 13.5. Specialisation coefficients of the four regions in the Netherlands.

	1950	1960	1970	1980	1991
North	0.15	0.13	0.14	0.19	0.18
East	0.09	0.09	0.09	0.14	0.15
South	0.13	0.15	0.11	0.15	0.12
West	0.23	0.20	0.17	0.15	0.19

South and West can be regarded as the economic hart of the country and North and East are more the peripheral regions. However, the differences are not very big so one has to be careful drawing conclusions.

The picture becomes more clear if the European regions are grouped according to their location. Five groups are distinguished according to their regional potential (Keeble, 1986). The method that is used is based on the determination of the regional product (brute) of each region combined by these values of the regions surrounding this region. So the economy of each region is combined with its location. In this way Europe can be deviated into five groups of regions:

inner central
outer central
intermediate
inner peripheral
outer peripheral

Table 13.6 shows the specialization coefficients of these five groups.

The picture now is very clear. The highest initial specializations can be observed at either end of the scale. There is a general trend towards de-specialization of regions.

Table 13.6. Specialisation coefficients of five groups of region in Europe.

	1950	1960	1970	1980	1990
Inner central	0.17	0.15	0.11	0.09	0.08
outer central	0.10	0.08	0.07	0.05	0.03
intermediate	0.03	0.03	0.03	0.04	0.03
inner peripheral	0.08	0.07	0.07	0.05	0.03
outer peripheral	0.19	0.19	0.15	0.12	0.11

4.0 THE DEVELOPMENT OF EMPLOYMENT OF SECTORS IN EUROPE

From section 3 it was found that sectors tend to be located in an increasing number of regions. The development of employment in the EU seems to be more equally distributed. The regional development is directly connected to the sectors located in it. In this section sectoral development of groups of European regions is studied. At first the three mean sectors: agriculter, industry and services are distinguished. The shares of these sectos in each of the five groups of regions is showed in Table 13.7.

Table 13.7. Shares of three sectors for five groups of regions in Europe.

Group	1950	Agriculture 1960	1970	1980	1990
Inner central	0.13	0.07	0.04	0.03	0.02
Outer central	0.20	0.13	0.07	0.06	0.03
Intermediate	0.32	0.22	0.12	0.08	0.05
Inner peripheral	0.37	0.26	0.15	0.11	0.07
Outer peripheral	0.49	0.40	0.27	0.20	0.13
EU-total	0.30	0.21	0.12	0.09	0.06
Group	**1950**	**Industry 1960**	**1970**	**1980**	**1990**
Inner central	0.47	0.48	0.46	0.38	0.32
Outer central	0.46	0.49	0.49	0.41	0.34
Intermediate	0.37	0.42	0.45	0.38	0.33
Inner peripheral	0.33	0.38	0.40	0.33	0.29
Outer peripheral	0.27	0.32	0.34	0.30	0.28
EU-total	0.38	0.42	0.43	0.36	0.32
Group	**1950**	**Services 1960**	**1970**	**1980**	**1990**
Inner central	0.40	0.44	0.50	0.59	0.66
Outer central	0.34	0.38	0.44	0.54	0.62
Intermediate	0.31	0.36	0.43	0.54	0.62
Inner peripheral	0.30	0.36	0.45	0.56	0.64
Outer peripheral	0.24	0.29	0.39	0.50	0.59
EU-total	0.32	0.37	0.45	0.55	0.63

Bron: Ereco (1995), Molle (1980), eigen uitwerking

Looking at the shares each sector will be described:

1. Agriculture

During the observation period the employment in this sector has decreased by 25 million workers. The inner and outer central regions are clearly underrepresented, the intermediate group shows a picture which represents Europe and the peripheral regions show an increasing overrepresentation.

In Figure 13.4 the negative growth for all groups is presented. Especially in the period 1960-1970 the decrease in this sector is very high.

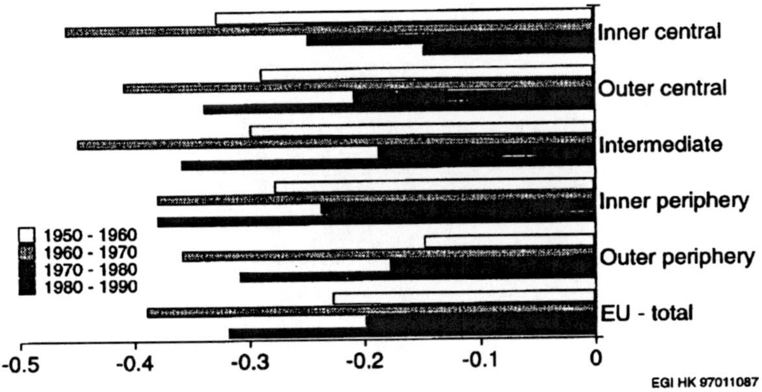

Figure 13.4. Growth of agriculture in five European groups of regions.

2. The industry

Industry shows a remarkable picture during the observed period. The growth from 1950 to 1970, becomes decline for all groups from 1970 to 1990. The initial growth is very equally distributed over the regions; the inner central regions show the highest increase. The decline in the second half of the period is high for the inner central regions as well. A filtering down process can be observed here. The growth of the sector is moving to the outer regions. The inner and outer peripheral regions show a higher than medium growth from 1960-1970, and the decline from 1980-1990 is relative small.

3. Services

This sector shows explosive growth during the observed period. The loss of jobs in the other sectors, agriculture and industry, is more than compensated by this development. At first the inner and outer central regions grow fast and later this growth is concentrated as the inner and outer peripheral regions. During the period 1970-1980 the service sector grows with more than 30%!

In general, all groups show an increasing part of their employment in the service sectors and a declining part in agriculture. The differences between the groups are declining and convergence tendences can be observed.

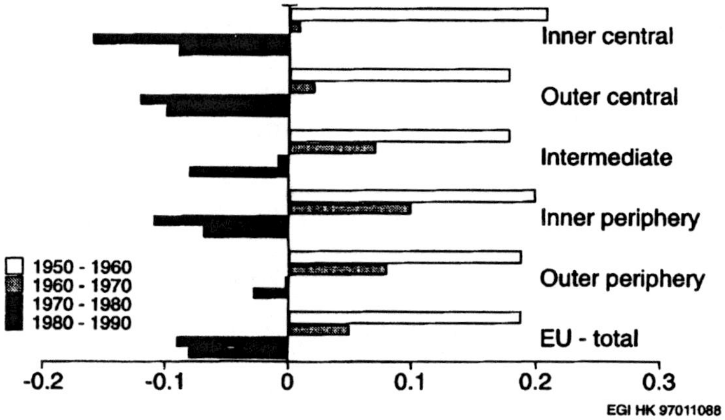

Figure 13.5. Growth of industry in five European groups of regions.

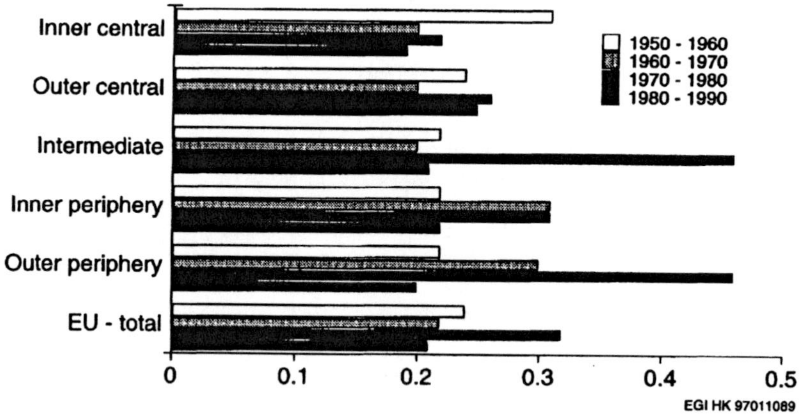

Figure 13.6. Growth of services in five European groups of regions.

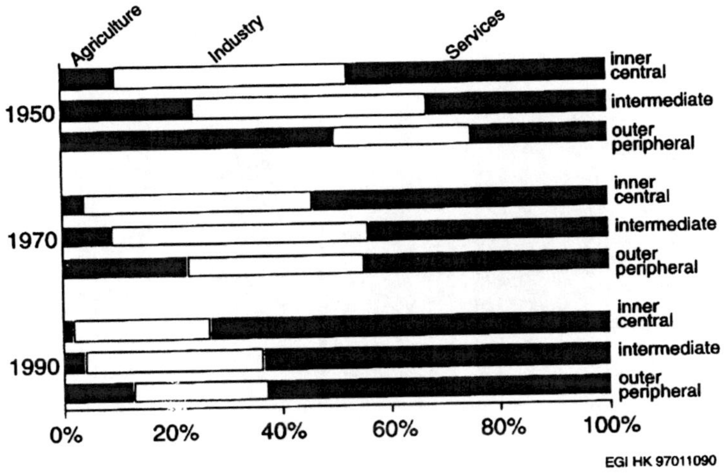

Figure 13.7. Shares of inner central regions, outer peripheral regions and intermediate regions in the main sectors

5.0 CONCLUSION

At the start of the observed period there is a big difference between the central and peripheral regions; prosperity is declining as the distance from the region to the centre is growing. This difference becomes smaller during the observed period. Prosperity is distributed more equally over the regions. Still at the end of the period in 1990, the difference between the central regions and the peripheral regions is big (127 versus 69). As an indicator for the development of prosperity, Figure 13.8 shows the regional product per head of the population for the five different groups of regions. The mentioned tendencies seem to be clear.

Besides the development of the prosperity, the development of the degree of participation is an important indicator for the development of labour productivity. If labour productivity shows converging tendencies in Europe, both indicators have to be studied more closely in order to determine which one is the most important for this development. In Figure 13.9 the development of the degree of participation is illustrated.

Figure 13.9 shows a less clear picture compared to Figure 13.8, concerning the regional production. Differences are almost the same during the period. The inner central regions show a small increase and the outer peripheral regions a small decline. It is difficult to explain these development as many factors could be determining this degree of participation.

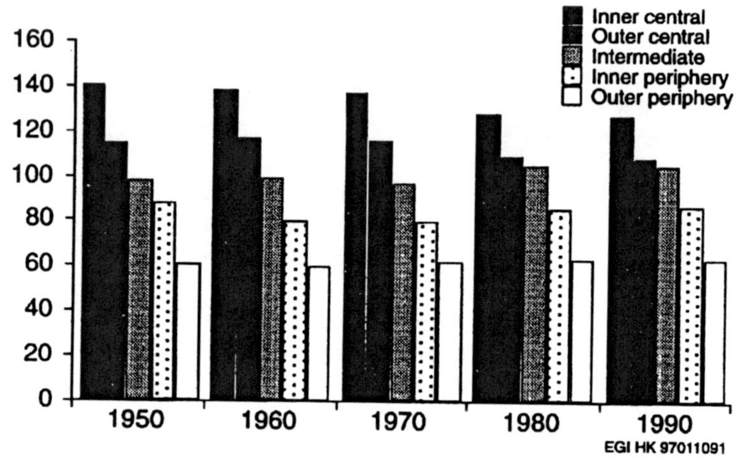

Figure 13.8. Regional product (gross) per head of the population of five groups in Europe.

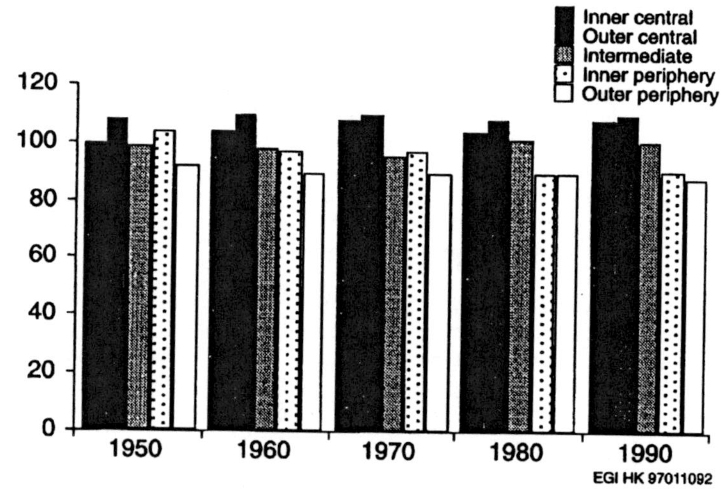

Figure 13.9. Development of the degree of participation in five groups.

Finally, the development of labour productivity is showed. This indicator is determined by the previous observations (the prosperity and the degree of participation). Figure 13.10 shows the development for all groups during 1950-1990. The differences of the labour productivity between the regions appears to be smaller than the differences in prosperity (Figure 13.8). At the start differences are very big. The last observations (1990) show the smallest differences. The outer central group and the intermediate group show comparable developments and a remarkable development can be observed in the inner peripheral group; these regions almost bridges the differences with the two groups mentioned. As the end three groups show almost equal labour productivity values, and the outer peripheral regions are coming closer (from 68% to 78%).

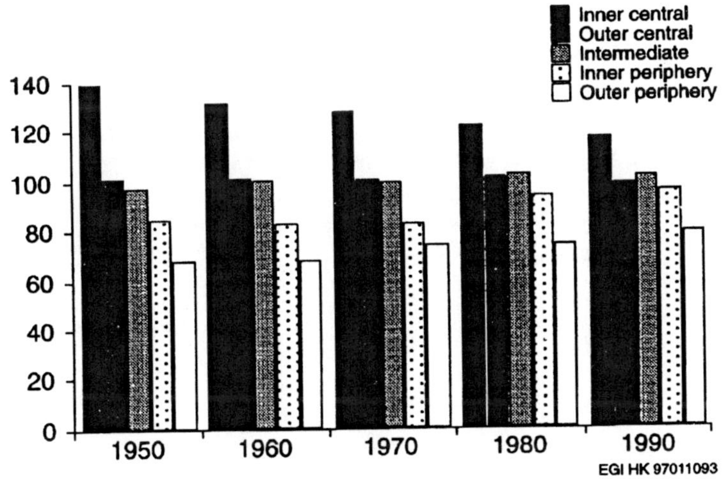

Figure 13.10. Development of gross regional product per worker for 5 groups (index).

6.0 SOME FINAL REMARKS

In this paper the regional development of the European Union from 1950-1990 is studied; differences between regions and the development of these differences are important for the member states. At this moment there are 15 member states and there is a tendency towards growing (Eastern European Countries, Turkey).

In Section 2.0 models explaining regional development are mentioned. Tinbergen-Bos models explain optimal location patterns in space. These models show where sectors locate which sectors concentrate and explain regional differences. The second type of models (FLEUR) explain regional development in time. Depending on different conditions one can expect regional differences to decline or to increase. In Section 3.0, first the development of economic sectors in Europe is described. Remarkable is the growth of the employment in the service sectors and the decline in agriculture. Looking at the distribution of sectors in space it was clear that regional differences are declining.

Technical improvement, development and increase of markets and the congestion in economic centres, leads to a dispersal of activities. Differences in efficiency between regions also stimulate the movement of factors. Regional differences always will remain because of different conditions; it is hard to forecast how far this convergence tendency will continue.

REFERENCES

Ancot, J.-P. and J.H.P. Paelinck. (1983). "The Spatial Econometrics of the European FLEUR-model." In *Evolving Geographical Structures*, edited by D. Griffith and A. Lea, pp. 229-246. Den Haag: Martinus Nijhoff Publishers.

Keeble, D., J. Offord and S. Walker. (1986). *Peripheral Regions in a Community of Twelve Member States: Final Report.* Department of Geography, University of Cambridge, Cambridge.

Kuiper, F.J., J.H. Kuiper and J.H.P. Paelinck. (1993). "Tinbergen-Bos metricised systems: some further results." *Urban Studies*, 30, 1745-1761.

Molle, W.T.M., B. Van Holst and H. Smit. (1980). Regional Disparity and Economic Development in the European Community, Farnborough.

Paelinck, J.H.P. (1985). Elements d'Analyse Economique Spatiale, Editions Regionales Europeennes, pp.143-183.

Table B.1. Specialisation coefficients of regions and member states.

		$SC_{.r}$ 50	$SC_{.r}$ 60	$SC_{.r}$ 70	$SC_{.r}$ 80	$SC_{.r}$ 91
Schleswig-Holstein	R11	0.12	0.11	0.1	0.1	0.06
Hamburg	R12	0.3	0.25	0.21	0.16	0.14
Niedersachsen	R13	0.12	0.08	0.07	0.08	0.06
Bremen	R14	0.3	0.26	0.21	0.17	0.13
Nordrhein-Westfalen	R15	0.17	0.16	0.14	0.12	0.11
Hessen	R16	0.06	0.09	0.1	0.08	0.09
Rheinland-Pfalz	R17	0.17	0.09	0.08	0.08	0.08
Baden-Wurtemberg	R18	0.12	0.12	0.13	0.14	0.15
Bayern	R19	0.11	0.1	0.09	0.11	0.09
Saarland	R1A	0.25	0.22	0.18	0.17	0.13
Berlin (West)	R1B	0.32	0.25	0.21	0.17	0.1
Ile de France	R21	0.28	0.21	0.15	0.16	0.13
Bassin Parisien	R22	0.15	0.12	0.1	0.06	0.08
Nord-Pas-de Calais	R23	0.21	0.19	0.15	0.11	0.09
Est	R24	0.1	0.1	0.09	0.07	0.1
Ouest	R25	0.3	0.27	0.22	0.14	0.13
Sud-Ouest	R26	0.28	0.22	0.18	0.11	0.11
Centre-Est	R27	0.13	0.1	0.09	0.07	0.06
Mediterrance	R28	0.14	0.16	0.17	0.14	0.12
Nord Ovest	R31	0.12	0.11	0.13	0.12	0.09
Lombardia	R32	0.17	0.17	0.19	0.16	0.14
Nord Est	R33	0.2	0.17	0.14	0.14	0.13
Emilia-Romagna	R34	0.28	0.2	0.15	0.14	0.13
Centro	R35	0.26	0.24	0.2	0.16	0.18
Lazio	R36	0.21	0.18	0.15	0.14	0.1
Campania	R37	0.23	0.25	0.21	0.18	0.14
Abruzzi-Molise	R38	0.45	0.38	0.31	0.24	0.15
Sud	R39	0.38	0.37	0.3	0.23	0.17
Sicilia	R3A	0.28	0.29	0.23	0.18	0.18
Sardegna	R3B	0.31	0.3	0.24	0.2	0.18
Noord	R41	0.15	0.13	0.14	0.19	0.18
Oost	R42	0.09	0.09	0.09	0.14	0.15
Zuid	R45	0.13	0.15	0.11	0.15	0.12
West	R47	0.23	0.2	0.17	0.15	0.19
Vlaams Gewest	R51	0.15	0.12	0.09	0.11	0.09
Region Wallonne	R52	0.2	0.15	0.13	0.14	0.12
Bruxelles-Brussel	R53	0.21	0.19	0.16	0.19	0.17
Luxembourg	R60	0.16	0.21	0.22	0.24	0.2
North	R71	0.28	0.2	0.14	0.12	0.06
Yorkshire & Humberside	R72	0.24	0.18	0.13	0.11	0.07
East Midlands	R73	0.23	0.21	0.16	0.14	0.08
East Anglia	R74	0.13	0.11	0.09	0.08	0.08
South East	R75	0.29	0.23	0.17	0.14	0.15
South West	R76	0.23	0.18	0.14	0.12	0.08
West Midlands	R77	0.3	0.25	0.22	0.17	0.1
North West	R78	0.26	0.19	0.14	0.11	0.08
Wales	R79	0.27	0.21	0.16	0.13	0.07
Scotland	R7A	0.18	0.13	0.09	0.08	0.08
North Ireland	R7B	0.19	0.18	0.15	0.16	0.12
Ireland	R80	0.19	0.23	0.19	0.15	0.12
Denmark	R90	0.1	0.11	0.1	0.12	0.15
Deutschland	R1	0.05	0.07	0.07	0.07	0.08
France	R2	0.08	0.07	0.06	0.05	0.06
Italian	R3	0.19	0.18	0.13	0.1	0.1
the Netherlands	R4	0.12	0.1	0.11	0.13	0.15
Belgium	R5	0.15	0.12	0.08	0.09	0.07
Luxembourg	R6	0.16	0.21	0.22	0.24	0.2

Continued table B.1

		$SC_{,r}$ 50	$SC_{,r}$ 60	$SC_{,r}$ 70	$SC_{,r}$ 80	$SC_{,r}$ 91
United Kingdom	R7	0.2	0.15	0.1	0.07	0.08
Ireland	R8	0.19	0.23	0.19	0.15	0.12
Denmark	R9	0.1	0.11	0.1	0.12	0.15
Europe (9)	R	0	0	0	0	0

Bron: NEI/ERECO, eigen uitwerking

CHAPTER 14

TOWARDS A « SPATIALIZED » COST OF CAPITAL CONCEPT

Michel Mignolet

1.0 INTRODUCTION

The economic literature has long been concerned with the location of productive activities in space. The investor is viewed as selecting the region that yields the highest expected value of after-tax profits. The firm considers, among others, the intrinsic characteristics of regions (the factor endowments) as well as any net agglomeration benefits[1]. By the clustering of activities, externalities are exploited that modify the comparative advantages of regions. Agglomeration economies add to the attractiveness of some locations[2]. However as firms congregate competition among users may bid up local factor prices (land, in particular) lowering the advantage of congested zones. The individual maximization decision also accounts for any subsidies granted in the different regions and the tax burden on the income from invested capital.

In the neoclassical tradition, the investment demand (the setting up of a new firm, for example) is explained by the cost of capital. This indicator expresses the minimum rate of return (the marginal revenue productivity of one monetary unit of capital) the investment project must yield before taxes in order to provide the saver with an attractive net of tax return. It captures in a summary statistic the financial cost, the effective economic depreciation, all tax devices, and investment incentives that directly affect the return on capital. Today the models become more and more realistic. For instance, they are able to integrate the different systems of international double taxation, if any, when the investment is cross-border, the different regimes alleviating the economic double taxation of dividends and the complex interplay of both[3]. A large number of financing arrangements can also be taken into consideration as can be the risk related to a particular asset.

This approach has widely proved its relevance and its usefulness for comparing various location choices. The numerous applications give some evidence of that[4]. While commonly used, this approach is not exempt of criticisms. In particular the plausibility of the main assumption is questioned : *undifferentiated space*. This hypothesis renders the marginal productivity of an investment project being absolutely the same wherever it locates. The

1 This way of setting out the location process does not exclude the possible part of history accidents that the recent literature showed to have influenced the past geographical pattern of activities.
2 They are largely due to cost reductions in the exchange of intermediate inputs.
3 See for instance Alworth (1988) extending the commonly used methodology of King and Fullerton (1984).
4 See O.E.C.D. (1991), C.E.E. (1992), Jorgenson and Landau (1993), E.B.R.D. (1993) and Shah (1995) respectively for developed (the first three references), in transition and developing countries.

assumption mentioned above entails other undesirable consequences of diverse importance, too:

- the undifferentiated space involves that (fixed) capital has not to be split up into plant and equipment on the one hand, land on the other hand. Pricing both components is not required. Any difference in land price, for example, across space is therefore ignored;
- the framework of competitive analysis is no longer the most appropriate one.

The fact that some input suppliers are located closer to any locator than others is notably responsible of that.

The object of this paper is *to extend the cost of capital framework by accounting for space*. The theoretical base of this paper is derived from two main fields of the economic literature :

- a first inspiration source refers to the effective tax rate on income from capital theory in the neoclassical tradition of investment theory;
- a second branch of the literature belongs to regional and spatial science. Two topics are especially useful here : the spatial differences in productivity and the differential land prices.

Our approach draws on elements from both sources.

The present paper is made up of two main sections before concluding. The first one - section 2 - introduces the basic model when space is undifferentiated. In order to consider an investment composed of plant and equipment on the one hand and land on the other hand, the analytical expressions of capital cost are successively presented respectively for a depreciable asset, a non-depreciable asset and a combination of both. In section 3 the assumption of undifferentiated space is relaxed by including gradually spatial productivity differences, land differentiated prices and imperfect competition.

2.0 THE COST OF CAPITAL : THE A-SPATIAL CONCEPT

In the literature about effective tax rates on income from capital, two rates of return are distinguished :

- the pretax real rate of return on the investment and,

- the posttax real rate of return for the finance supplier (called the saver).

The first one corresponds to the (user) cost of capital. It is defined as the minimum rate of return[5] an investment project must yield before any taxes in order to provide the saver with the same net of tax return he would receive from lending at the market (risk-free) interest rate. This is the second rate of return mentioned above .The analytical expression of the capital cost is derived from an explicit optimizing framework[6] on the investment decision of the firm.

[5] Eventually adjusted for risk (see McKenzie , 1994).
[6] The representative firm is assumed generally to maximize its equity value in the tradition of Hall and Jorgenson (1967). Alternatively Auerbach (1983) calculates the cost of capital when the value of both equity and debt is maximized.

Let us consider in turn a depreciable asset, a non-depreciable asset and a combination of both.

2.1 The Depreciable Capital Case

The standard expression (Boadway and Shah, 1995) of the gross cost of capital for a depreciable asset is reproduced in (1). Let us admit that perfect competition holds in all markets and denote the useful variables as follows : P and P_{dK} respectively are the prices of output and of investment goods, π and π_{dK}, the inflation rate and the real capital gains on the depreciable asset[7], A_{dK}, the present discounted value of any grants and tax allowances[8] given for the same asset, ρ, the nominal financial cost, τ, the corporate tax rate[9], δ, the economic depreciation and f'_{dK}, the marginal productivity of capital. The cost of capital expression for a depreciable asset, c_{dK}, can be written as follows :

$$c_{dK} = \frac{P.f'_{dK}}{P_{dK}} = \frac{1-A_{dK}}{1-t}.\left[(\rho-\pi)+(\delta-\pi_{dK})\right] \qquad (1)$$

Equation (1) shows that the cost of capital is the marginal value productivity of one monetary unit of capital. When public policy is neutral ($A_{dK} = \tau$), the cost of capital, c_{dK}, reduces to a sum of two terms :

- the real financial cost (ρ - π) plus,
- the effective economic depreciation rate (δ - π_{dK}).

The financial cost, ρ, most often differs in a world of distortionary taxes according to the source of financing. For domestic arrangements, King and Fullerton (1984) calculate separately the cost of capital for different financing methods. Boadway, on the contrary, measures a weighted average of financing mix (Boadway, 1987; Boadway and Shah, 1995). Transnational arrangements are considered by Alworth (1988)[10].

---

7 π_{dK} expresses the difference between the growth rate of the investment price and the inflation rate.

8 Including any tax savings due to the future depreciation deductions.

9 In a cross-border financial arrangement, τ is representative of the net tax burden resulting from tax regimes in host and home countries (i.e. the potential international double taxation and any relief methods).

10 In order to illustrate the measurement of financial costs, only the case of a closed economy will be considered here for the sake of simplicity. Moreover the finance supplier is supposed to be a domestic household. Since nominal interest payments are tax deductible for the company, the financial cost for debt finance is $\rho_E = (1-\tau).i$ where i is the interest rate. If ψ expresses the nominal after-tax rate of return required by existing shareholders on retained earnings, the financial cost of retaining profits ρ_R is equal to ψ / $(1-m_g)$ where m_g is the shareholders' personal tax rate on capital gains (transformed into an effective rate on accruals). If one assumes that σ is the required return to new shareholders (which may differ from ψ for generality), the financial cost associated to a new shares issue ρ_S becomes $[\ \sigma + \pi\ (m_g - 1 + [\ 1-m_d\ ].\ \theta)\ ]\ /\ \theta.\ [\ 1-m_d\ ]$, where θ and m_d respectively denote the opportunity cost of retained earnings in terms of gross dividends forgone and the personal tax rate on dividend remittances (see King and Fullerton, 1984; Boadway and Shah, 1995). θ is greater than 1 when methods of alleviating economic double taxation of dividends (the imputation regime, for instance) are implemented. The term $(m_g - 1 + [\ 1-m_d\ ].\ \theta)$ is representative of the net tax penalty attributable to the fact that a purely nominal return is taxed at θ rate but escapes from any capital gains tax.

2.2 The Non-Depreciable Capital Case

Transposing the cost of capital expression for land (a non-depreciable asset) is straightforward : economic depreciation and capital allowances for tax purposes are put equal to zero (see Boadway and Shah, 1995). Accordingly the cost of capital for land, c_L, becomes :

$$c_L = \frac{P.f'_L}{P_L} = \frac{1-A_L}{1-t}.\left[\rho - \pi - \pi_L\right] \tag{2}$$

where P, ρ, τ and π have been defined above. P_L, f'_L, A_L and π_L can be interpreted in the same way as the corresponding variables P_{dK}, f'_{dK}, A_{dK} and π_{dK}. They express, respectively, the land price, the marginal productivity of land, public advantages[11] and the real capital gain on land.

2.3 An Investment Made Up Of Depreciable And Non-Depreciable Assets

When the capital stock consists of depreciable assets and land, the expression of capital cost becomes more complicated. For the sake of simplicity, one assumes that the production technique is fixed in terms of depreciable capital and land wherever the investment is located[12]. Without loss of generality, this hypothesis can be expressed as follows : an additional unit of investment, dK, is composed everywhere of one unit of depreciable asset (dK_d = 1) and one unit of land (dL = 1). As shown in (3), the investment expenditure in value, P_k.dK, is equal to the sum of expenses for the purchase of depreciable asset, $P_{dK}.dK_d$, and land, P_L.dL :

$$P_K.dK = P_{dK}.dK_d + P_L.dL. \tag{3}$$

In an a-spatial universe, there are no transportation costs. Moreover, under perfectly competitive conditions - the standard framework for the cost of capital study - every firm is a price-taker. Factor prices are therefore fixed and equal wherever the investment location.

As $dK = dK_d = dL = 1$, equation (3) reduces to :

$$P_K = P_{dK} + P_L . \tag{4}$$

Let us define λ as the part of land in the total capital expenditure, namely

$$\lambda = \frac{P_L}{P_K} . \tag{5}$$

King and Fullerton (1984) consider an arbitrage mechanism in such a way that the saver is indifferent between the three financing choices. In order to obtain this result the authors impose that $\psi = \sigma + \pi$ (m_g - 1 + [1-m_d]. θ) = (1-m_i). i where m_i is the personal tax on interest.

11 The scale of public advantages for land, A_L, is weaker than for a depreciable asset because the only aids are potentially a subsidy and an investment tax credit.

12 This hypothesis will be discussed below when the undifferentiated-space assumption is relaxed.

I am now in a position to derive the cost of capital expression for a mix of depreciable and non-depreciable assets. Using (1), (2) and (4), one can write

$$P_K.c = \frac{1-A_{dK}}{1-\tau}.[(\rho-\pi)+(\delta-\pi_{dK})].P_{dK} + \frac{1-A_L}{1-\tau}.(\rho-\pi-\pi_L).P_L. \qquad (6)$$

Integrating (5) into (6),

$$c = \frac{1-A_{dK}}{1-\tau}.[(\rho-\pi)+(\delta-\pi_{dK})].(1-\lambda) + \frac{1-A_L}{1-\tau}.(\rho-\pi-\pi_L).\lambda. \qquad (7)$$

Now let us examine how the cost of capital expression is modified when the undifferentiated-space assumption is relaxed.

3.0 THE COST OF CAPITAL IN A DIFFERENTIATED SPACE

In Section 2, I provide an overview of the standard model measuring the cost of capital. This model enables us to calculate the minimum rate of return an investment must yield in order to be implemented. The variables included in the analytical expression of capital cost may differ from region to region. It is the case of general environment variables such as interest rates or inflation rates. It is also the case of public variables namely the investment incentives and the tax parameters and regimes on income from capital. The indicator defined in (7) turns out to be valuable as well for the investor as for public authorities : it enables us to compare performances of various investment locations in terms of capital cost with respect to the variables taken into account. It may also be used in order to simulate alternative public policies aimed at fostering investment : the differentiated efficacy of some tax devices or capital grants may, for example, be examined by this method.

While pertinent, this approach comes up against some limitations : it is, for instance, unable to determine if a regional policy generates a sufficient or an insufficient differential cost of capital to attract new plants. Space is indeed not undifferentiated. The productivity of any production technique may be higher in one region and lower in another because of natural endowments or agglomeration (dis)economies. One can reasonably assume that firms take the spatial differentials in productivity into account in their location decision making. At the opposite side, the productivity advantages of some regions are offset to some extent by higher factor prices (land, labour, plant or equipment) that must be paid.

This section sets out to integrate progressively space-specific variables into the cost of capital framework. One will successively examine an accounting for differential productivity between regions, consideration of differences in factor prices, and finally - because one cannot presume firms to act in an environment characterized by perfectly elastic demand or supply in all markets - an imperfect economic environment. Through the transformations, the cost of capital is progressively converted from a general factor explaining investment demand into an actual indicator of interregional attractiveness.

Let us consider that N regions apply for the location of the investment project. In each region, any location site is supposed to face the same conditions about factor endowments and prices so that location and region are here considered to be interchangeable.

3.1 Accounting For Differences In Regional Productivity

Spatial productivity differentials are more often apprehended in the specialized literature by estimating production function models[13].
A general expression is given in (8). Output in region r, Q_r, is represented by a homogeneous production function of degree h :

$$Q_r = A_r f(K_r, L_r) \lambda^{hr} \tag{8}$$

where K_r and L_r denote the capital stock and labour input in region r, respectively. Differences in productivity from region to region are generally[14] captured by the Hicks-neutral shifter term[15], A_r, by returns to scale[16], or by both[17].

In contrast with factors enhancing only the productivity of one given factor of production, regional factors are supposed to affect output in general[18]. Accordingly they are absorbed by the independent shift parameter. A_r refers therefore to *business milieu*. It accounts for differences between regions due to site specific characteristics (e.g., proximity to transport nodes as well as to cities, land topography), local infrastructure, metropolitan structures, climate[19], natural resources endowments, industry mix, and so on. In this first approach, A_r is estimated by econometric methods, assuming that $f(.)\lambda^h$ is the same in every region.

Agglomeration economies, in the standard classification due to Hoover (1936) are composed of three terms : (i) **scale economies** internal to the firm depend on the firm's scale of production; (ii) **localization economies** external to the firm but internal to the industry relate to the size of the industry; and, (iii) **urbanization economies** benefiting all industries link to the scale of the city. Localization and urbanization economies originate in large pools of skilled

13 Some studies rely on the general framework of the Constant-Elasticity-Substitution production function. Others use the Cobb-Douglas or the translog forms. Because capital stocks series are not generally available at the regional level, most studies estimate a labour demand equation derived from a CES production function. See for example Carlino and Voith, 1992.

14 Alternatively to this standard approach based on the average production function, Beeson and Husted (1989) use a frontier production function approach. Spatial productivity differentials are then measured by the deviations from the "best practice" frontier (e.g., the maximum output achievable using that vector of inputs).

15 See for instance Sveikauskas (1975). Recent examples are provided by Moomaw and Williams (1991) and Carlino and Voith (1992).

16 See Shefer (1973) and Carlino (1982).

17 See Beeson (1987). Catin (1991) applied her approach to French regions.

18 That factors are supposed to be captured by f (.). Some richer specifications of the production function include efficiency terms affecting K and L : the age of the physical stock or educational attainment and experience. See for instance Ke and Luger (1996). If the function is poorly (richly) specified, the shift parameter will concentrate the effect of a large (small) set of variables not captured by f(.).

19 In a broadened sense, climate incorporates social climate, enterprise culture, presence of innovative milieux, and so on.

labour, entrepreneurial talent, wholesalers of specialized items and specialized business services, and inter-firm technological spillovers. Carlino (1982) notes that agglomeration economies are technical in nature due to increasing returns[20]. Hence he comes to the conclusion that they may be more directly measured by h, the homogeneity degree of the function . So, through parameter h, he seeks to capture productivity differentials due to variation in increasing returns to scale. In this second approach, for estimating differentiated returns to scale over space Carlino must assume that A is constant across locations.

The border separating variables affecting A_r and h is not absolute. Moomaw (1983), for example does not follow Carlino. He classifies urbanization and localization economies into the Hicks-neutral shifter term, putting forward the argument that these effects are outside the firm's control.

Lastly, spatial productivity differentials may be apprehended by the combination of shift parameter and returns to scale. Both factors are then allowed to vary between regions. Expressed in an additive framework, the total factor productivity growth is measured by the sum of the growth attributable to both terms.

Whatever the method, the literature provides interesting solutions for measuring the differential productivity supplied by every region. From any three approaches it is *a priori* possible to build an index expressing productivity in the *r*th region relative to a benchmark entity (the nation, for instance). In order to illustrate the method, for the sake of simplicity, only the first approach will be considered here. Following Moomaw (1983), A_r is assumed to capture all factors explaining productivity variation across locations, namely interregional differences in factor endowments on the one hand, localization and urbanization economies related to the number of nearby firms, on the other hand.

Let us define $\hat{A}_.$ and $\hat{A}_r$ as the Hicks-neutral shifter terms measured by estimating a homogeneous production function of degree h respectively for the benchmark entity and the region r[21]. Hence the productivity index[22], α_r, for region r equals :

$$\alpha_r = \hat{A}_r / \hat{A}_. \qquad (9)$$

If one assumes that the productivity index, so estimated from past data, is representative of the contemporaneous differential of productivity for any new investment in region r, one can incorporate it into (7). The neo-classical theory states that the firm decides to invest up to the point where marginal productivity of capital is equal to its additional cost. At present, the marginal product of

20 In connection with this, Fujita and Thisse (1996) stress the essential role of increasing returns to scale for explaining the geographical distribution of productive activities.

21 Carlino and Voith (1992) for instance use a three-stage estimation procedure. First, they estimate $\hat{A}_r$ for every region r. A second model is fitted in order to explain $\hat{A}_r$ by a set of region-specific variables (e.g. industry mix, human capital characteristics, public investment in infrastructure, metropolitan structure). Thirdly the average productivity shift (for the benchmark entity), $\hat{A}_.$, is measured by the linear combination of estimated parameters from a regression in the second step and means for every region-specific variable.

22 When variables representing business milieu are industry-specific, it may be desirable that the estimation be made at the industry level, i. In such a case, productivity indexes by region and by industry, α_{ir}, are to be estimated.

capital is affected by differential productivity provided by region r. Accordingly the first member of the equality is replaced by $\alpha_r.c$, such that

$$c^r = \left\{ \frac{1-A_{dK}}{1-\tau}.[(\rho-\pi)+(\delta-\pi_{dK})].(1-\lambda)+\frac{1-A_L}{1-\tau}.(\rho-\pi-\pi_L).\lambda \right\}.\frac{1}{\alpha_r} \qquad (10)$$

3.2 Accounting For Regional Differences In Factor Prices

Let us admit now that assets prices notably the land price may vary between regions. For every location choice r (= 1,...,N), the investment expenditure in value is equal to the sum of expenses attributable to depreciable asset, P_{dK}^r, and land, P_L^r, as follows :

$$P_K^r .dK^r = P_{dK}^r .dK_d^r + P_L^r.dL^r \qquad (11)$$

The hypothesis of fixed production technique[23] with each factor increment being counted for one unit allows us to omit suffix r attached to dK, dK_d and dL. This assumption is particularly strong ; it is made here for the sake of simplicity[24]. When land prices vary across space, if factors are substitutable, one would rather expect variable proportions of factors. In the standard models (under perfectly competitive conditions) « output is produced the less (depreciable) capital and labour intensely and the more land intensely the farther away from the center production takes place »[25].

Let us consider a particular region R as a benchmark. For region R, we have $P_K^R = P_{dK}^R + P_L^R$ because of the fixed-production-technique assumption, where each factor increment is counted for one unit. Following section 2, I define the proportion λ as the ratio of P_L^R to P_K^R and multipliers χ^r as the ratios of P^r to P^R for any subscript dK or dL. Accordingly for any region r the following equality holds :

$$P_K^r = P_K^R . [\chi_{dK}^r . (1-\lambda) + \chi_L^r . \lambda] \qquad (12)$$

and the cost of capital expression for region r, c^r, is defined as the marginal value product of one monetary unit of capital in the benchmark region R,

$$c^r = \left\{ \frac{1-A_{dK}}{1-\tau}.[(\rho-\pi)+(\delta-\pi_{dK})].(1-\lambda).\chi_{dK}^r+\frac{1-A_L}{1-\tau}.(\rho-\pi-\pi_L).\lambda.\chi_L^r \right\}.\frac{1}{\alpha_r} \qquad (13)$$

Let us turn now to the last extension of the cost of capital expression by taking into account the imperfectly competitive markets due to space.

[23] This is the Weber (1909)'s assumption. See Paelinck and Nijkamp (1975) p. 34.

[24] Relaxing this assumption can be only made at the expense of great complexity in the analytical expressions. The fixed quantity of factors could be replaced by a variable assortment. The best combination of factors would be provided for every relative cost between depreciable asset and land by the tangency of the isocost straight line and the isoquant curve in a partial equilibrium model.

[25] See Stahl (1987) p771 .

3.3 Accounting For Imperfectly Competitive Markets

Spatial competition is by nature oligopolistic (Gabszewicz and Thisse, 1986) so that the framework of competitive analysis used for measuring the cost of capital is not the most appropriate one. One would prefer the framework of strategic interactions between agents (Fujita and Thisse, 1996).

However let us remember the purpose of our paper, which is to determine an analytical expression for the cost of capital that accounts for **differentiated spatial characteristics**. The ultimate aim is to find an indicator empirically measurable able to compare the performances of various location choices. If market power characterizes the agents in a regional context any value chosen for elasticities of commodity demand or input supply[26] would be purely speculative. Furthermore, the same values have to be given *a priori* to the elasticity parameters, wherever the investment is located, in such a way that they are not discriminating across locations[27]. Even if the perfectly competitive context is less realistic, it provides a convenient benchmark that is every bit as good as any other hypothesis.

In order to illustrate how some market power may affect the analytical expressions for capital cost, I shall consider two limiting cases : a pure monopoly for the commodity market and a pure monopsony on the capital market[28]. When the firm acts as a pure monopolist, the price for the good is fixed at a higher level than it would have been in perfectly competitive conditions. Taking into account this case requires replacing P in expressions (1) and (2) by

$$P.\left[1-\frac{1}{\eta}\right] \quad , \tag{14}$$

where η denotes the (negative) elasticity of commodity demand to price (Boadway, 1987; Boadway and Shah, 1995). Symmetrically, when capital price (for instance, the land price) is sensitive to quantities of the input used, the expressions (1) and (2) have to be modified by replacing P_K by

$$P_K.\left[1+\frac{1}{\theta}\right] \quad , \tag{15}$$

where θ expresses the elasticity of land supply.

4.0 CONCLUSION

Regions step up efforts to stimulate the setting up of new plants : capital grants and tax incentives are abundantly used, for example, to foster investment formation. How should the impact of economic policy tools on the investment decision be assessed ? The economics literature on effective tax rates upon

26 Which would express the expected deviation from the perfectly competitive conditions.

27 Unlike the other extensions developed to the model in sections 3.1 and 3.2 : spatial productivity differences and differentiated land prices.

28 In each case, quantity is supposed to be a function of its own price and not of other prices.

income from capital provides convenient models able to measure the rates of return (after any taxes and public aids) required for the investment between regions. These models have been widely used at the national level or at the regional level, including for regional policy purposes[29].

While convenient and commonly used, this approach is bounded by some restrictive assumptions. The following example illustrates some of these limitations. In the standard model higher taxes increase the cost of capital. As a result investment is supposed to be deterred in all cases[30]. But those taxes may finance a more generous provision of public goods and improve the general productivity of a project. Including taxes on the capital income (and public financial aids) but ignoring the productivity gains due to public goods only gives a partial view of the regional attractiveness that may involve some misleading conclusions.

What lies behind such approximations ? In the standard models, space is not considered : it is supposed to be undifferentiated. The productivity of an investment project is absolutely the same wherever it locates. Land prices are also set equal across space.

This paper set out to integrate these factors within the cost of capital framework. It also examined, but more briefly, the question of the opportunity to consider imperfectly competitive market conditions due to space. So developed the model provides a first measure of a « spatialized » cost of capital.

Obviously this contribution does not exhaust the matter. Some further extensions could be thought of : the integration of adjustment costs following Goulder and Thalmann (1993) or Boadway (1987), for example, or the taking into consideration of irreversibility phenomena ; most location decisions involve an irreversible capital commitment.

REFERENCES

Alworth, J.S. (1988). *The Finance, Investment and Taxation Decisions of Multinationals.* Oxford: Basil Blackwell Ltd.

Auerbach, A.J. (1983), "Corporate taxation in the United States." *Brookings Papers on Economic Activity*, 2, 451-505.

Beeson, P. (1987). "Total factor productivity growth and agglomeration economies in manufacturing, 1959-73." *Journal of Regional Science*, 27, 2, 183-99.

Beeson, P. and S. Husted. (1989). "Patterns and determinants of productive efficiency in state manufacturing." *Journal of Regional Science*, 29, 15-28.

Boadway, R.W. (1987). "The theory and measurement of effective tax rates." In *The Impact of Taxation on Business Activity*, edited by J.M. MINTZ and D.D. PURVIS. John Deutsch Institute for the Study of Economic Policy, Kingston.

---

29 Some recent examples are given by Guiot and Mignolet (1995) and by Mignolet et al. , 1997.

30 Alworth (1988), O.E.C.D. (1991), Head et al. (1994) and more systematically Mignolet (1997) have already shown for cross-border financial arrangements that the deterrent effect of taxes on investment and even more the incentive effect of tax breaks are a function of tax regimes both in the subsidiary and in the parent countries.

Boadway, R. W. and A. Shah. (1995). "Perspectives on the role of investment incentives in developing countries." In *Fiscal Incentives for Investment and Innovation*, edited by A. Shah, pp. 31-136. Oxford: Oxford University Press.

Carlino, G.A. (1982). "Manufacturing agglomeration economies as returns to scale : a production function approach." *Papers of the Regional Science Association, 50, 95-108.*

Carlino, G.A. and R. Voith. (1992). "Accounting for differences in aggregate state productivity." *Regional Science and Urban Economics*, 22, 597-617.

Catin, M. (1991). "Economies d'agglomération et gains de productivité." *Revue d'Economie Régionale et Urbaine*, 5, 565-98.

C.E.E. (1992). *Rapport du comité de reflexion des experts indépendants sur la fiscalité des entreprises*, Bruxelles.

E.B.R.D. (European Bank for Reconstruction and Development). (1993). "Progress in reform." *EBRD Economic Outlook*, 46-54.

Fujita, M. and Thisse J.F. (1996). "Economics of Agglomeration." In *Economics of Cities...*, edited by J.M. Huriot and J.F. Thisse (forthcoming).

Gabszewicz, J.J. and J.F. Thisse. (1986). "Spatial competition and the location of firms." In *Location Theory*, edited by J.J. Gabszewicz, J.F. Thisse, M. Fujita and U. Schweizer, 1-71. Chur: Harwood Academic Publishers.

Goulder, L.H. and P. Thalmann. (1993). "Approaches to efficient capital taxation, leveling the playing field vs. living by the golden rule." *Journal of Public Economics*, 50, 169-96.

Guiot, S. and M. Mignolet. (1995). "La politique régionale européenne et le coût du capital : application à la Martinique et au Hainaut d'un modèle de taxation internationale." *Revue d'Economie Régionale et Urbaine*, 2, 283-300.

Hall, R. and D.W. Jorgenson. (1967). "Tax policy and investment behavior." *American Economic Review*, 57, 391-414.

Head, C.K., J.C. Ries, and Swenson, D.L. (1994). "The attraction of foreign manufacturing investments : investment promotion and agglomeration economies." *NBER Working Paper* 4878, October.

Hoover, E.M. (1936). *Location Theory and the Shoe and Leather Industries*. Cambridge: Harvard University Press.

Jorgenson, D.W. and R. Landau, eds. (1993). *Tax Reform and the Cost of Capital : An International Comparison*. Washington: The Brookings Institution.

Ke, S. and M.I. Luger. (1996). "Embodied technological progress, technology-related producer inputs and regional factors in a firm-level model of growth." *Regional Science and Urban Economics*, 26, 23-50.

King, M. and D. Fullerton. (1984). *The Taxation of Income from Capital. A Comparative Study of the United States, the United Kingdom, Sweden and West-Germany*. Chicago: National Bureau of Economic Research, University of Chicago Press.

Mignolet, M. (1997). "The multinational companies cost of capital : what is the impact of regional policy ?" In *New Models Explaining the Development of Regions, Essays in Honour of Jean PAELINCK*, edited by R. Giradi. Egea-Boconi, Milan (forthcoming).

Mignolet, M., T. Piraux, and A. Vereecke. (1997). "Le coût du capital et les politiques régionales : une application à six régions européennes." *Cahiers Economiques de Bruxelles*, 153, 51-115.

McKenzie, K.J. (1994). "The Implications of Risk and Irreversibility for the Measurement of Marginal Effective Tax Rates on Capital" *Canadian Journal of Economics*, August, 27, 604-19.

Moomaw, R.L. (1983). "Spatial productivity variations in manufacturing : a critical survey of cross-sectional analyses." *International Regional Science Review*, 8, 1-22.

Moomaw, R.L. and M. Williams. (1991). "Total factor productivity growth in manufacturing : further evidence from the States." *Journal of Regional Science*, 31, 17-34.

O.E.C.D. (1991). *Taxing Profits in a Global Economy : Domestic and International Issues*, Paris.

Paelinck, J.H.P. and P. Nijkamp. (1975). *Operational Theory and Methods in Regional Economics*, Farnborough: Saxon House.

Shah, A. ed. (1995). *Fiscal Incentives for Investment and Innovation*, Oxford: Osford University Press.

Shefer, D. (1973). "Localization economies in SMAs : a production function analysis." *Journal of Regional Science*, 13, 55-64.

Stahl, K. (1987). "Theories of urban business location." In *Handbook of Urban Economics*, edited by E.S. Mills , 759-820. Amsterdam: Elsevier Science.

Sveikauskas, L.A. (1975). "The productivity of cities." *Quarterly Journal of Economics*, 89, 392-413.

TO JULIETTE

AN EPILOGUE FOR A VALUED COLLEAGUE AND DEAR FRIEND

It is appropriate to end this book with some observations about the man whom it honors.

1.0 SCIENTIFIC RIGOR

The papers contained in this book represent a high level of scientific rigor that is appropriate given the man to which they are dedicated. Jean Paelinck is a gifted communicator with the language of mathematics, he is a brilliant econometrician and the father of something that is arguably more difficult than econometrics--spatial econometrics, and he is a thoughtful intellectual who understands the need to build bridges between scientific research and governmental and private-sector problem solving and decision making. Jean has spent much of his career moving effortlessly, or so it seems, between the twilight zone of basic research and the more immediate pressures of developmental research. He also has been a driving force in the *founding* of such specialized scientific fields as medicometry, oenometry, and restaurometry. Jean takes special pleasure in articulating new and innovative research agendas and in following the words of N. Boileau, who he is fond of quoting: "Ce qui se concoit bien s'énonce clairement et le mots pour le dire arrivent aisément"--if things are well conceived they can be clearly expressed and the words will come smoothly. This line, perhaps more than any other, expresses Jean's rigor in style, expression, and thinking.

Having said this, we feel compelled to look beyond Jean Paelinck the scientist and make explicit what those of us who know Jean take as implicit.

2.0 SCIENCE AND MUSIC

Jean is a man of many parts--he lives in a world where science, mathematics, language, literature, and music all have a regular and significant place in day-to-day life. His motto (or at least one of them ... "a model a day keeps the doctor away") carries over to his music too. Jean practices his piano regularly. He is familiar with the work of dozens of composers and he is a composer himself. Jean contributes his scientific work to scholarly congresses, to which he contributes his music, too. He composed "The March of the Western Regional Science Association" and he performed it at the opening session of the 1997 annual meeting held in Hawaii, USA. Jean not only wrote a march for the French Geography Festival that is offered each year in Saint Dié Des Vosges, France, but he also has organized and performed a complete musical program there.

3.0 A CITIZEN OF THE WORLD

Jean has a general interest in the world's places and the world's people. He is a geographer by inclination if not by training. His fluency in over a dozen languages gives him insights into the intricacies of Asian, African, European, Australian, and Latin American and Anglo-American social, political, economic, and cultural institutions, a stock in trade that can be claimed by few others. Jean works in the future and uses his knowledge of Latin and Greek to enhance his understanding of the past. Further, Jean has lived throughout the world and has always used these opportunities to become better acquainted with local subtleties in the life of the mind--and in life on the streets. Jean is not just an intellectual and citizen of the world; he also is an intellectual and a *street smart* citizen of the world.

Jean is warm, generous, and thoughtful. Jean is devoted to his family and unselfish with his colleagues. He is the perfect host--he puts his guests at ease and works hard to see that they are comfortable and that their needs are met. Those who have been house guests of the Paelincks certainly know this; but perhaps more significantly, even those who have only met Jean briefly and in a *business environment* have the same impression of him. Several of those who contributed to this book first met Jean when they were young scholars with at best localized reputations. Nevertheless, they all tell essentially the same story--when they met the "world famous Jean Paelinck" he was warm, he was genuinely interested in them as scientists but he was equally interested in them as people, he was upbeat, he was enthusiastic about his work, their work, and life in general, he was generous with his time, and he was generous with his ideas. He was never patronizing or too self-absorbed to be kind, considerate or to give a sincere and thoughtful response to issues and ideas introduced by others.

4.0 THE YEAR OF THE PAELINCKS

When we first started making plans for "The Year of The Paelincks" we had three goals: to contribute to several congresses by drawing together a selection of papers of exceptional scientific merit; to preview papers that would find their way into this festschrift volume; and, to create an opportunity for Jean to visit with old and new friends. We are confident that all three missions were accomplished. We identified five venues that would fit our criteria and Jean's interests, namely The Western Regional Science Meeting in Napa, California, The World Regional Science Congress in Tokyo, The European Regional Science Congress in Zurich, The French Speaking Association's Meeting in Berlin, and The North American Regional Science Meetings in Cincinnati and Washington, DC. These venues and conferences performed as anticipated. Old friends from around the world could easily accommodate geographic and scheduling preferences for participation. Young scholars found that barriers to participation were reduced. And all comers were able to engage in scientific discussions with Jean who, traveling with Juliette, not only attended virtually each and every session, but played a central role in sessions as a discussant and source of fresh ideas and innovative solutions to complex problems. Of equal important were the opportunities for old friends to get together and for those who know Jean less well to become more familiar with him.

Given his exceptional talents it is not surprising that the demands on Jean's time have been heavy. Despite these pressures Jean can always find time for an early morning walk just about anywhere in the world, for a bicycle ride in coastal Belgium or for skiing in the French Alps. But most important of all to Jean is the time devoted to his family. There may be short-term dislocations, but in the intermediate- and long-term, family has come first. Juliette has always been a major force and now that the children have grown and she has retired from her own teaching career, she has become increasingly conspicuous throughout Europe, and in Asia and North America, too. Jean stops short of approaching total strangers to discuss his children and grandchildren, but he never misses an opportunity to bring friends up-to-date on the accomplishments of his children, Claudette, Marc, and Geneviéve, or those of his grandchildren. While Jean is an exceptional talent, he leaves no doubt that first and foremost he is a family man.

5.0 NEW CHALLENGES

Early in his career Jean left the University of Namur, where he received his last earned degree, and was given his first regular professional appointment. Leaving was not easy; Jean still has a special place in his heart for Namur. Still, Jean left to take on new challenges and opportunities. Now Jean has left Erasmus University, where he spent much of his professional career, and has taken up headquarters at the Tinbergen Institute, Rotterdam. Again Jean has left a special place but again he is moving on to new professional challenges and opportunities. He remains an active scientist, a teacher at Asian, European, and North American universities, a major force in the management of regional science institutions, a contributor to the arts, a mentor to young scholars, a valued colleague and dear friend, and a dedicated and enthusiastic husband and father. Incredibly, Jean may become even more active internationally now that he no longer has the same day-to-day obligations at Erasmus. If Jean were to be asked, "have you lived in Europe all your life?" he might answer, "not yet." In the years ahead we look forward to maintaining close ties with Jean and Juliette, and to spending time with them when they are at home in Europe, or visiting Asia, North America, Africa or wherever else family, friends, or an interesting project take them.

From Jean's experiences we can better understand the world of science and we can learn essential lessons about life. We can again write the words of Clearque d'Ai-Khanolim: "ΓΝΩΘΙ ΣΕΑΥΤΟΝ, Gnâthi Seauton"--teach yourself about yourself.

Antoine Bailly
University of Geneva
Switzerland

Lay James Gibson
University of Arizona
U.S.A.

INDEX

Advanced Studies in Theoretical and Applied Econometrics

1. J.H.P. Paelinck (ed.): *Qualitative and Quantitative Mathematical Economics.* 1982 ISBN 90-247-2623-9
2. J.P. Ancot (ed.): *Analysing the Structure of Econometric Models.* 1984 ISBN 90-247-2894-0
3. A.J. Hughes Hallet (ed.): *Applied Decision Analysis and Economic Behaviour.* 1984 ISBN 90-247-2968-8
4. J.K. Sengupta: *Information and Efficiency in Economic Decision.* 1985 ISBN 90-247-3072-4
5. P. Artus and O. Guvenen (eds.), in collaboration with F. Gagey: *International Macroeconomic Modelling for Policy Decisions.* 1986 ISBN 90-247-3201-8
6. M.J. Vilares: *Structural Change in Macroeconomic Models.* Theory and Estimation. 1986 ISBN 90-247-3277-8
7. C. Carraro and D. Sartore (eds.): *Development of Control Theory for Economic Analysis.* 1987 ISBN 90-247-3345-6
8. D.P. Broer: *Neoclassical Theory and Empirical Models of Aggregate Firm Behaviour.* 1987 ISBN 90-247-3412-6
9. A. Italianer: *Theory and Practice of International Trade Linkage Models.* 1986 ISBN 90-247-3407-X
10. D.A. Kendrick: *Feedback.* A New Framework for Macroeconomic Policy. 1988 ISBN 90-247-3593-9; Pb: 90-247-3650-1
11. J.K. Sengupta and G.K. Kadekodi (eds.): *Econometrics of Planning and Efficiency.* 1988 ISBN 90-247-3602-1
12. D.A. Griffith: *Advanced Spatial Statistics.* Special Topics in the Exploration of Quantitative Spatial Data Series. 1988 ISBN 90-247-3627-7
13. O. Guvenen (ed.): *International Commodity Market Models and Policy Analysis.* 1988 ISBN 90-247-3768-0
14. G. Arbia: *Spatial Data Configuration in Statistical Analysis of Regional Economic and Related Problems.* 1989 ISBN 0-7923-0284-2
15. B. Raj (ed.): *Advances in Econometrics and Modelling.* 1989 ISBN 0-7923-0299-0
16. A. Aznar Grasa: *Econometric Model Selection.* A New Approach. 1989 ISBN 0-7923-0321-0
17. L.R. Klein and J. Marquez (eds.): *Economics in Theory and Practice.* An Eclectic Approach. Essays in Honor of F. G. Adams. 1989 ISBN 0-7923-0410-1
18. D.A. Kendrick: *Models for Analyzing Comparative Advantage.* 1990 ISBN 0-7923-0528-0
19. P. Artus and Y. Barroux (eds.): *Monetary Policy.* A Theoretical and Econometric Approach. 1990 ISBN 0-7923-0626-0
20. G. Duru and J.H.P. Paelinck (eds.): *Econometrics of Health Care.* 1990 ISBN 0-7923-0766-6
21. L. Phlips (ed.): *Commodity, Futures and Financial Markets.* 1991 ISBN 0-7923-1043-8

Kluwer Academic Publishers – Dordrecht / Boston / London

Advanced Studies in Theoretical and Applied Econometrics

22. H.M. Amman, D.A. Belsley and L.F. Pau (eds.): *Computational Economics and Econometrics.* 1992 ISBN 0-7923-1287-2
23. B. Raj and J. Koerts (eds.): *Henri Theil's Contributions to Economics and Econometrics.* Vol. I: Econometric Theory and Methodology. 1992 ISBN 0-7923-1548-0
24. B. Raj and J. Koerts (eds.): *Henri Theil's Contributions to Economics and Econometrics.* Vol. II: Consumer Demand Analysis and Information Theory. 1992 ISBN 0-7923-1664-9
25. B. Raj and J. Koerts (eds.): *Henri Theil's Contributions to Economics and Econometrics.* Vol. III: Economic Policy and Forecasts, and Management Science. 1992 ISBN 0-7923-1665-7
    Set (23–25) ISBN 0-7923-1666-5
26. P. Fisher: *Rational Expectations in Macroeconomic Models.* 1992 ISBN 0-7923-1903-6
27. L. Phlips and L.D. Taylor (eds.): *Aggregation, Consumption and Trade.* Essays in Honor of H.S. Houthakker. 1992. ISBN 0-7923-2001-8
28. L. Mátyás and P. Sevestre (eds.): *The Econometrics of Panel Data.* Handbook of Theory and Applications. 1992 ISBN 0-7923-2043-3
29. S. Selvanathan: *A System-Wide Analysis of International Consumption Patterns.* 1993 ISBN 0-7923-2344-0
30. H. Theil in association with D. Chen, K. Clements and C. Moss: *Studies in Global Econometrics.* 1996 ISBN 0-7923-3660-7
31. P.J. Kehoe and T.J. Kehoe (eds.): *Modeling North American Economic Integration.* 1995 ISBN 0-7923-3751-4
32. C. Wells: *The Kalman Filter in Finance.* 1996 ISBN 0-7923-3771-9
33. L. Mátyás and P. Sevestre (eds.): *The Econometrics of Panel Data.* A Handbook of the Theory with Applications. Second Revised Edition. 1996 ISBN 0-7923-3787-5
34. B. Assarsson, D. Edgerton, A. Hummelmose, I. Laurila, K. Rickertson and P.H. Vale: *The Econometrics of Demand Systems.* With Applications to Food Demand in the North Countries. 1996 ISBN 0-7923-4106-6
35. D.A. Griffith, C.G. Amrhein and J-M. Huriot (eds.): *Econometric Advances in Spatial Modelling and Methodology.* Essays in Honour of Jean Paelinck. 1998 ISBN 0-7923-4915-6

Kluwer Academic Publishers – Dordrecht / Boston / London

Printed in the United States
59938LVS00001BB/25

9 780792 349150